Understanding Your Customer

What Every Automotive Salesperson Needs to Know About their Customer

By

David Lewis

Understanding Your Customer
Copyright 2013 by David Lewis

ISBN Number: 978-0-615-82663-9

First Edition: August 2013
Published in North America by DTM Publications
Printed in the United States of America

This book is dedicated to my two children, Taylor & Mitchell, who provide me with their endless support, love and understanding while I travel around the country training and learning.

Table of Contents

CHAPTER 1
WHAT IS A CUSTOMER?

According to the dictionary, a Customer is, "a person, company, or other entity which buys goods and services provided by another person, company or other entity." You can't get a more simple explanation than that.

From an Automobile Salesperson's point of view though, it is a bit more specific: To me a Customer is someone who spends money at my Dealership allowing me to receive the income I need to pay my bills and afford for myself and my family the lifestyle we are living or we desire. Without Customers, I don't sell cars. If I don't sell cars, I don't make a living.

We are all Customers to someone. Everyone living in the real world buys and sells products on a regular basis. Most tend to buy from businesses that offer good products and services at a fair price and have a good reputation. The same is true when it comes to purchasing an automobile.

People living in America depend on their automobiles to a degree that has made the automotive industry fundamental to our way of life. Though Americans today cross the whole spectrum of style, price and type of vehicle, the one constant is their ongoing need for a car. Less than 6% of American households have no vehicle in their driveway, while over 67% have 2 and nearly 20% have 3 or more. As you can see most Americans are car Customers.

These days the average Customer is someone who buys for different reasons than they did in days of old and what is important to them has changed drastically. In today's economy, a Customer is someone who primarily buys something to eliminate a pain they are experiencing. Whether it's a need for economy, space, luxury, reliability, durability or price, the smart Salesperson today zeroes in on what will meet their Customers' needs and takes away their pain.

No matter how you put it, Customers are the most important people in our trade and learning how to take good care of them, either in the sales process or after the sale, is probably the most valuable business decision you can make to better your own life and build a successful career. But let's take a closer look at what a Customer brings to our business at the Dealership.

On any given day, a single Customer who comes to your Dealership may end up purchasing a new or used vehicle, leasing a new vehicle, trading in a used vehicle, financing their new or used vehicle, purchasing a service contract, buying additional aftermarket options, servicing their car in the service department and/or purchasing parts in the parts department. Considering that the average Customer will buy or lease nine vehicles in their lifetime, isn't that quite a good reason to develop a relationship with your Customer for life?

Add to this purchase history, the family and friends they will refer to you as their friendly, trusted and diligent car Salesperson, you can see how this can quickly add up to a substantial amount of revenue that is all related to just one Customer who chooses to do business with you. Let's see what the numbers have to say about that.

The average cost of a new vehicle purchased in 2011 was $30,748. The average price of a used car purchased at a franchised Dealership during the same period was $16,138. With that in mind, developing a solid relationship with your Customers can be a highly profitable investment of your time and talents. Experts will tell you that over a 15 year period just one Customer will come in contact or influence 30 other people in their car buying process. And each of them will purchase 3 cars over the same period of time.

Using the above figures, those 30 Customers will represent an average of nearly $2 million in vehicle purchases. Add to that the same vehicles being traded back in and you have another $650,000 of used car sales being made available to you through those same 30 Customers.

Now let's take into consideration the commission that will be earned. Assuming the average commission is $250 that one Customer will generate over $22,500 of commission in that same time period. Remember that started with only one Customer.

You can see how that can add up over a nice long career in the business. Since the average Automobile Salesperson in America sells 125 cars per year, just do the numbers on that and you have a substantial amount of potential business through your personal efforts to develop good Customer relationships.

As you well know, each Customer you meet has a unique personality and a specific need to fill. They come to you looking for someone who can help them buy what, for most people, is the second most expensive purchase they will make other than their home. They have understandable expectations and fears that go along with spending that amount of money and because of this, they are looking for someone that is professional and has the experience and expertise to help them find what they want and need, and at a price they can afford. On top of that, they want their Salesperson to respect them and do their best to treat them honestly and fairly.

No two Customers are alike. Some are mild mannered and easy to deal with, while others are boisterous and overpowering people who seem to know exactly what they want and expect you to make sure they get it. Some are outgoing and friendly and have no problem talking to a Salesperson, while others come to the Dealership with a suitcase full of fears and negative expectations that require a lot of unloading before you can get to a place of trust and communication.

How well you come to know and understand your Customers will make all the difference in your ability to develop a long lasting and profitable relationship with them over the life of your career. Believe it or not, they are looking for just that. If you can deliver that kind of quality experience for them they will not only come to you when they want or need their next vehicle, but they will look forward to the opportunity and you may also earn a friend for life.

Apparently, there are a large number of Customers who prefer pre-owned vehicles. Used car Customers outnumber new car buyers 7 to 1. Although new car purchases represent the highest prices paid per vehicle, more than twice as much is spent annually buying used cars. Even though everyone would probably prefer to own a brand new car, the cost difference, as well as letting someone else take the initial depreciation hit of a new car, seems to make buying used vehicles the choice most Customers make.

Customers seem to be getting older too. Over the 4 year period from 2007-2010 the average age of car buyers in America increased from 50 to 55 and during that same period, new car purchases by Customers over 65, increased from 5.7% to 7.6% of the car buying public in America. Knowing this, you may want to give a little more heed to the seniors that call or visit your lot. They often bring low mileage trade-ins and have less difficulty with financing or paying cash.

That does not mean that all Customers are up in age. The bad news for American automakers is that Generation 'Y' (Customers born in the 80's and 90's) prefer to buy Asian imports over others. In fact in 2011, 52% of Customers from 18-27 years of age purchased an import over a domestic car.

Here are a few interesting statistics about recent vehicle buying trends:

➢ Over 75% of Customers now start their car buying experience online before going to a Dealership

➤ They tend to buy within 5 days of starting their shopping process
➤ 80% of buyers will take their new car home on the day of purchase
➤ 70% of new parents buy a new car due to the birth of a child
➤ Customers who allow more profit to the Dealership tend to be happiest with their vehicles
➤ 60% of Customers buy something different from what they came looking for in color, model, etc.
➤ Customers biggest complaint about Dealerships is the pressure applied to them by the Salesperson
➤ Customers overwhelmingly state their purchasing decision was based mostly on the product versus the price they paid

It is easy to see why selling a car is not something you should decide to do just because you can't find another job. It takes a serious effort to become a professional in this business and that's the way it should be. That doesn't mean that it requires a college education. Some of the most successful people in our business don't possess a high school diploma, but they have learned the value of becoming knowledgeable in the business, the process and the Customer. Those who do this can look forward to a growing career with great potential for the future.

An average Automobile Salesperson can earn in excess of $50,000 annually and those who become experts can and will exceed $100,000 in annual compensation. This makes the Customer the most valuable commodity you have and well worth the time, money and effort you invest to advance your skills to the highest level.

Today's Customers are savvy and come well informed. It only stands to reason that you should do the same if you want to earn their business.

The most important thing to know about Customers is that they are the heartbeat of our business. Serving them is the name of the game and learning how best to do that is both enjoyable and profitable. The Salesperson who masters the art of Customer Satisfaction is setting in place a practice that will help them develop the most of what this business has to offer in both financial reward and career potential.

Customer satisfaction is not always what takes place after the sale; it also takes place during the sale.

The key failure point in most Automobile Salespeople is that they truly do not understand the Customer. They think they do, but they really do not. If they did, then they would not be utilizing some of the sales processes, objection responses, closing techniques and sold Customer follow-up procedures that they do.

When surveying Customer's, most will state they do not enjoy the car buying experience. Many relate it to the pain and suffering of getting a root canal done. If these are their thoughts and beliefs, then why do we promote, present and sell in that manner? Why have we not learned from our Customers and made the appropriate changes and enhancements? Why are we still utilizing the same selling steps that we used in the 1970's?

The reason to all of these questions is simple, we have

only put our focus on what we, as an industry, thinks is best, and we have not studied our Customer. You know, the one who buys our product, the ones whom we come to work every day to serve and the ones who provide us with the income to support ourselves and our family.

Nobody likes change, but unfortunately it is time for change. That is, if you want to grow and get better at what we do, which is sell cars.

There are not many guarantees in life, but there is one guarantee I can state to you with confidence and that is, if you are satisfied with the results you are getting in your Dealership or personally in your sales career, then stay the course, and your existing results will remain your future results. But, if you are like me, and want to keep getting better at what you do, then the place to start is with studying your Customer and developing a sales process and follow-up system that they like and respect. If you do, your results have no place to go but up.

CHAPTER 2
UNDERSTANDING YOUR CUSTOMER

Satisfying your Customer is the most important priority that you have as an Automotive Sales Representative. The value of everything else that you do in your position hinges on your ability to have a successful working relationship with those who come to you to purchase or lease their vehicles. No matter how good you are at any other part of your business, if the Customers needs are not met, you will most likely not make a sale. With that in mind, any effort you take to better your understanding of how best to serve them, will only enhance your success and grow your earnings in this business.

The tendency for some Salespeople to rely upon outdated methods of pressure and manipulation is going the way of the 'all buyers are liars' concept. Those who view their Customers in this way and treat them accordingly, will soon find it difficult to work in reputable Dealerships. The truly professional Automobile Salesperson not only respects the Customer, but highly values them and truly desires to meet and exceed their buying expectations.

To start with, the best way to learn how to understand your Customers is to put yourself in their shoes. How would you want to be treated if you were coming to a Dealership to invest tens of thousands of dollars in a vehicle? Would you expect to be treated respectfully? What would you want the Salesperson to be concerned about first, their commission or meeting your wants and needs? Would you want them to focus on what was best for them or what is best for you? When you can truthfully answer these questions, you are at the beginning of understanding your Customer.

The simple rule is to do for your Customers what you would want a Salesperson to do for you, plain and simple. Starting from that premise, what do Customers want when they come to you?

A research firm recently surveyed 7,000 consumers asking them what their main motivations were for considering the purchase of a new car. There were 14 primary reasons that stood out in the responses to their survey. At the top of the list was their car had high mileage. Over one third of the respondents said that this was their main reason for looking for a new car. Coming in second, were those who said they were tired of their old car and wanted something new. That was closely followed by the third group that claimed their car always needed repairs and had to be replaced.

From there, it went down through things like a desire to have the newest safety features, better gas mileage, good financing opportunities, new technology gadgets, etc. What the survey clearly showed was that they all knew why they were looking for a new car and very few of them were just driven by emotion or a sudden urge to buy. They had problems or needs, and getting a new car was viewed as an important part of solving those issues.

In a future chapter, I will share with you the Customer's actual factors of what they buy and from whom they will buy it from.

Understanding what is driving your Customer to shop for a new vehicle is essential to your ability to help them find what they want. The most important part of that process takes place after your initial Meet and Greet, when your Customer responds to your first questions and you start the process of listening. The more you listen to what they have to say, the better chance you will have of understanding what they want and need. Though this is hard for some Salespeople to accept, too much talking will get you in trouble right from the start. The key to understanding your Customer is to let them tell you who they are and what they want. Once they see that you are listening and they drop their natural defensive mechanisms, you can then begin the process of serving them and meeting the needs which led them to your Dealership.

Since most of today's Customers have already started shopping online before coming to you they already have a sense of what they are looking for and they often bring that information with them when they shop. With that in mind, knowing your inventory and being familiar with what your product offers is an important part of your job. It is never good if the Customer knows more about your cars than you do. But don't make the mistake of telling them a lie to answer something you don't know. It's always better to take a few minutes to find the right answer when that happens. If they think you have lied to them, you will never gain their trust.

Many Customers go to a Dealership already expecting

the Salesperson to take advantage of them. They may have had a bad experience before when trying to buy a car or they have heard some of the horror stories that are always floating around about car Salespeople. Some fear they will be cheated on the value of their trade-in or pressured to buy something they don't really want. There are many reasons that may cause Customers to have a natural distrust or fear when coming to look at buying a car.

You must not react to this in a critical way or the process of selling will become a burden when it can actually be a lot of fun for both you and your Customer. Your ability to be enthusiastic and excited about helping them find what they are looking for can play a big part in whether or not they will be relaxed and trusting in you as their Salesperson. Your commitment to giving them your full attention will often make the difference between you and other Salespeople they may have spoken to, or will speak to, at another Dealership.

Regardless of why Customers are defensive, one of your most valuable tools for success is learning how to disarm their reluctance, and how to respond to them in a way that will lower their resistance and help you build trust. I will cover this extensively in another chapter, since it is a critical part of your skill set as a professional Automobile Salesperson.

Another matter where Customers may require some adjusting to is in the area of 'sticker shock.' Seeing how much car prices have risen compared to when they made their last purchase can often be mind boggling and, believe it or not, they may at first want to blame it on you. If they haven't bought a new car in 10 years they will find that prices have risen over 32% on average. This can be quite a shock for some and learning how to present the value of what you offer is not something that you can take for granted. There are good reasons why the costs have risen and you need to be able to understand what those are and how to present them to your Customers in a way that adds value to the vehicles you sell.

American's spend a lot of time in their cars today. Over 11 billion miles are driven each day on our roads and highways. That's an average of 40 miles per driver each day. And most of us are driving those miles in much smaller vehicles than our parents had, yet we expect the same level of luxury and performance. Thanks to advanced technologies in comfort systems, safety features, fuel economy and sophisticated electronics we can have that, but it costs money to develop such things and thus the prices rise. Cars were once expected to go 100,000 miles before being traded in, are now expected to go nearly twice as far, and they do. But those advancements come at a cost. Make sure you let your Customers know these things and you can save yourself a lot of backing up during your presentation.

Though once considered a cutthroat business by many, our industry is now working hard to turn that reputation around. The credit for this goes to those Dealers, Managers and Salespeople who place their focus squarely on Customer satisfaction. Those of us who accept the challenge of achieving excellence in this business have a unique opportunity to advance what these Leaders have started. Reversing the negative feelings that many people have about the car buying experience is not easy and will take place one Customer at a time. But it can be done, and understanding what Customers really want is where it all begins.

In reality Customers are just people. People like you and I. They want to know that their hard earned money brings value to their lives and helps them achieve a measure of security, prosperity and enjoyment. Because transportation plays such a big part in the life of the average American, it is important that they can depend upon their vehicles to take them where they want to go, when they want or need to go there. Whether it is for work, pleasure or just getting their kids safely to school or to the ball game, they don't want to be stranded when they turn the key to start the engine.

As a Salesperson, you are an important part of the equation. Customers want to have confidence in you that they are being taken care of in a manner that shows genuine concern and understanding, and that you respect who they are and what their wants and needs are. The more you learn about your Customer, the better prepared you will be to deliver a product and service to them that will exceed their expectations.

Your Customers are worth it, I assure you. Every effort you spend to learn how best to help and serve them will bring a return to you over the years of your career. Not just in finances, but in the respect that comes from doing your business with integrity and honesty.

Successful Salespeople who have been doing this right for years often talk about their 'Customer Family' being made up of those who come to them whenever they have a vehicle concern or are in the market for a new vehicle. They refer their friends, business associates and family members to this Salesperson, because they know they will be treated with the same respect that they have come to expect through years of doing business together.

This is exactly what makes understanding your Customer worth the effort. When you learn to excel in this area you will find that Customers are no longer intimidated about coming to your Dealership when they need a car; instead they are excited. They are excited because they know that you will look out for their interest and be concerned that they receive value for the hard earned money they are spending with you. And you will have the pleasure of knowing that you are in a growing business, with a great future, as you build a Customer base that will keep you prospering in the years to come.

CHAPTER 3
HOW TO JUDGE THE
CUSTOMER'S BEHAVIOR

The value of a good impression cannot be overstated when dealing with a Customer for the first time. The Meet & Greet is so critical because everything they initially perceive about you will be established within the first few moments of contact. How the Customer behaves will be directly linked to their perception of you in those first few minutes. How natural and professional you come across will make all the difference in the world as to how they will respond to you.

A Customer's behavior often reflects the stigma they have attached to the car buying experience. When people come to your Dealership expecting to be treated a certain way they will behave in a manner that reflects how they think they will be treated. If they believe that you are going to try to take advantage of them, they may be cautious or timid, and reluctant to cooperate with your initial questions or inquiries about their needs. Some may come across as aloof or act as though they are not in need of any assistance, while others may even be a bit nervous and unable to clearly express what they are looking for.

Learning to understand what your Customer's behaviors are telling you is the mark of a true professional Salesperson. It is a learned ability and not something that is necessarily a natural gift.

One of the great misconceptions about sales is that it depends upon being a 'Born Salesperson', someone who is naturally outgoing and has a dynamic personality that attracts people to them. Though this is certainly true about some people, the reality is that a true professional is someone who works hard at their trade and develops their gifts and abilities through the process of learning, doing, changing and growing.

There are many actions that take place in a sales dialogue that are open to interpretation. Learning how to understand body language and voice inflections can be a tremendous help in your quest to understand a Customer's behavior. Do they look away when answering your questions or turn away when you are trying to ask questions or start to converse with them? Do they fidget and act nervous when you are trying to make inquiries about their wants and needs, and what brought them to the Dealership? All of these are normal defensive postures that take place when a Customer is unsure of how to interact with a Salesperson.

Some Customers may respond aggressively when you are attempting to speak with them as though you were being pushy or trying to control the situation. This usually reflects fear or a past experience they may have had with another Salesperson. All of these are important signals that you must learn how to interpret if you are to help them get through the initial emotions that often arise when communicating with a Salesperson.

How you, as a professional, deal with these responses from your Customer are critical for the success of your presentation. It is important to assess your own attitude to make sure you don't become aggressive or defensive or even overly confident or critical in response to their behaviors. This can only create a combative situation that leads nowhere.

Some of your Customers may be perfectly at ease when buying a car. They understand how business works and expect you as a Salesperson to do your best to earn their business. They may be confident in their own abilities to deal with the process and understand that not only do they want to get the best deal possible, but they also respect your need to be compensated and the Dealership's need to make a profit. Learning how to work with this type of Customer, without taking the sale for granted, will also be an important part of your negotiation and presentation skills.

The old mindset of car sales was based upon controlling the Customer. The new and better way is for you, as a professional Salesperson, to learn how to control yourself. When you can demonstrate self control in these situations you are better able to break through the fears and defensiveness of your Customers and to move toward an effective process for helping them accomplish what they came to do: find a vehicle that meets their needs and fulfills their desires.

Ultimately, people just want to be happy. Because we spend so much time in our cars these days having one that is a pleasure to drive, is dependable and does what we need it to do can make at least some difference in our lives. Don't underestimate the value that you bring to someone by helping them find a good car. If any professional trade requires a unique set of disciplines and skills it is selling, because we deal with every different personality imaginable, learning how to present oneself in a way that helps the Customer is not necessarily an easy thing to do. It is a skill and it is developed by doing.

The job of an Automobile Salesperson is even more so. Why? Because Customers come with preconceived ideas of what to expect and in many cases these are not positive. The fact that most people would rather go to the dentist for a root canal than go to a car Dealership validates what I am saying.

One of the most important factors in your ability to assist the Customer is to understand your own motives. If you are only doing what you do for the money that will come through in your presentation and reinforce the Customer's fear and apprehension. Do you truly desire to serve the Customers? Are you genuinely concerned about their well being and about helping them find the vehicle that is just right for what they want and need?

If not, why not? Isn't that the essence of your business? Isn't your career choice in life supposed to be meaningful for both you and for those you do business with? If it's not, it should be!

Being an Automobile Salesperson is not something to be ashamed of unless you are doing things that you *should* be ashamed of. Like any other career, you have people who do things poorly and those who do them well. Our industry certainly has both types. But it is up to you how you choose to view and handle your business.

Learning how to judge your Customer's behavior is not a negative thing, it is positive. When a professional Salesperson makes judgments on a Customer's behavior, it is not so they can figure out how to outsmart them. It is for the purpose of discovering how best to help them. They realize that unless they can understand what motivates and drives their Customer to purchase a new vehicle, they cannot properly know how to guide them in the right direction.

It is important that you believe in yourself and what you can offer to your Customer. Are you truly certain that you will do your best to serve them better and in a more professional manner than other Salespeople whom they might meet? If so, then relax in your selling process and enjoy it. When you can do that, you are likely to find that your Customers will respond in the same way.

So, instead of focusing on trying to sell your Customers, try to inspire them by being the opposite of what they expect. If you sense that they are intimidated or defensive, make an effort to release that posture with verbiage that they will find comforting. Just as it is important for you to see your Customers as normal people, it is just as important that they perceive you in the same way.

Two of my favorite types of Customers are ones that many Salespeople choose to run from. I call them 'The Engineer' and 'The Scarecrow.' When these two come through the front door they are often passed to a new guy, because some seasoned Salespeople would rather not deal with them.

The 'Engineer' is totally caught up in the specifications and technical details of vehicles. If it's a hybrid or electric car they are looking for, they want to know if the vehicle has things like Regenerative Braking and how the process works to recharge the battery. They may ask if it is a Motor Generated (M/G) process with a Pancake system like the Prius. The Engineer may want to know about the latest safety features in Stability Control, Lane Departure Warning Systems or Continuously Variable Transmissions (CVT's).

You can quickly see why some Salespeople would rather not bother with this type of Customer, but learning how to get on their good side can be very profitable for you. For one thing, they know that the latest technologies have a price tag that goes with them, and they don't necessarily expect you to keep all that information in your head. If you can learn how to talk with them and know how to find the specs in your factory brochures, they will often sell themselves for you. And don't forget about your Service Techs. They can come in handy at a time like this. Having your Customers spend a few minutes with them can put you in good position for selling the Engineer.

The 'Scarecrow' on the other hand, is afraid of their own shadow. Their defensive posture is so high, they typically make statements like, *"Is it OK if I walk around alone"*, *"I am just looking"*, *"I only have a limited amount of time"*, *"All I want is a brochure"* and

"What is your best price on that car over there." This individual is so apprehensive that they want to be left alone or will only consider your guidance if they can control the process. Most Salespeople fail to truly understand what this Customer is stating and end up responding with verbiage that fails to lower their posture and in most cases, ends up raising it even higher.

Whatever types of behavior your Customers display, the fact that they have come to your Dealership usually means they are looking for a car. You can either mark them down as tire kickers or let someone else sell them. If you learn how to deal with their unique ways of communicating and find a way to help them, they will usually make a buying decision and you will make a commission.

All of us have our own personality and unique ways of dealing with the situations that make up our life experience. If we only deal with people who are just like us, we will have a very narrow view of the world and the people in it. Selling automobiles is a fun and challenging occupation and it's the people that you serve that often bring the most joy to the process. Learning how to judge your Customer's behaviors can go a long way to helping you broaden your road to success and you will most likely find yourself growing and changing along the way.

CHAPTER 4
WHY CUSTOMERS ARE SO DEFENSIVE

To become successful as a Retail Automotive Salesperson, you must learn how to deal effectively with Customers who are operating from a defensive posture. Though there is no single reason why Customers act this way when visiting an automobile Dealership, it often stems from the negative reputation that has become a part of our business.

Whether it is deserved or not, is not the primary question. Whether you can effectively separate yourself from the negative stigma that goes along with being a car Salesperson, is what really matters. Here is the good news: you don't have to think about that if you are doing the right things. By being honest, professional, enthusiastic and helpful to your Customers you can successfully remove yourself from any preconceived list they have in their mind about negative behaviors to expect from a car Salesperson.

One goal is to always do the unexpected. Most Customers expect certain levels of behavior from a Salesperson. They expect slick sales lingo, fancy and confusing pitches, and pressure to buy immediately. By being different and not falling into the typical sales presentation, you catch your Customers off guard, and this in turn will lower their defensive postures.

Though it is true that you must learn how to properly address the objectives and natural defensive postures that you will often encounter in your initial conversations with your Customers, it is also accurate to say that you can learn how to do that so effectively that they will eventually come to trust you without question. In later chapters of this book, I will cover proven and proper ways to deal with Customer objections, obstacles and defensive postures at great length.

One of the most common reasons why Customers are so defensive when they visit a Dealership is they feel powerless when dealing with a professional Salesperson. Though today's Customers are more informed than ever before, they still believe that you know something they don't and there are many different ways you can win at their expense. Though they may have done minimal research on trade values and the dealers cost of vehicles, they know they have probably only seen the tip of the iceberg when it comes to all that is involved, and they are sure that you, the Salesperson, are aware of that. Because of this, they fear they will be taken advantage of in some way.

Knowledge is power for sure, but feeling they lack knowledge can make Customers very defensive when dealing with a Salesperson. Though they may have spent a lot of time conducting some research on the Internet, they might also feel overwhelmed by too much information and will be reluctant to show themselves as being weak in this area. Knowing how to put what they have learned from their research into an effective conversation with a Salesperson, may become confusing to them and add to their defensive postures.

Sometimes Customers have had a previous experience at a Dealership that may have made a negative impact on them. This alone can assign you, as a Salesperson, to the category of *crook* before you even get to say *"Hello."* Though most people know this is not really true and that no two people are alike, it may create at least a temporary sense of suspicion that you will need to overcome. When this happens, the Customer may be cautious in giving information and somewhat cynical in their responses until you have sufficiently shown yourself to be worthy of some level of trust.

Many will make initial statements like, *"I am just looking, can I walk around alone, I only have limited time, I am not buying a car today* and *All I want is a brochure."* These initial statements are made to gain control of the process and display a presence of understanding. Understand that they know what you are going to try to do, and that they will not accept that behavior.

More than any other fear that drives a Customer to become defensive is the fear of being ripped off. Today the Internet may be a helpful tool for selling or buying vehicles, but it is also heavily populated with websites that warn car buyers of all the bad things to expect when they go to a Dealership. This of course is understandable when you look at some of the negative reputations that have been a part of our history, but if you were to believe what many of these information websites say, you would think our business was run by the devil himself.

You can't do anything about the negative baggage a

Customer brings to the Dealership when they first arrive, but the way you handle yourself and your presentation can clearly provide an opportunity to release their posture and present you in a different light.

People by nature would normally prefer to trust than to fear. In our business you have to earn trust and sometimes you are earning it on the heels of some other Salesperson or Dealership that shipwrecked the Customers trust in the past. Your integrity and care for the Customer will eventually pay off if you make a concerted effort to ease their fears and disarm their defensive posture through your professional sales process.

Often the emotion that is involved in buying a car can put Customers on the defensive. They know that they are excited about getting a new vehicle, but they may fear exposing that to the Salesperson will make them more vulnerable to being taken advantage of. This is understandable and should not be something that you take personally or it will hinder your own enthusiasm.

If you had the ability to listen to Customer conversations before they got out of their car, you might hear a husband telling his wife that no matter how much she likes what they see, she's not to get visibly excited as it would weaken their ability to remain objective and would give the Salesperson too much ammunition. I have been on test drives where one person wanted to express their excitement and the other one kept trying to put cold water on it. Make sure you don't respond to this by becoming frustrated or defensive yourself. Never pit them against each other thinking this might win the day.

It won't!

You will learn in later chapters that lowering the Customer's defensive posture is actually very easy. It begins with you understanding the Customer and then presenting yourself in a manner that is unexpected by the Customer. In these chapters I am going to share with you proven responses that will take that Customer who is so defensive they do not even want you around them and within 15 seconds develop a relationship of understanding and ease. I will teach you statements that will create an environment of trust and companionship, and will allow for a two hour presentation and demonstration that you can't beat.

And if you don't believe me, then keep reading. And if you want to find out how, again, keep reading. Either way, you have nothing to lose.

CHAPTER 5
HOW THE CUSTOMER VIEWS US

In a 2003 Gallup Poll on honesty and ethics in various professions, nurses received the top ranking while Car Salespeople were at the very bottom, just below HMO Managers. A similar poll done again in December of 2012 had replaced HMO Managers with Members of Congress as the 2nd lowest rated while Car Salespeople were still at the very bottom of the list.

If you accept such things as a valid measurement of public opinion, the last decade hasn't made much of a dent in our industries poor standing with the public. We still have a lot of work ahead of us if public opinion is going to change.

It would be incorrect though to think that all Customers have a negative view of people in our business. In fact, many professional Car Salespeople have tremendous relationships with their Customers who depend upon them for reliable information when they need it and a fair business transaction when they are looking for a car. Of course, this doesn't happen by accident and is usually the result of someone working hard to serve their Customer and earn their business.

Many of the negative stereotypes assigned to Car Salespeople come from the fact that someone who has had a bad experience is more inclined to complain. It's the old adage, 'No news is good news.' In other words, satisfied Customers don't usually go out of their way to publish their experience, so you rarely hear about it unless it's from someone who is unhappy.

While it is true that you can't please everyone, the fact is that if you do your best to meet your Customer's needs and expectations, you won't have to spend that much time worrying about those who complain. If you see this business as a positive profession that provides a good living with a potential for long term success, you will implement those practices that lead to good Customer relations. If that's what you want to do, this book was written for you. As you practice the methods and processes I will teach you, you can avoid being viewed by your Customers as anything but a trusted professional.

Many people view a Car Salesperson as someone who haggles for a living and they feel unprepared to beat them in this combative process. The complexity of everything that goes into a typical car purchase leaves them feeling that they have no other option but to be ready for a battle when they need a new car. Thus, they come to the Dealership expecting to have a fight to the finish until someone wins.

Often, Customers believe that a Car Salesperson has a lot of tricks up their sleeve and make their living by out-smarting the buyer. When the public is asked to give their opinion of Car Salespeople the term most often heard is the word 'slick.' If you Google the words *Car Salesman* on the internet, the images that come up first will depict someone who looks like a shyster smoking a cigar and holding a set of keys with a sly *'you can trust me'* grin on their face. This is a long held view of people in our business and as hard as it is to believe, there are still some Salespeople out there who work hard at being slick.

Unfortunately, as you can see in the Gallup Poll ratings, the negative reputation that has followed our trade has caused many to fear or distrust us before they even have a chance to meet us. They have heard that we are out to get them, so they often come to the Dealership expecting to get robbed in some way or another. Like it or not, there are good reasons for this.

Listen to some of the typical radio ads that run in large metropolitan areas where the competition is thick. You might get the idea that no matter what your credit is like, or what condition your current vehicle is in, you'll be able to get the best deal at the lowest interest rate and thousands for your trade, even if it has to be towed to the Dealership. Some even tell you a paystub is all you need to be qualified for a loan. But at the end of all of these ads there is always a legal disclaimer that is read so fast you couldn't possibly understand it unless you were The Rain Man.

These, of course, are in large part targeted for a certain segment of the population that are driven by emotion or have credit problems and are willing to accept the possibility that it might be real and that the deal is too good not to at least go in and have a look. In many ways the public view of a car Dealership is formed by such promotions. The results often leave Customers feeling that they were deceived by slick ads to bring them in and then pressured to buy once they were there.

Though the average person who manages their finances well and can afford to pay cash or has decent credit will view these ads as something for suckers, they obviously produce a lot of business or Dealerships wouldn't spend the money they do to make them.

How Customers view a Car Salesperson is often related to how Car Salespeople view Customers. If we view the Customers as ignorant sheep to be fleeced, they will certainly respond with suspicion, mistrust and the type of opinions that have been laid at our doorstep for decades.

In a perfect world a Customer would withhold their judgment until they go to a Dealership and meet with a Salesperson. The way that they were treated at that time, and the way they perceived the experience would be based upon that initial encounter. What the Salesperson projected to the Customer at that time would be the basis for how the Customer views them.

Of course, we are not living in a perfect world, but you as an individual Salesperson with integrity and professional training can develop a process and style that puts you in place for this type of business reputation. Stick with me and I will show just how that is done, just as it has been for many other professionals who have studied my materials and put into practice the things we teach in our Training Programs at David Lewis & Associates.

Many opinions of Car Salespeople and Dealerships are handed down from generation to generation as a protective warning to friends and family members. Those who have a good relationship with a Salesperson will obviously send their friends and relatives to that person. Those who don't have such a relationship may be quick to point out the dangers that await anyone who dares to venture on to a car lot carelessly.

Statements like, *"Don't sign anything until you call me,"* or *"Get a second opinion of your trade-in before you do anything"* are typical warnings given to help family and friends avoid being taken advantage of. Someone who has experience in dealing with Car Salespeople will often be recruited to go along to make sure they get a fair deal.

In the case of used car sales, many Dealerships today offer Carfax™ reports or other such things to help eliminate this fear and put the Customer somewhat at ease. The whole idea of 'Certified Pre-Owned Vehicles' was developed as a way to ease used car Customer fears of the prospect of being sold a 'Lemon.'

The Internet has done a lot to change how people prepare to buy a car and in some cases how they actually make the purchase. The fact that so much information is available online today doesn't necessarily mean that Customers feel equipped to engage directly with a Salesperson without being cheated. As much as the industry has been trying to move beyond the negative reputation that has followed us, it is not that easy, as the Gallup Polls clearly show us. Just a few bad apples can upset the effort and rekindle the old fears that things are still the same as they were before.

Here's the good news: you can't do everything, but you can do something. The vision of our Company is to contribute to the growing host of Leaders in our industry who want to change the way we are viewed by the car buying public. But the purpose for this book is to equip you, the working Salesperson and Manager, on how to separate yourself from those who have a negative public opinion. To become one who is a recognized professional known for your skills and integrity, and sought out by buyers looking for someone who will treat them with respect and dignity.

Do you believe that you can be that person? I mean do you really believe it? I do! I am committed to help you become just that, so that you can build a career you will never need to apologize for, and you can have a Customer base that will keep you busy enough to help you accomplish the kind of success that you can be proud of, one that will grow exponentially in the years to come.

CHAPTER 6
HOW WE VIEW THE CUSTOMER

Now that we have looked at how the Customer views us, we need to examine how we in the trade have traditionally viewed the Customer. It stands to reason that the two are directly linked. By that, I mean that the way Customers view the Car Salesperson is a direct result of the view we have held of the Customer. Because of the often cynical adversarial view we have had in the past we sometimes worked the sales process in such a way that the Customer did not feel safe, and instead felt threatened and distrustful. This helped create the negative reputation our business has in public opinion.

Though we have all heard it said that 'buyers are liars', it would be unfair to categorize all Salespeople as feeling that same way. There are many who have always seen themselves as professionals and have viewed their Customers as an integral part of their success. At the same time, it would be dishonest of me to ignore the fact that most Salespeople often harbor a cynical view of the Customer.

Of course, we know that all Customers are not liars, but for those Salespeople who want to justify their shady practices this has worked to alleviate their guilt for a long time. Those of us who plan to make a career in this business would do well to remember that without satisfied Customers we can't accomplish our goals for success.

The best way to view a Customer is to see them through the value they place on what they are trying to achieve in their purchasing decision. Never look at them through your own goals and desires or you will miss what they are trying to tell you about themselves. You must devote yourself to listening to the Customer and continuously reaffirming what they are saying so that you can have a clear picture of what they want and are trying to accomplish it. You can then match that to what you and your Dealership have to offer and it will become a win/win situation.

The next important view you must hold of your Customer is to view them as a friend. Just as you would not want an adversarial relationship with someone who is a friend in your personal life, neither would you want one with someone who is a business acquaintance. If you view your Customer as a friend, you will treat them in a friendly fashion and in most cases they will respond with kindness. People normally respond in respect to how they are treated and it is no different in our business. When a Customer perceives you as a friend they will drop their defensive mechanisms and allow you to better serve them. When this happens, the process becomes a more pleasant and helpful experience and the Customer will give you all the time you need to help them accomplish their goal.

Many sales training methods teach the Salesperson to view Customers through the prism of numbers. In other words, if the average Salesperson closes 20% of their potential Customers and their goal is to sell 15 cars that month, they just need to talk to 70 people and the numbers will work. Though that is a reasonable method of planning when it comes to setting daily goals, the trouble is that the closer you get to the end of the month the more you will tend to churn through Customers, not giving them the proper time to make a great impression and presentation.

Customers are not numbers. They are unique people with specific personalities and specific wants and needs. The more you take the time required to meet those needs, the better your chances of making the sale. Three Customers treated well are worth more than ten that were given a quick run through and rejected as tire kickers.

Always keep in mind that Customers are your bread and butter, and if you view them as such, you will treat them the right way. You don't make anything until the Customer spends their money, and it is a proven fact that most people who come to your Dealership looking for a vehicle will buy one somewhere. Outside of the specific brand they are looking for, you are the next most important factor in their decision making process.

How you view your Customer will not only develop your presentation, it will also develop you as a Salesperson, good or bad. Learning how to put yourself in the Customer's shoes will always be a great help to understanding how best to help them accomplish what they are trying to do. In spite of what many people say about Salespeople, it is not the ability to persuade that wins the day and builds a good career, it is your ability to meet the Customers expectations and by doing so in a way that makes what you do a satisfying experience for both them and you.

When you can do this, you can approach every Customer with confidence and enthusiasm, and you will come to work every day seeing potential for your future and a growing ability to reach your goals as a professional Automobile Salesperson.

CHAPTER 7
PERCEPTION EQUALS REALITY

For the past two chapters I have been dealing with how the Customer and the Salesperson view each other. I hope you have come to appreciate the value of how you present yourself in the process of selling. Everything in life is seen through the filter of our own ideas, and because of this, our reality is based upon our perception of the things around us. There is a quote that truly represents this thought, *"We do not see things as they are. We see them as we are."*

This is especially important when your profession in life requires you to present yourself in a way that is acceptable to those who come to you for such an important business transaction, such as buying a car. Though you may be great in all of the principles and knowledge that your job requires, whether or not your Customers choose to purchase from you will often be decided based on how they perceive you as a person.

If they perceive you as genuine, enthusiastic, knowledgeable, honest and so forth, that goes a long way to determine how much they will open themselves to you so you can correctly discover their wants and needs. Without this, selling cars is like shooting ducks with a blindfold over your eyes. The results will be hit or miss. And it is likely that they will mostly be a miss.

In a very real sense, selling is acting. Not in the negative sense of being something you are not, but in the positive sense of learning how to respond to the other players in a way that is clear, well timed, knowledgeable and rehearsed.

"Rehearsed?" you might be thinking to yourself, "Isn't that fake and phony?"

Not at all! In fact just as great actors will rehearse their lines over and over to make sure they capture what the writer is trying to say and how best to say it with meaning and emotion, so must a great sales professional perfect their knowledge and presentation in such a way that it becomes second nature and requires little acting after a while. This is what separates the professionals and top achievers in our business from those who operate merely to a level of mediocrity. Talent is good, but often talented people come across as entertaining rather than someone with professional excellence. If you, as a Salesperson, are perceived to be acting, you will not impress your client where it really matters.

Selling, like acting, often requires that you adapt some of the emotions and nuances of the Customer, so that you can have a conversation that is natural and effective. If you come across as someone who has just memorized certain lines for information or effect, the Customer will realize this and respond accordingly. In the same way if you are disrespectful and just carry on your own presentation without regard to what the Customer is trying to say or tell you about their wants and needs, you will be seen as self absorbed and not interested in helping them accomplish their goals.

This is not to say that you are to shoot from the hip from Customer to Customer. That is why we help our Salespeople to create effective Word Tracks that are personalized and creative, which will allow the Customer to connect with the Salesperson on a deeper level. These are not only helpful, but they can become a key ingredient of a professional presentation once they become natural and are adapted to fit any circumstance that might occur.

Apart from how the Customer perceives you, it is also critical that you properly perceive your Customer's actions and mannerisms of speech and body language. They too, are often acting out a part they have convinced themselves was necessary to protect them from a Salesperson who might try to outsmart them or convince them to buy something they don't really want or need. Your ability to see past the fears and apprehensions of your Customer will be an important part of your ability to relax the process and make it something that the Customer will perceive as non-threatening and comfortable. This cannot be overstated nor should you underestimate its value to you as a professional Salesperson.

Much like the famous Indian story by John Godfrey Saxe, where he tells of six blind men trying to describe an elephant, depending upon where they stood in relation to the elephant each had a different picture in their mind of what the elephant was like. The first man fell against the elephant's side and described it as a giant wall. The second touched its tusk and described it as a spear. The third man grabbed its trunk and said it was like a snake. One after another the six blind men gave their perception of the elephant and each described only the part that they came in contact with. Each had a valuable insight of the part they touched, but all were wrong as to what the elephant was like as a whole.

Like these men, when we first approach the Customer, we are blind to anything except the very basic perception of them that we have from first glance or initial greeting. We must be patient and allow the Customer time to reveal themselves to us from every angle through the questions they ask and by the way they carry themselves. The way that we respond to our perception of the Customer will create the way that the Customer perceives us.

Too often, as Salespeople, we speak and act too quickly before gaining the right perspective of how the Customer wants to be treated. Often, they will at first, come across as aggressive and very stern in their attitude. This is a self-defense mechanism triggered by fear or pre-determined expectations. If you settle for this, your entire presentation will be like a stuttering man trying to debate a professional linguist. You will quickly fall into a pattern of yes/no answers that lead nowhere and inspire no emotion or provide any real information. You will also most likely be perceived by your Customer as inept and after a few short rounds of this behavior they will say thanks for your time, leave for another Dealership and probably buy a car from someone else.

Selling cars is an art form, and it must be treated as such. It is a highly advanced art form that requires patience, practice, communication, dedication and learning. If it becomes just a game of numbers, the numbers will usually disappoint. When that happens, your job becomes a grueling exercise in futility and you will drag yourself to the Dealership every day viewing your Customers as enemy combatants to be defeated so you can earn your daily bread and pay your bills.

On the other hand, those who develop the skills of learning how to create their perception of the world, and themselves, will usually have great success at whatever they do. This is why for our online video students we recommend that the courses be viewed in the morning before leaving for work. Why? Because your ability to start your day with enthusiasm, creative ideas and confidence can create a positive perception that will carry you through your day and affect you and everyone you come in contact with in a positive way.

Some may view this idea as hocus pocus, but the truth is, you are what you eat. The input that you have in your daily life will affect and create who you are and how you perceive life. This is not psycho babble. It has been proven over and over again by great achievers throughout history.

Your world is what you make it and how you perceive yourself, your life and your career will determine the way others perceive you and ultimately the level of your success you will achieve in life. To quote our industry's founder Henry Ford, *"If you think you can or you think you can't, you are right!"*

Learning to take command of your own mind and emotions, and to control yourself rather than trying to control the Customer, can open up a great door for success and achievement in your life and career. When this happens on a regular basis you can truly enjoy this business as a pathway to your own goals and a genuine platform for helping those you serve as Customers.

CHAPTER 8
FAILING TO UNDERSTAND
CUSTOMER POSTURES

The study of the sales process is not rocket science, but it certainly is scientific in nature. If you didn't do so well in your school science class though, don't get nervous; I'm not going to give you a test. To be truthful, every encounter with a Customer is a test of sorts. Remember the ABC's (Always Be Closing). Either they are selling you or you are selling them. It is easy to misunderstand their intentions if you rely only upon the words they speak to communicate. The body speaks and a person's posture is the first major influence on the impression they make.

In the initial contact with your Customer, it is important to realize that just as you are trying to read their words and behaviors to understand what they want and need, the Customer is also checking you out, as well. They want to know that you are someone they can deal with who is honest, knowledgeable and truly helpful. If they are going to spend tens of thousands of dollars with you, they have a right to know that you will have their interest at heart. Of course, it is of real importance that you do have these character traits of honesty and propriety if you want to have a quality and lasting business relationship with your Customer's.

Understanding how posture communicates what someone is feeling, is very important. There are sitting and standing postures, and both have unique information they will tell you about the Customer's mind-set or emotional state. The handshake is also an important part of a person's communicating posture. Knowing what these mean can give you an advantage for understanding how best to assist your Customers in having a comfortable and beneficial experience with you. Failing to understand what these actions are saying, can hinder your ability to respond properly in your own dialogue and behaviors.

Many body language experts and sources claim that 50-80% of all human communications are non-verbal. With that in mind, it becomes very important to understand at least the basic knowledge of how posture and body language convey meaning in a conversation.

For instance, how close a person will stand to you is an important indication as to whether they are comfortable or not. It is common for someone to keep a bit of distance when first meeting, but if they get closer as the conversation continues it usually indicates they are becoming more comfortable with you and feel less cautious or threatened. If they continue to keep their distance it says that they are uncomfortable and still questioning your intentions.

A perfect example of this is when the Customer states, "*I am just looking*" or "*is it OK if we look around alone.*" This is both a verbal and non-verbal posture. The Customer is telling you that they are scared, apprehensive and very defensive. The manner in which you respond will now be critical. If you respond in a manner that makes them more defensive all you are doing is pushing them farther away. Whereas, if you respond in a manner that releases those fears, they are more likely to come closer and let you spend some time with them.

If they have their arms crossed when you are speaking this generally indicates a defensive emotion or that they are waiting for you to finish talking before deciding how to act. It can also mean disagreement or a sense of helplessness, depending on the situation. Sometimes, while standing, they may place their hands in their pockets or have them tightly clasped at their sides indicating nervousness, insecurity or anxiety. This is a sign that you should take a pause or give them an opportunity to express themselves before going on. If they start pointing their legs or feet in another direction they are ready to move on or get away from what you are saying, you have lost their interest.

When someone wants to keep themselves in check or contain their emotions they will often clench their fingers in a closed hand at the front of their belt or below the stomach area showing they are trying to be patient. If they rest their open palms on their hips or in their back pockets, they are ready for you to stop talking or to move on to another topic.

When their hands are closed in a fist on their hips, it may be a sign of frustration or that they are feeling isolated or are fixed and narrow in their opinion. This can be an important sign that they are not interested in your ideas or suggestions, but desire that you give them what they want no matter what you think. For instance, you may think a woman with several children needs a mini-van and you try to talk her out of the sportier car model she is looking for. If she reacts in this way, you may want to move to the section of the lot that has the sporty model vehicles that peak her interest and quit trying to convince her otherwise. Remember, it's about what they want and not what you want them to have or what you think their budget will allow. As sales champions, we tend to think we know it all. Don't forget this is a buyer initiated sale.

When a man stands with one fist on his hip this is called 'locking horns' and shows that he thinks you are being disrespectful or insulting his intelligence; especially if he is with his wife or loved ones. However, when a woman makes that same gesture she is in the 'tell me more' mode. This is normally a time to capitalize on the moment, because you have her full attention and have found a hot button. This is time to drive the sale home.

Postures that are displayed when someone is sitting are also very informative and important to the process. If someone is leaning forward when you are speaking, it shows they are interested in what you are saying. If they tend to lean back in a reclining posture they are relaxed and comfortable, but not necessarily sold. It may also mean they may be losing interest and this says you are talking too much. When that happens you might want to focus on a point of interest like a special feature of the vehicle or ask them something about their favorite topic; themselves. Three statements that can draw them back into the conversation are, *"Did you know?"*, *"What do you think?"* and *"How about this?"*

Men tend to sit with both feet parallel on the ground when they are comfortable and women will generally cross one leg over the other with their hands in their lap when they feel the same way. On the other hand when someone lacks confidence they will lower their torso towards the ground a bit and let their hands fall in front of them resting on their legs. This means that they lack information and you have more work to do.

If they are leaning slightly forward with their chin resting upon their closed hand, it signifies serious thinking, planning or decision making. At this time you may want to ask something about any points you have already covered or if they have questions about them. But this is also a time to be cautious, because this is when their true objections normally will come out, and you don't want to talk too much. Questions are always objections at this point, and they are always looking for a way out. Don't worry, you have them sold. Just don't talk, let them do the talking. This is where the old adage, *"He who talks first loses"* comes in.

Tactical table positioning is also critical and very simple. Always sit close to your gender and never in between, or close, to the opposite sex. A mistake a lot of Salespeople make is to try to earn points with the client by spending 'way too much' time with their children. This shows weakness. Recognize them and put them in the picture, but don't lose focus on why the Customer is there.

Body language, facial expressions and eye contact are

important signals that can help you understand someone's mood or how they are feeling about your conversation or a given situation. Learning how to interpret these things can be most helpful to you as a Salesperson. You must be careful to consider them collectively, rather than just to take each individual posture and assign a meaning to it.

You don't want to get too obvious when studying your Customers body language to the point where you appear to be examining them. This can be annoying and rude, and they may put forth false impressions to cover up what they are truly thinking or feeling. A simple look in the eyes sometimes will do the trick.

As you can see, your understanding of body language and postures is critical. But remember this: it all starts before you even shake hands. By the time you meet the Customer they have already made some assumption, of whether they will trust you or not, so always assume they don't and you will win every time.

CHAPTER 9
PUT YOURSELF IN YOUR
CUSTOMERS SHOES

As a Salesperson, you must always remember that your most powerful tool is your ability to satisfy the Customer. When you have studied your craft, work hard and do your best to meet the needs of your Customers, you can earn a good living and feel good about the trade you have chosen as a career.

Empathy is a powerful force for good. When you have a genuine desire to see others succeed and want them to experience fulfillment, you are on the right road to your own happiness and success. The best way to experience that is to take the time to see how someone else's shoes feel when they are on your feet.

In the car business, there are a lot of opportunities to do the right thing, but they are often passed over for fear of loss. The important part that the automobile plays in the typical American life is indisputable, except for a very small portion of people in our society who are opposed to things like progress or modernization. Without a car, you become very restricted in what you can do in modern America. With that in mind, your job as a car Salesperson plays an integral part in helping those who come to you looking for a vehicle to experience pleasure and a sense of fulfillment in their lives.

Does it sound too heroic to think that your job has a very important part to play in helping others find happiness and peace in their life? If you have ever had to live with a vehicle that was continuously letting you down or was not dependable, you understand exactly what I'm talking about. Life can be very stressful when you have car problems, especially when you can't get to the places you need to go to make your life work.

On the other hand, some people just buy a new car because they feel like it's time for a change. Helping them is just as important, because they are trying to do something that adds perceived value to their lives and they are asking you to help them do it.

"But how do I put myself in someone else's shoes to see how that feels?" you might be asking. The truth is, in most cases the Customer is already showing you their shoes. But you're so busy working your sales process and trying to get them to wear the shoes you want them to wear, that you don't have time to try theirs on. From the moment a Customer shows up on the lot most Salespeople have one thought that dominates their mind and their actions: *"What do I need to do to sell this person a car today?"*

I'd like to help you change that. If you let me, I guarantee you will be glad that you did. How do I know? I have talked to Dealers, Managers and yes, Salespeople all over North America and I've found something that is quite amazing: Salespeople who see their position as one of helping the Customer reach their goals generally go home at night feeling like they have done something worthwhile and they usually make a good living in the process.

There's no better way to accomplish this than to put yourself in the shoes of the person that you are trying to help. To listen so well to what they are saying and be so committed to meeting and exceeding their expectations that you actually know what their wants and needs are, because they have become your wants and needs for them as well.

That's not saying that you don't do your part as the Salesperson. You still want to greet the Customer with all the confidence and enthusiasm that you can muster up, so you can believe in what you are doing. Remember, it's not about you, it's about them! They come to your Dealership looking to meet their needs, not yours. When you take that on as your personal mission your needs will be met too.

When you make your selling process about meeting your Customer's needs you will find that you too get what you are looking for. Do you want to make a good commission? Of course you do and satisfied Customers are proven to be more profitable both at the time of purchase and in the long term residual business they represent. Do you want to build a lasting and growing career? Of course you do, and the best way to do that is one satisfied Customer at a time.

When this happens, you have put on their shoes and you will know how they feel: You're not going to sell them something that isn't a good fit, like a pair of shoes that doesn't fit right. They may feel okay for a few days, but after a while your feet start hurting and you realize they are the wrong size, shape or style for you. So it is with a car that was pushed on someone who really wanted and needed something different, but succumbed to the Salesperson's power and ability to convince them otherwise. It happens every day and it helps to reinforce the negative opinion that many have of those in our business.

It doesn't have to be that way. Trying on someone else's shoes often starts with looking at the old pair they wore in. If they have a vehicle they plan to trade-in what does it say about them? What do they say about it? Are they trading it in because they liked it so much they drove it until it wouldn't go anymore and now they need another one that will serve them in the same way? Or maybe the car they bought ten years ago was before they had children and now they have three. Do you think they may be looking for something different? Put yourself in their shoes and ask yourself, *"What would I want if that was me?"*

On the other hand, maybe they have just sent their last kid off to college and they are ready for a little fun time for themselves. Don't assume because they are past fifty that they want a four door sedan. They may want a sporty model that will give them a chance to feel young again. They've earned it, haven't they? Let them tell you what they want and need, and when you help them find it they will appreciate you for a job well done. They will come back to you when they need to buy again and will send family and friends your way as referrals. You will become *their* Automobile Salesperson.

Listen, affirm, ask, and listen!

Listen to what they have to say. Affirm that you have heard them correctly. Ask questions that will give you more information. Listen for what more they have to tell you. Each step of the way you put your feet a little deeper into their shoes and pretty soon they fit so well you can tie the laces. You know what they like and you know how it's going to make them feel: It's going to be the same way it would make you feel if you were in their shoes.

That doesn't mean that you won't sell them a convertible just because they have kids. If that's what they want, do your best to make them happy. Just make sure it's what THEY want rather than what YOU want to sell them.

Remember, selling and telling are two different things. When you *listen* to your Customers you have a much better chance of finding out what it is that they really want. If you spend your time *telling* Customers what they want you may find yourself always in need of new Customers, because the ones you had before don't come back to see you again. Their feet hurt too much from the last pair you talked them into and they will choose to look elsewhere for a better fit the next time they go shopping for shoes.

.

CHAPTER 10
THE 5 VARIABLE CONDITIONS

Understanding your Customer is critical to developing the proper approach to your sales process. Learning how to differentiate between negative and positive emotions and responses will be a critical tool for having a successful and lasting relationship with your Customers.

As I have already mentioned, one of the great misconceptions about sales is that you have to be a great talker in order to succeed. While this is not necessarily true in the way it is often depicted, your ability to be inspiring and creative in the use of words and unique verbiage begins with understanding how Customers view your presentation and why they respond the way that they do. If your words and actions are perceived as 'slick' and 'manipulating', they will become defensive. If, on the other hand, they perceive you as professional and informative, they will be open and inspired.

With this in mind, there are certain conditions that occur during the sales process that you must be aware of that are connected to what you say and how they respond, and they are:

- Pressure
- Defensiveness
- Control
- Posture
- Impulse

Do these conditions affect your sales? Of course they do. Pushing through a sales presentation without properly understanding its impact on your Customer can drastically reduce your level of success.

Do they affect Dealership profits? Yes! There is plenty of industry research and documentation that shows that pressured Customers are harder to sell, pay less for their purchase and are less likely to return to the same Dealership to buy again.

So, let's take a look at each of these conditions and see how they affect the Customer and the potential for a successful sales experience.

➢ *Pressure*

The potential for pressure words and actions to hinder a successful sale cannot be understated. From the Customer's point of view, pressure is the primary problem when dealing with car Salespeople, and in many ways it is central to the negative reputation our industry has had with buyers.

The best way to avoid this is to put yourself in the Customer's shoes and imagine how you would feel being approached in the same way. It is not a pleasant experience for sure and usually will result in a combative Customer or one who goes elsewhere to purchase.

How do we define *pressure* in relationship to the sales process?

• Pressure is *the exertion of force* used on the Customer to get them to do what you want. Though it may manifest itself in many ways throughout a sales presentation, it will always make the Customer uncomfortable and defensive. Putting pressure on your Customer will just reinforce the negative stereotype people have of the car Salesperson.

• Pressure is also defined as *a moral force that compels.* This does not necessarily mean that it is a negative moral force, but it can be, and it is often used that way in our business. Trying to persuade the Customer to purchase something that is not what they are looking for is an example of the negative use of this kind of pressure. Often the ability to do this is considered a 'gift' in a Salespersons skill-set, but it usually results in an unhappy Customer who later has buyer's remorse.

• A third definition of pressure is *an urgent demand.* It is not uncommon in car sales for a Customer to be presented with a 'today only' deal that forces them to make a decision they are not ready to make. Many Salespeople and Managers alike often use such tactics to motivate the Customer to make a decision through fear of loss. There are many ways to use this type of pressure, but all of them show a lack of consideration for the Customer's true wants and needs.

• Finally, pressure can be *a burdensome condition that is hard to bear.* This can be a pressure that does not necessarily initiate with the Salesperson, but is related to a feeling of necessity that is forcing the Customer to buy. It may be that their current car is not meeting their needs, has too many miles or is broken down and needs expensive repairs that make it necessary to buy another, even though they weren't really planning to purchase a new vehicle at the present time.

All of these types of pressures can create tension between the Customer and the Salesperson. If you do not properly know how to relieve these pressures your ability to make a presentation that results in a satisfied Customer will be jeopardized.

How do we relieve the Customers pressure?

Your ability to relieve the Customers pressure will depend upon how well you discern what pressures they are experiencing. You can lower them by listening to what the Customer wants and needs before making your presentation. The words you use and the questions you ask must be directed at helping them achieve their goals and inspiring them with your professionalism and genuine desire to help.

Avoid pressure words like *now* and *today* in your presentation. Ask their permission to proceed during each step of the sales process and show them respect by the way you address them with your unique and inspiring verbiage. Make your presentation more like a conversation and less like an interrogation process.

Give the Customer the appropriate time and attention to experience what you have to offer without forcing them into your process. Stay away from questions about price, payment or credit. Instead focus on those things that are important to them and thoroughly demonstrate the benefits offered by your product, your Dealership and by you, their Sales Representative.

Understanding your Customer is essential for lasting success in this business and correctly interpreting their words and actions is critical as well. The natural result of not doing so brings us to our next condition:

➢ *Defensiveness*

When a Customer senses or feels they are being pressured by the Salesperson they will become defensive and resist every effort to make a thorough presentation and successful sale. They may lie about their intentions or give only partial information in response to your questions.

Defensiveness as it relates to the sales process can be defined as:

• The act of protection

• The goal of resisting an attack

• To guard against pressure

• A position or attitude

When a Customer is defensive they are attempting to protect themselves from something they feel can be dangerous. They may feel helpless or unable to compete with an experienced Salesperson. If they perceive you as a force to be reckoned with, they will set up their defensive mechanisms to guard against you as an enemy attacker. This may include adopting a position or attitude that makes it hard to discover what their wants and needs are so you can help them.

All of these defensive conditions are natural responses to the fears and apprehensions that Customers bring with them when they come to an automobile Dealership. There are certain questions and statements that must be avoided or they will increase the Customer's defensive posture and limit your ability to lower their defenses. Questions and statements like:

• Are you buying a car today?

• Who else will be involved in the buying decision?

• What is your budget?

• Park the car in the sold line.

• If we can come together on terms and numbers, are you ready to buy a car today?

• What is your phone number? (when requested too early during a phone up)

Though common to the typical sales presentation, they are harmful to your ability to develop trust and communications with your Customer. They must be avoided if you are to help them relax and become less defensive and more open to your process.

There are certain statements you can make that will

help you relieve the Customer's defensiveness. These are:

- Information gathering

- Give you brochures and prices to take home

- Shopping process

- You can control the clock

All of these show your interest in the Customers well being and recognition of their right to be treated with respect and integrity. They will set you apart from other Salespeople and create an atmosphere of trust and comfort that will lower their defenses and allow you to make a professional sales presentation. But do not misunderstand me, you will still ask for the sale at the end of the presentation, that is, when you have earned the right to do so.

This now leads us to the next condition:

➤ *Control*

The third factor that creates a negative environment for selling is the issue of *Control*. The following are definitions of control as it relates to the sales process:

- To exercise restraint or direction over

- To dominate

- The act of regulating

When Customers feel that you are trying to control them
or their purchase decisions, they will automatically
resist your efforts to do so. The reason this is important
to them is because they fear that losing control will
cause them to:

• Make an impulsive decision

• Make a decision they will later regret

The best way to overcome the Customer's fear of losing
control is to do everything you can to let them believe
they are actually in control. This is accomplished by
listening to and confirming that you have a correct
understanding of what they are hoping to accomplish;
and doing your best to help meet their needs and
desires.

Your ability to be understanding and informative will
allow them to feel as though they are in the decision
making process and you are there to help them
accomplish their goals. The next condition is:

➤ *Posture*

As I have already mentioned in a previous chapter, a
person's posture can tell you a lot about how and what
they are feeling. In the sales process, posture is defined
as:

• A state, situation or frame of mind

• An affected or unnatural attitude

- A mental or spiritual attitude

- A developed policy or standard

Learning how to correctly read body language and facial expressions can help you recognize what the Customer is feeling or experiencing during your presentation. Often, Customers come into a Dealership with a pre-determined state of mind that makes it difficult to gain enough ground in the conversation to help them. Your ability to recognize these things can help you to empathize with the Customer and find a way to show them that you understand and have had similar experiences or feelings yourself.

What would make someone have a pre-determined posture when first coming to your Dealership?

- Past experiences

- News clips, articles or movies

- A friend, family member or co-worker

There are many reasons why some Customers come to your Dealership already prepared to resist your presentation and attempt to help them. Often Customers are reacting to a previous negative experience and that has given them an affected or unnatural attitude.

They may have read or heard something negative about car Salespeople or even watched one of the movies that depict them as shysters and cons. They may have had a negative report coming from a family member or friend who had a bad buying experience.

What is the best way to lower their defensive posture under this situation?

• Do the unexpected

• Be unique and inspiring

By taking an inspiring and positive approach you can help unwind the negative threads that are binding them and reassure them that you are someone who can be trusted to protect their interest. You can reduce their defensive posture by catching them *pleasantly off guard* and by your unique and inspiring attitude and presentation. The final condition is:

➢ *Impulse*

Impulse as it relates to the sales process would be defined as:

• The influence of a particular feeling or mental state

• A sudden involuntary inclination prompting action

• A compelling action or force

We know that 70-80% of automobile purchases are made on an impulse. We also know that the one step people fear that will increase their impulse to make the purchase is the Demonstration Drive. Unfortunately, our percentage of Demonstration Drives only hovers around 60%. Yet we all know that the odds of selling someone a car are greatly increased if a Demonstration Drive is done.

Ironically, many people are fearful of taking a Demonstration Drive. Their fear is based around the concerns that they might like the car and then want to buy it, and they will then make an impulsive decision to do so.

You will learn in Chapter 16 that there is actually a step that you can add to your sales process that will actually make that defensive fear go away and greatly increase your odds of them taking the car for a drive. Once on the drive how you act, communicate and respond to any questions or comments can now make or break how their impulses will react.

CHAPTER 11
THE CUSTOMERS VIEW OF OUR SALES PROCESS

Have you ever wondered what it feels like to be a Customer looking to purchase a vehicle? What are their thoughts, concerns and worries? Sure they're excited, but why are they so defensive? What makes them so scared and nervous?

Well the answer is simple: we do. As Salespeople we utilize a process that is designed to make them defensive. Our sales process often creates an environment of concerns and worries that makes them feel uncomfortable and needing to protect themselves.

Consider this very common scenario:

A Customer pulls into the lot with the intentions of starting their shopping process for a new car. They are NOT ready to buy today, but plan to make a purchase within the next couple of weeks. Upon arrival, and usually before they are out of their car, a Salesperson approaches them ready to start the sales process. There's a brief introduction and then the typical barrage of questions: *"What are you looking for? What is your budget? Do you have a trade? How much do you owe on your trade? What do you think your trade is worth? Are you paying cash or financing?"*

All of these questions only mean one thing to the

Customer: the Salesperson wants to sell them a car. Not in a couple of weeks like they had planned, but today. Thus, you now have a Customer whose defensive posture is reaching for the heavens.

No matter what the Customer had already planned to say or do at this point, they've been knocked off center and will often respond with something like, *"Oh, I'm just looking"* or *"Is it OK if I just walk around and look at what you have?"*

At this point, the Salesperson may say, *"Sure! I'll walk with you just in case you see something you like and have any questions."* Now the Customer has become even more defensive. Why? Because the Salesperson is not listening to their request. The more defensive they become, the more likely the Salesperson is going to continue with this approach, because the Salesperson is getting resistance to their request, with no concern about the Customers request.

At this point they would like to be left alone, but the Salesperson is following them around the lot asking even more questions, such as, *"What is your timeline for making a decision?"* or *"Is there anyone else that will be involved in the buying decision?"*

Without even knowing anything about the Customer's true wants and needs, they have been made to feel like they are being interrogated to see what they can afford. As most Salespeople have been trained, it is all about their budget. Why waste time showing them a car they cannot afford?

Now their defenses keep rising and they would probably like nothing better than to get out of there before being pressured into doing something they don't want to do. If nothing else, they would like to be left alone while they look at your inventory, but they already realize you're part of the deal by now.

The fact finding mission continues with a repeat of the earlier questions. *"Will you be trading in your car today?" If you want, I can get my Used Car Manager to do an appraisal to see what it is worth." Do you have any idea what you want for it?"*

"I'm not sure what I'm doing yet" states the Customer, *"but I don't like to make rash decisions so let me just look around to see if there's anything I like."* The frustration rises as they feel like they are in the grip of someone who is relentless.

"We have so many vehicles on sale today," states the Salesperson, *"why don't we go into my office and sit down and I can go over the list of what's on sale and make it a lot easier for you. Once I know what you are looking for we can eliminate a lot of time and energy and find one that suits you. Depending on your credit you can probably drive out today with a great deal in the payment range you're looking for today."*

The Salesperson has now put them on the spot and asked questions they are not ready to answer. This practically guarantees that the Customer will give untruthful responses while they figure out how to get out from under this pressure. If they do come into the office they now are so set in a defensive mode that everything the Salesperson does or says will seem to them like they are in mortal combat.

Now put yourself in this Customers shoes. All the Salesperson has done so far has created red flags that just confirm everything they expected to hear from someone whose only desire is to make a sale today. From here on out, anything the Salesperson does to diffuse the emotional pressure will be like fighting an uphill battle.

Let's not forget the trial closes which are sure to increase the pressure even more. Like the most common one, *"If we can come together on terms and numbers are you ready to buy a car today?"* Sometimes this is stated before the Customer even drives the car.

Maybe they have managed to get the Customer to take a test drive and as they pull back on to the lot the Salesperson says, *"Why don't you park the car in the sold line over there so no other Sales Representative can sell it before we get a chance to work out the numbers for you and negotiate the price."*

All of these phrases and methods are designed to control the Customer and each time they are utilized it actually diminishes the chances of making a sale. They certainly weren't created to establish a great working relationship or build Customer friendship and loyalty. With things like the 'Manager Turnover' still ahead and the likelihood of having their trade low balled, is it any wonder people have such a low opinion of the car sales process?

Think of how this would make you feel if you were in the Customer's shoes looking to buy a car and some Salesperson treated you in the way this Customer was treated. They left their home excited about the prospect of shopping for a new car and instead they had an experience that made them feel like they narrowly escaped alive.

If you do not think that your sales process mimics this one you might want to take an honest look at how you do it. I think you will be very surprised.

As a Salesperson, one of your primary goals is to knock down barriers, not build them up. Our existing process is what creates these situations, not the Customer. Ironically, people want to be sold; they just don't want to be pressured.

We already know that most Customers arrive at the Dealership in a very defensive mode. The goal of our sales process must be designed around lowering that posture, not raising it. The lower it becomes, the easier it will be to close the deal. The lower it becomes, the higher the gross will be. I cannot tell you how many times I have seen awesome presentations, ones that are truly inspiring, yet the Salesperson cannot understand why they did not make the sale. The reason is simple: they just did not get their Customer's posture down low enough when it came time to ask for the sale.

Let's use a 1 – 12 posture scale, and place 12 as the highest defensive level. Let's say that most Customers arrive on the lot with a posture scale of 8. The

Salesperson does a cordial Meet & Greet, is well dressed and groomed, and appears to initially be honest and sincere, so the Customers posture drops to a 7.

Next, come the qualifying questions: *"What is your budget? Are you paying cash or financing? Do you have a trade? How much do you want for your trade? What do you owe on your trade?"* And finally, *"What is your timeline for making a purchase?"*

Well guess what? Those questions have made the Customer even more defensive, so now you are up to a defensive posture of 9.

Why do these questions make the Customer more defensive? Because they are questions that relate to making a sale; questions about their budget, their trade, and especially the one about their buying timeline. Remember, most Customers visit the Dealership in a shopping and investigative mode. Sure, many will make a purchase if they find a car they love, but their intent when they make their initial visit is that of a shopper, not a buyer.

Two things are now going to happen. The Customer will either answer the questions or they will deflect the questions with a demand.

If they answer the questions they will most likely reply with false information; especially to the question about their budget. Why do they do that? Again, it is out of fear. Fear of trying to obtain the best deal possible. I know if my budget was $400 per month and you asked me for that figure I would low ball you and state that it was $300 per month.

Now, with that false budget the Salesperson invests the next hour or so presenting and demonstrating cars that only fit that budget amount, without any regard to what the Customer actually desires. Guess what happens now on the defensive posture meter? The Customer is now at a 12, and the odds of selling anyone over the level of a 4 are virtually impossible.

What about the Customer who makes the demand after all of those qualifying questions are asked? You know the demand like, *"We are just looking, is it OK if we walk around alone?"*

How have we been trained to respond? With this comment: *"I would be happy to walk around with you as I know the inventory very well and this way if you have any questions I will be present to answer them for you."*

You now have a Customer that has again risen to a 12 on the defensive meter. Why? Because you are not listening to them, they want to walk around alone and you are forcing yourself on them.

But let's assume you have done a good job with the Meet & Greet, Qualification and Selection steps. The Customer appears to be enjoying their experience so far and thus their posture has dropped to a 5 on the defensive meter. Then when it comes time to ask them to drive the car, they are reluctant. So you make a statement like, *"Well you wouldn't buy a pair of shoes without trying them on first, would you?"*

Not only have you compared the purchase of a car to buying a pair of shoes, but you have also applied pressure. Most Customers are very fearful of taking a Demonstration Drive as they do not want to actually fall in love with the car since they did not come in today to actually make a purchase. So now you have applied pressure again and the Customer is back up to an 8 on the defensive meter scale.

Assuming the process goes your way, the Customer does decide to drive the car, and during the drive they truly start to fall in love with the car. That new car smell is exciting them; they love the comfortable seats and can actually visualize themselves owning the car. With this level of enjoyment the Customer now drops back down to a 5 on the defensive meter scale.

Unfortunately, most of us have been trained to talk during the Demonstration Drive and we ask questions like, *"How does it drive? How does it handle? How is the visibility? Where will you be taking your first trip in your new car?"* and finally, *"Who will be the first person you will be showing your new car to?"*

BAM! Their defensive posture is now back up to an 8 on the meter.

To make matters worse, upon arriving back at the Dealership you tell the Customer to park the car in the sold row, that way no one else will look at the car while we negotiate the price. Guess what, you are now back up to a 12.

Next, comes the Walk Around presentation, which in most cases will again lower their defensive posture. If you have done a great job, maybe it comes down to a 7 or 8 on the defensive meter. Now, comes that infamous trial close: *"If we can come together on terms and numbers are you ready to buy the car today?"* What do you think happens now to their defensive posture? YUP...right back up to a 12 again.

This is not the process of a truly professional Salesperson. This is the process of a Salesperson who pressures 8 – 10 Customers a month to buy a car. This is a process that builds barriers instead of working to knock them down.

Make a commitment to yourself not to be the Salesperson I have just described. If you already are selling like this, make the decision to change and take the actions needed to do so. You are already half way there by reading this book. Go the rest of the way and adapt the principles I teach here into your style of selling. Take ownership of them and they will become yours in no time at all.

I assure you I did not pick these methods out of the air just so I could write a book about understanding Customers. I have lived them and proven them in over thirty years of being in the car business and I know they work. I have taught them in Dealerships and seminars across North America and have seen how they impact the success of those who are willing to learn, practice and apply them to the process of selling cars. They will not only propel you upward as a professional

Salesperson, but more importantly, they will make your Customers glad to do business with you, knowing that you have their best interest at heart.

When you can stop selling and telling, and can focus your efforts on lowering your Customer's anxiety's and fears about the car sales process, guess what? You win! If they were planning to buy, they will buy from you, and when they buy again they will come back to you knowing that you will treat them with respect. So always do your best to make their experience one they can truly enjoy.

This is the mark of a true professional. This is what makes those who experience real success in our business so valuable to the Customers they serve.

CHAPTER 12
WHY SHOULD I BUY A CAR FROM YOU?

So far, we have looked at things like the Customer's mindset, postures and defensive actions, as well as, the Salesperson's response to these things. We have discussed the Customer's view of our business, our sales process and our view of the Customer as well. We've observed the behaviors of our Customers and shown that reality is whatever someone perceives it to be in their mind. Hopefully, you are getting a clearer picture of the things that you must prepare for if you are going to reach the goals you have for success in your career. Certainly understanding your Customer is at the heart of everything you do as a professional Salesperson.

It should be obvious to you by now that earning a Customer's business is not something that just happens. It is the result of a quality presentation based upon a clear understanding of what the Customer wants and needs, followed by a commitment to do your best to deliver just that. To do this, you must not only respect the Customer and the opportunity you have been given to serve them, but you must also understand the value of a professional approach to doing this business. Unless you are certain that you will do more for the Customer and treat them better than anyone else they may encounter at another Dealership, you have not done everything you can to earn their business.

Does this mean you can't sell a car unless you meet all of these qualifications? Not necessarily. But it does mean that you are not ready to become a Leader in the profession you are working in. Leaders always want to do their best and never settle for second best. They know the value of loyal Customers and they treasure them for what their business brings to their life and career.

What better way to understand what it is like for the Customer who has come to your Dealership looking for a car than to ask yourself the question, *"Why should they buy a car from me?"* Have you ever asked yourself that? Do you truly have a good answer that isn't just another sales pitch you've picked up along the way? I mean, if it's just the price or the model line-up that you offer, they certainly can find that somewhere else. Since most Dealerships work from the same price structure or wholesale trade-in books it is likely that they could work the same deal you are offering them at a number of other Dealerships. Most can get the same finance rates, factory incentive programs and option packages that you offer them. So what is the difference that would make them buy from you?

When I visit Dealerships I always ask the Salespeople, *"If I lived in your area, stopped in to shop for a car at your Dealership, why should I buy a car from you?"* And consistently they state the same things. They say, *"Because you will like me, because we have a great product, a great selection, a great service department, we are a community oriented Dealership and because I will take care of you after the sale."*

Well that all sounds wonderful, but I hate to be the bearer of bad news. You see, everybody states those reasons. Every time I ask, I get the exact same response. If everybody is stating the same reason, what sets one Salesperson or Dealership apart from another one? The answer is NOTHING.

We all sound alike. We all state the same thing each and every time. The reason being, we all studied from the same playbook. And the worst part of all is this play-book was written over 30 years ago. We have all been stating the same reasons why a Customer should buy from us for years. We sound like a broken record.

I happen to be a big poker player. I love the game. I think it is because you don't have to have the best hand to win. You just have to utilize the best strategies.

Now for you poker players, would you ever consider playing a game of poker with me with your cards face up, and my cards face down? Of course not. Why? Because that would give me a competitive edge over you. If I can see your cards I can develop a more beneficial strategy.

Unfortunately, the Customer who visits your Dealership already has that same competitive edge over you. The reason being, our cards are already face up. They already know what we are going to say, when we are going to say it, and how we will be saying it. Thus, they are able to strategize in advance of their visit to the Dealership.

The reason I should buy a car from you is because you are unique and different from the other Salespeople I will or have visited in my shopping process. Because you don't say the same things that the others state, and you surely do not make the statements or ask the questions the Customer will expect.

There is really only one answer to this question of *"Why should I buy a car from you,"* and I hope by now you are getting the picture. The one thing they can't get anywhere else is YOU; a Salesperson who is different, unique and inspiring. A Salesperson who does not state the expected, and who presents their product, personality and Dealership in a manner that was not what the Customer expected.

With that in mind, it might be a good time now to review your sales process. What are you thinking about when you first approach a Customer who is coming to your Dealership? Are you sizing them up for a knockout punch or looking for an opportunity to find out what they want and how you can help them find it? When you see that they are defensive at first do you think of ways to take advantage of their vulnerability or do you look for ways to help them become more comfortable and less threatened? Do you recognize that the better you serve your Customer, the better the chances are that you will make the sale and get a fair profit in the process?

Today it's not enough to have the cheapest price or the slickest ads. You have Customers who know what they want and most have done their research online before ever coming to your Dealership. They may have already been to several other Dealerships before yours and have been treated poorly, giving them an even more defensive posture than you would normally expect. Are you prepared to be the difference that makes the difference?

If you want to make it to the top in this business there is no better place to start than where you are right now. When you take a personal inventory of your own skills, methods and Customer care philosophy, how do you rank yourself? On a scale of 1-10 where would you place yourself if you were a Customer coming to buy a car from you? If you can't answer this with some factual basis for your rating, it is time to start finding out where you stand. Only then can you take the necessary steps for improvement.

Today, if you call most companies or make an internet purchase they will often ask your permission to do a brief survey at the end of the call or online experience. Why do they do this? They want to know that their representatives and website are delivering the kind of service their Customers expect and deserve. They know that if they aren't doing that they will lose business to other competing companies. That's smart. We should have the courage to adapt that to our business. But even if the Dealership doesn't do it, you can do it for yourself.

Have you ever thought of asking your previous Customers how they felt about their dealings with you as a Salesperson? It might take a little bit of convincing at first, but if they feel you are sincerely trying to find ways to improve the buying experience for your

Customers they will probably be honest with you. Don't just do it off the cuff, but take the time to put together several questions that might help you evaluate the service you offer.

Take a tip from some of those companies who have surveyed you. They usually ask questions that could have a realistic impact on a Customer. Here's a few that I might want to ask if it were me:

- Was I polite and courteous to you when you came to our Dealership?

- Did you feel that I answered all of your questions in a clear and concise manner?

- Did you feel I was genuinely concerned with helping you find the vehicle you wanted?

- Did you feel I was pressuring you in any way during my presentation?

- Did I explain the features and benefits of the vehicle to your satisfaction?

- Was the Demonstration Drive and Walk Around helpful in making your decision?

- Is there anything I can do to improve the Demonstration Drive and Walk Around?

- On a scale of 1-10 (10 being the highest) how would you rate my service to you as a Sales Representative?

- On the same scale how would you rate your overall experience at our Dealership?

- What suggestions would you have for me that can help me better serve you as a Customer?

- Would you want to do business again with me in the future?

Again, we can see the value of putting yourself in the shoes of your Customer. Learning what makes them tick and what motivates them in the area of their transportation wants and needs will put you far above the competition and improve your chances to satisfy your Customers and achieve personal success and a growing Customer base.

As Salespeople we often rely upon the next person coming to the lot to be the sale we are looking for. We sit and wait and expect the next Customer to provide an opportunity for our success. That's not the way of a winner. Winners create opportunities by making the best of every chance they have to turn their Customers into loyal satisfied clients for life. They realize that the people coming to their Dealership have a need to fulfill and they eagerly work with their Customers to help them accomplish that plan.

Discovering the things about yourself and your sales process or presentation that can help you become better at what you do for a living makes perfect sense, but it doesn't come easily. Sometimes it requires outside help as it is often difficult to see things about ourselves that need to be improved.

That is why I write the books that I write and travel the

country trying to help others learn and develop the things I have learned in this business. Our training programs come from not only my experience in the business, but from other professionals who work with me to develop the best and most current materials available on the market. We monitor the industry on a daily basis to find ways to improve what we do, and we recommend that our Dealership clients do the same.

Don't ever settle for the status quo when it comes to your own life and career. Find out how to be the best and put forth every effort you can to improve your skills and to achieve all that you can in this business. When you have done that, you can look any Customer in the eye and give a clear explanation as to why they should buy a car from you. They should buy a car from you because you guarantee that you will do your very best to be professional and knowledgeable at what you do and will make every effort to help them accomplish their purchase goals. They should buy a car from you because you are committed to meeting and exceeding their every expectations and will work harder than anyone else to earn their business.

When you truly mean this and can communicate that to your Customers in your words and in your actions, the potential for your success in this business is really unlimited.

CHAPTER 13
OBSTACLES VERSUS OBJECTIONS

We are now going to look at some of the Obstacles and Objections that all Salespeople must prepare for if they are to expect any real success in this business. It is natural for Customers to put Obstacles in front of us until they are sure that they trust the person they are dealing with. These are different from the Objections that will occur later during the closing process, but they are just as powerful for dismantling your presentation and, when not dealt with properly, they can stop you from ever getting to the Close.

Often when a Customer first comes to an Automobile Dealership, they are reluctant to cooperate in any way. They know they want or need to purchase a car, but they have fears and concerns that cause them to put roadblocks in front of the Salesperson until they can figure a strategy that will allow them to accomplish their goal and get what they want.

Whether these fears and concerns come from past dealings that they had with other purchases or just from the perceptions that many have in their minds about car Salespeople and Dealerships, it doesn't matter. What matters is whether you as a Salesperson are able to overcome these Obstacles and move forward in the process of earning the Customers business. Until you are able to break through by being unique and inspiring, and can start to lower the defensive mechanisms the Customer has in place, you cannot truly begin your sales process.

For many people, buying a car is like going to war. They would rather not do it, but the resources that they need to carry on their life are in this foreign country (the Dealership), under the control of an enemy (the Manager), and in order to get them they have to do battle with an opponent (known as a Salesperson).

Like anyone headed into a battle for the first time, they may have some idea of what they think will occur, but often, when they get there, things are not exactly like they had imagined so they have to regroup and make a new battle plan. It is during this time of re-strategizing that they throw obstacles in the path of their opponent, to give them time to evaluate the situation and decide how best to win the war.

If you, the Salesperson, are able to convince them that you are not the enemy, they will give you the opportunity to earn their business. Until you do so they will try to keep a safe distance from you by throwing Obstacles in your path. If you aren't able to convince them that you are not the enemy, their defensive posture will never reach a point of where they will fall in love with a car, get low enough to actually make a sale, and if either of these things does not occur, they will just leave and go to another Dealership.

As in a battle, a Salesperson can often seem like an enemy charging the field when they first approach the Customer. When that happens, the Customer will throw out an Obstacle like, *"We're just looking, can we just walk around by ourselves to see what you have?"* When this happens, how you respond will make the difference as to whether they will allow you to make your presentation and continue on, or whether they become more defensive and ultimately go somewhere else to shop.

Customers state Obstacles for 3 reasons:

1. Fear of losing control
2. Defensive reasoning from past experiences
3. Expected comments and behaviors

In the next Chapter, I will deal specifically with the most common Obstacles that Customers put forth during the initial Meet and Greet. I will also provide several responses that are proven to have a better result than those which have been a part of the standard Obstacle responses that have been taught in our industry for many years.

As the title of this chapter indicates, there is a definite difference between Obstacles and Objections. As I said, Obstacles come during the initial time with the Customer, the presentation & demonstration, and must be dealt with effectively for you to proceed with a structured sales process. An Objection, on the other hand, is a part of the negotiation process, and is stated after they have decided they like a vehicle and are ready to work toward making the purchase.

There are 4 primary things that cause Customers to have Objections:

1. A natural impulse when making a big purchase

2. Fear of making a long term commitment or lack of trust in us

3. They don't like the price and want to get it down lower

4. They don't like you or your Dealership

In the case of the last item there is nothing you can do and the likelihood of their leaving to go elsewhere is very high. Either way, Objections are not something to fear, as they are either buying signs or signals the deal is coming to a negative conclusion.

There are also several different types of Obstacles and Objections that must be studied and understood if you are to be successful in countering them in a logical and informed way.

The first type comes when the Customer refuses to follow our process, and they are typically Obstacles. They make statements like, *"I don't need to drive the car? I'm in a hurry? How much can you knock off the sticker price? I want your best price right now? What's the best interest rate I can get on this car?"*

These are the most difficult types and must be handled cautiously. Be careful not to act like you are offended or become confrontational with the Customer. This can put you at a disadvantage and can later affect your game plan in a negative way.

The second type are defensive statements and they too

are typically Obstacles, like, *"We're just looking? We're just shopping for the best price? This is last years' model and it's already old? This should be considered a used car since you have already given demos in it."*

These are easy to overcome and can give you a good advantage if you have a logical response prepared for the Customer.

Finally, the third type is a refusal to purchase or delay of making a decision, and those would be considered Objections, statements such as; *"Your payment or price is too high? You're not offering me enough for my trade? I don't want to put any money down? I've already got that deal beat somewhere else."*

These Objections always occur after the sales presentation has taken place. Your ability to overcome them will depend upon how good of a job you have done in your presentation process. By being unique and inspiring, you can lower the Customer's defenses and reduce any other Objections they may have. If they are sold on the vehicle, as well as on you and the Dealership, these will be easier to overcome and will enable you to hold your grosses to a higher level.

Learning to prepare properly for Obstacles and Objections will make both you and your Customer less confrontational. You will no longer fear dealing with them in the process of selling. In fact, with a commitment to the learning process you will eventually be able to turn them to your advantage.

It is natural for people to want to feel like they have control of any process that involves spending or making a big commitment of their time and money. Though they may have Objections and Obstacles that must be overcome, that in no way means they are not genuinely planning to make a purchase. It's the skills and abilities that you develop as a Salesperson to respond to these that will make the difference between the success or failure of the deal.

We all have stories of 'Lay Down' Customers that came to our Dealerships and bought a car without even haggling or any long negotiations, but all of us know this is very rare. So our planning must be based on preparation for any and all Obstacles and Objections, and if a Customer does 'Lay Down', then so be it, lucky us.

On the other hand, most Customers you will see during the normal course of your day will more than likely offer you the chance to earn their business, but will still come with Obstacles and Objections that must be overcome with skill and preparation. Those Salespeople who are serious about making every opportunity count will learn to overcome these with logical and unique responses that answer the Customer's questions and fears without pressure or manipulation, and in a straightforward professional manner.

In the next chapter, I will share with you some of the common Obstacles that you can expect from Customers in your daily routine and how best to respond to them in a manner that is logical and unique. This will provide both you and the Customer with the necessary confidence to proceed and with less fear or need for taking a defensive posture. In Chapter 17, I will share with you how to effectively handle Customer Objections in a professional and responsible manner.

CHAPTER 14
OBSTACLE RESPONSES

Our industry, like all others, changes with time and adapts itself to keep up with the times. Many of the methods of selling and dealing with Customers that made up the 'Old Way' were largely responsible for the negative view the public often holds of our business. Learning how to move on from those to develop processes that are more conducive to building better Customer relationships is a critical part of what we teach at David Lewis and Associates.

Understanding your Customers and what makes them respond to you as they do is probably the most important part of the learning process for successful Salespeople. Because there are attitudes and behaviors that often accompany a Customer when they first arrive at your Dealership, how you react to them can make the difference one way or the other. Learning how to be unique and inspiring is the key to whether you can break through their fears and defenses, and turn their vehicle shopping into a positive experience and an eventual sale.

Before I deal with each specific Obstacle, it is important to note that as a professional Automobile Salesperson you have a responsibility to treat every Customer with dignity, respect and professional courtesy. This is at the heart of "Understanding Your Customer" and earning their business. Without a genuine desire to help your Customers accomplish their purchasing goals and enjoy the benefits of what your product and Dealership have to offer, you cannot expect them to respond to you with loyalty and appreciation for what you do.

Your ability to understand and properly assist your Customer starts with the initial 'Meet and Greet' and your success in making an inspiring first impression. When you introduce yourself graciously and do your best to establish respect with your Customers by your unique verbiage and professional courtesy, you are already on your way to overcoming those natural fears and inhibitions that often make a Customer defensive when they first talk to an Automobile Salesperson.

As we look at several of the common Obstacles that Customers bring up, we will examine both the typical responses previously taught (Old School) and those we now teach. The latter have proven to be successful for lowering Customer anxiety and allowing the Salesperson to make a professional and non-threatening presentation leading to a sale.

Obstacle #1 – *"We are just looking, is it OK if we walk around alone?"*

This indicates a lack of comfort and a defensive distance that the Customer wants to keep until they have figured out how to gain control of their emotions. The typical playbook move for this Obstacle is to question the Customer on what they are looking for and offer to walk with them in order to answer any questions they may have. This tends to make them even more defensive, as they feel you are already beginning to pressure them and attempting to establish control of the situation.

I have found that the key to lowering their defenses at this point is to do just the opposite. That is, to offer a response that is unique and unexpected, and one that catches them pleasantly off guard.

In developing this response I wanted to utilize verbiage that they do not expect and am sure that others will not be using. I also never say *"no"* or disagree with the Customer, as this will obviously make them even more defensive.

The following is my response to:

"We are just looking, is it OK if we walk around alone?"

Of course you can, everybody has to start their shopping process somewhere. So does that mean you do not have to buy a car today? (No, not today) *Great, that actually takes all the pressure off me as a Salesperson. I would be happy to show you around, why don't we consider today to be purely an informational gathering event. Now, if you do see a car you like, we can still take it for a drive, and then before you leave I would be happy to provide you with brochures and pricing for you to take home and consider during your shopping process.*

This unique and unexpected response will almost certainly be different from what they were anticipating and if they have already been to other Dealerships it is very likely to set you apart from the common reply of other Salespeople. More importantly, this response will lower their defensive posture to a level that will allow you to now spend some time with them.

Let me now break down this response in greater detail for you.

Of course you can, everybody has to start their shopping process somewhere. This initial sentence starts the process of catching them off guard, because you are agreeing with them. It lets them know you understand shopping is part of their process.

So does that mean you do not have to buy a car today? (No, not today) You never want to ask a question that could result in an answer you do not want to hear, and this question will get the answer you want to hear almost every time, and that is, no....not today. Again, this removes pressure by them making clear that they will not be buying a car today.

Great, that actually takes all the pressure off me as a Salesperson. This sentence displays a sense of relief on the part of the Salesperson that again acknowledges the fact that a buying decision will not be made today.

I would be happy to show you around, why don't we consider today's visit to be an informational gathering event. By stating informational gathering it tells the Customer that they can take their time, collect data and no pressure will be placed on them.

Now, if you do see a car you like, we can still take it for a drive, and then before you leave I would be happy to provide you with brochures and pricing for you to take home and consider during your shopping process. This last sentence is in essence the "cherry on top". It lets the Customer know that if they find a car they like, they can still drive it. More importantly, once they are done looking, you will be happy to provide them with brochures and pricing, to take home to consider. You should also note that I specifically used the phrase *'shopping process'*; to again demonstrate a posture of understanding and agreement.

Remember, your only goal with this very common obstacle is to release their defensive posture so you can spend time with them. If you cannot do this, then most will walk around alone, and as soon as you take your eyes off of them they will leave.

Now, we all know at the end of this process we are still going to ask them to buy the car, but only after we have done a professional presentation and demonstration. Most would expect you to ask them to buy. Ironically, most will buy, that is, if you have done a great job releasing their defensive posture, have sold yourself, your product and your Dealership. Who wouldn't?

Obstacle #2 - *"I'm not going to buy a car today"*

When a Customer tells you, *"I'm not going to buy a car today"*, they are letting you know that they don't want you to pitch them and they aren't ready to answer a bunch of questions. This defensive statement is to stop you in your tracks before you start pressure selling them.

The "Old School" approach would be to give them reasons why they should reconsider: special prices, factory discounts that would be gone after today, special interest rates, etc. *"What will it take to get you to buy a car today"*, is a common pressure statement Salespeople use at times like this. In some cases Managers would chastise a Salesperson if they let the Customer leave without bringing them in to meet the Manager.

Also, keep in mind, that sometimes this statement is just a common expected reflex most think they should state.

Regardless of why they state it, you must respond in a manner that acknowledges their statement, or all you are going to do is make them even more defensive. Why build barriers? When you can tear down barriers.

The following is my response to:

"I'm not going to buy a car today"

I understand, shopping is a very important part of the process. Why don't we do this, let's make today solely an informational gathering visit. I would be happy to show you all the cars we have in stock. If one catches your eye we can take it for a drive. Then, before you leave, I would be happy to give you some brochures and pricing on the cars you liked for you to take home and consider during your shopping process.

You probably realized that this response was very similar to the one I use on, *"We are just looking, is it OK if we walk around alone?"* And it is. I utilized the same concept;

all I did was remove the question, *so does that mean you do not have to buy a car today?* There is no need to ask that question, they have already stated they are not buying a car today.

The only addition I made was, *I understand, shopping is a very important part of the process.* Again, agreeing with them. Why disagree? If you disagree or start to overcome their logic, all you are going to do is make them uncomfortable and more defensive.

Obstacle #3 – *"What is your best price on that car over there?"*

This statement clearly tells us that the Customer wants to be in total control of the sales process. Most will be inquiring about pre-owned cars on your front line, and were just driving by. Typically, this type of buyer is an impulse buyer and if the price is right, will buy.

Your goal with this individual is to get them into your sales process. We all know that nobody buys a car without first driving it. So getting them to drive the car must be our utmost thought. But you have to be careful, any wrong statements and this Customer is leaving.

Most of us have been taught to ask the Customer if they would like to drive the car first, and most will say NO. Then we ask them if they would like to come inside so we can get some information, and most will again say NO; stating they will stay outside and wait for you to get them the price.

Now, left with no alternative, the Salesperson heads inside hoping the Sales Manager is in a good mood. We all know what they will say, *"I am not giving them a price until they drive the car."* And this gets us nowhere.

You need to slow this Customer down, but in a manner that does not arouse suspicion.

The following is my response to:

"What is your best price on that car over there?"

I am not sure, let's walk over to the car so I can get the stock number and get that price for you right away.

Action 1: Walk over to the car and get the stock number (and we all know the Customer will follow you).

Action 2: Go inside the Dealership

Upon returning state: *My Manager is tied with a Customer right now, he said it would only be a few minutes and he will have that price for us. While we are waiting for him, I brought the keys out so you can take a minute and check out the interior of the car.*

In essence, I have accommodated this request and moved the Customer into the sales process.

Let's review it line by line.
I am not sure, let's walk over to the car so I can get the stock number and get that price for you right away.

The Customer has asked for the price, and I am going to accommodate them. My initial goal was to get them over to the vehicle, and I have done that by telling them I needed the stock number. Now that I have the stock number the action comes into play, which is to leave the Customer and go into the Dealership.

The Customer is now under the impression that they are in control, and you are doing what they have requested. Once inside the Dealership you need to get the keys and head back out. But, do not go back out too fast; remember you want the impression to be that you are speaking with the Manager for the price.

Upon returning I stated:

My Manager is tied with a Customer right now, he said it would only be a few minutes and he will have that price for us. While we are waiting for him I brought the keys out so you can take a minute and check out the interior of the car. Immediately after stating this, open the vehicle door, start it up, pull it ten feet out and invite them to sit in the car. Most will do so.

You now have this Customer in your sales process. Spend a few minutes going over the internal features, then look over your shoulder and state, *it looks like he might be just a few more minutes, since we are in the car would you like to take it for a short ride? I am sure that by the time we get back he will be free and have that price for us.*

Will everyone agree to take a drive? Probably not, but

some will. Those that do are now even deeper into your sales process. And isn't that the goal, to get them into your sales process?

Obstacle #4 – *"I don't have much time"*

This particular obstacle is a catch 22, as some truly only have a limited amount of time and others may just be stating this as a defensive format. Whether it is a true statement or not, the last thing we want to do is acknowledge any type of formal time line.

If not true, there are two reasons why it has been stated. First, as a form of control. Like most defensive postures the Customer wants to control the sales process. They know our goals and do not want to allow us the opportunity to take advantage of them. The other reason, which is similar to the first is, they want an exit strategy. If they are feeling pressured or uncomfortable they want a valued excuse as to why they would want to leave early.

Regardless of why they have made this statement, you must respond in a manner that acknowledges their stated limited time, but does not set a firm deadline for their visit. It is imperative that you utilize verbiage that will release their defensive posture, and demonstrate your understanding of their time.

You will find that this response is again, very similar to the first obstacle, which is, *we are just looking, is it OK if we walk around alone,* but adds one small enhancement.

The following is my response to:

"I don't have much time"

I fully understand, but I am glad you still stopped in. So can I assume due to your limited amount of time that you do not have to actually buy a car today? (No, not today) *Great, that actually takes all the pressure off me as a Salesperson. I would be happy to show you around, let's consider today to be an informational gathering event. Now if you do see a car you like, and time permits, we can still take it for a drive. What I am going to do is let you control the clock, just give me 5 minutes notice before you need to leave so I can gather up some brochures and get you some pricing to take home and consider.*

Again, you have probably noticed that this response is very similar to *we are just looking, is it OK if we walk around alone* and *I'm not going to buy a car today.* Why? Because in essence they are all directly related to a posture statement.

My goal is not different. It is to be unique, inspiring and to lower their posture so I can make a great presentation and demonstration. The only difference is that I have added one statement and enhanced another.

The added statement is, *what I am going to do is let you control the clock.* This throws indirect control over to the Customer. It allows them to believe that I realize they have a time constraint and at any moment during the process they are going to need to leave. Which also makes them responsible for having to decide when to leave.

The enhanced statement is, *just give me 5 minutes notice before you need to leave so I can gather up some brochures and get you some pricing to take home and consider.* Again, restating that they are in charge of the clock, and that I am prepared to provide them brochures and prices to take home.

This entire response is effective whether they truly have a time limit or not. Those with time limits will let me know when they need to leave, and for those that have just stated it purely as a defensive posture as an exit strategy, should they need one. And if your presentation is inspiring, this obstacle will become a mute issue, as they will now follow your sales process to its entirety.

Obstacle #5 – *"I'm on my lunch hour"*

Many times the Customer will purposely visit the Dealership to look for a car during their lunch hour. The reason being, to both control them and the Salesperson. Controlling us is nothing new, but controlling them is.

One of the few areas that most have trouble controlling is their urge and excitement to buy. They fear making a snap decision and then regretting it at a later date. Purposely showing up at the Dealership to look at cars during their lunch hour will indirectly control that desire to buy now. It forces them to leave and consider whether they like the car, you, and the Dealership, as well as, a cooling off period for themselves.

How often do you think Customers have made an instant purchase, and then later regretted it? We all know this is called Buyer's Remorse.

The two things to realize as a Salesperson when dealing with a Customer who is only on their lunch hour is, do not rush the process, and realize they will not be buying now.

Too many times I have seen Salespeople try to jam a two hour presentation into 30 minutes, resulting in the inevitable bad presentation. No value, no mental ownership and no sale. By taking your time and being inspirational, you will give the Customer a reason to return.

The following is my response to:

"I'm on my lunch hour"

That is not a problem, so can I assume with such limited time you do not need to buy a car now? (No, not now) *Great, that actually takes all the pressure off me as a Salesperson. I would love to spend whatever amount of time you have available now showing you some cars. We will use this time as purely an informational gathering opportunity. Now if time permits and you do see a car you like, we can still take it for a drive. What I am going to do is let you control the clock. Just give me 5 minutes notice before you need to leave so I can get you some brochures for you to take home and review.*

Again, you should have noticed that my script is very similar to *we are just looking, is it OK if we walk around alone* and *I'm not going to buy a car today.* It is almost an identical script to *I don't have much time.* The only difference is in this response, I did not make any comments about getting them prices.

If a Customer enters the Dealership around the lunch hour, and appears to be dressed for work, maybe a uniform or business attire, the odds are they are telling the truth. Now, that does not mean they are, but for the most part they will be.

The critical thing to remember about the Customer is again, not to rush the process. Actually, the best thing to do is to time the process out so that they need to leave just before the Demonstration Drive step. By doing this, you will be giving them a reason to want to come back to the Dealership.

Some of you may want to offer the Customer the opportunity to drive the car back to work with them and then return later in the day, and that is a great idea, but it would have to depend on your Dealership's policy. Also, be sure not to ask any of those nasty pre-trial questions like, *what is your timeline for buying a car* and *will there be anyone else involved in the buying decision.* All these questions do is make the Customer more defensive and then they may not return.

Sometimes, we have to accept the fact that either time or their posture will not permit them to buy the car now. But if they took this posture with you, then they took it with all the others they have or will be visiting in their shopping process.

Obstacle #6 – *"All I want is a brochure"*

In most cases, this obstacle, *all I want is a brochure*, is actually a buying sign in itself. You just have to be patient. The problem is, patience is not a strong quality of most Salespeople. We want instant gratification, with most of us not able to see past the end of the day or week, and definitely not past the end of the month.

A Customer that states this is typically just starting their shopping process and will be very diligent in the process and will normally buy when they are ready, and cannot be persuaded differently.

Your initial goal while they are at the Dealership is still going to include your attempt to get them into your sales process. And if you can, there is always that chance they may buy today, but for the most part, all you will be doing is planting the seed that you are different and unique. Demonstrating that you are the one they will want to return to visit when the time is right.

In most cases, this buyer typically makes a purchase within 30 days, so the time invested today could produce a tangible result within a short period of time. You will notice in my response that I am still going to attempt a more immediate result.

The following is my response to:

"All I want is a brochure"

Action: Start walking towards your desk (they will follow).

Absolutely, I would be happy to get that for you right away. Just like most companies we are going green, so I will be ordering you a brochure online and have it sent directly to your email address. What is the best email address to reach you at? (jsmith@yahoo.com)

Action: Start walking the Customer out the door as if they were now leaving.

While you are here, would you like to invest a few more minutes to look at some of the cars we do have in stock. This will give you an opportunity to see the colors we have in stock, determine the different options and accessories that are available, plus give you an opportunity to look at the sticker so you can get an idea of price. I think it will make viewing the brochure later today much more informative.

My only goal with this response is to get them over to the cars. You do not want to offer them that option first, as that will definitely raise their defensive posture. By doing it after the fact, it comes across more sincere.

I started out my response by acknowledging I would be happy to get them a brochure. *Absolutely, I would be happy to get that for you right away.* I had a valid reason for requesting their email address and that was to let them know I would be emailing them the brochure, *Just like most companies, we are going green, so I will be ordering you a brochure online and have it sent directly to your email address. What is the best email address to reach you at?* (jsmith@yahoo.com)

If the Customer did not have an email address, or would rather have a paper brochure, and we had one available, I would have retrieved one for them.

I purposely allowed them to think the process was over as I start to walk them back outside, but I am really just beginning. Once outside my next statement was: *While you are here would you like to invest a few more minutes to look at some of the cars we do have in stock? This will give you an opportunity to see the colors we have in stock, determine the different options and accessories that are available, plus give you an opportunity to look at the sticker so you can get an idea of price.*

Most who are truly interested in your product, will accept this offer. It is non-threatening and comes across in a sincere manner. The most important part of this statement is the last sentence, which is, *I think it will make viewing the brochure later today much more informative.*

It is very important to add this phrase, as this will clearly send the message you understand they will be leaving shortly to retrieve the email to consider. If at any point in time the Customer thinks that you may attempt to sell them something today, this entire process will come to a halt and the Customer will leave.

Once at the car, you now have the Customer in your sales process. If done properly, after a few minutes you can invite the Customer to sit inside one of the cars and before long they will be driving the car and falling in love with it.

Obstacle #7 – *"My Spouse is not with me"*

This final Obstacle is often something that has been pre-planned by the Customer in order to keep them from making an impulsive decision if they find something they like. Obviously, most married couples do confer with each other on large purchase decisions, so for the most part this is probably a very valid obstacle.

The old way of handing this would be to pressure the Customer to call their spouse or even suggest they take a car to them at work or at home. Whatever it took to get the other decision maker there 'let's get it done!'

This is only a formula for disaster. Especially if brought up early on in the process. Your only goal must be to let them know you understand and respect the situation. Keep in mind that if they have used this approach with you, they have probably, or will probably use it with the other Salespeople, at the other Dealerships; they will come in contact with.

The following is my response to:

"My Spouse is not with me"

I understand and appreciate that. On such an important

decision as purchasing a vehicle you certainly want to have your spouse with you. Knowing that you do not have to make a buying decision today actually takes all the pressure off me as a Salesperson. Let's consider today's visit to be purely just an informational gathering event. We can look at all the cars we have in stock, and if time permits and you find one that catches your eye, you can even take it for a drive. Then before you leave I can provide you with some brochures and pricing for you to take home and share with your spouse.

It is so critical that you understand that 99% of the time this obstacle is stated, they are not going to purchase a car without their spouse being involved. Now, I am not advocating that at the end of the process we don't at least ask them to buy, we would be foolish not to, but that must be our secondary goal. Our primary goal is to make a presentation that is so inspiring, that they want to return with their spouse.

Just consider where their defensive posture is after you have made this statement, now knowing that you understand they are not buying today.

Some of you are probably saying to yourself, *"Why don't you offer to drive the car to their spouse"* or *"Have them take the car themselves to show their spouse"*, and that is an option. I must warn you; the minute that thought is proposed it has now become a sales environment. Once the Customer recognizes that, they will start to become more defensive again.

If you want to bring up those options be sure to bring

them up at the very end. Not during the sales process. This offer should only be made once the Customer is fully engaged in a thought process of loving the car, you and the Dealership. If you bring it up during the Demonstration Drive you lose those benefits of being unique and different. The best time to offer that option is once the entire sales process has come to an end.

As you can see my entire thought process with Meet & Greet Obstacles is all based around what is best for the Customer. This is not the time to be thinking about a sale or commission. It is all about the Customer, their defensive posture and how to release that posture.

CHAPTER 15
TWO EARS, TWO EYES, ONE MOUTH

Ask most people what it takes to be a successful Salesperson and they will probably state that you have to be a good talker. While the ability to speak well is obviously beneficial in sales, the wisdom to know when not to talk is just as essential for success in this business. Learning how to balance the two is where the real potential lies. For that however, one must develop the art of listening.

Nature itself instructs us on these things, if we take the time to think about it. The fact that we have two ears and two eyes, but only one mouth should tell us something; obviously we are meant to spend more time listening and looking, and less time talking. That's a lesson that sometimes takes a long time and many lost commissions to learn.

Any experienced Salesperson knows how easy it is to shipwreck a deal by talking too much. But often the Customer leads us to believe that they have little or nothing to say, so we pick up the ball and run with it. When this happens, we start selling and telling, rather than listening and learning.

For a Customer just arriving on the lot, there can be few things that are more frustrating than listening to a sales pitch when you are trying to tell the Salesperson what it is you came in for. To understand your Customer, you must first give them the time to tell you what it is they want. For this, you have to listen closely and learn to ask the right questions at the right time.

Studies tell us that by the time today's Customers come to look for a car, they already have a good idea of what they are looking for. Industry surveys show that nearly 85% of today's buyers do their research online before ever coming to the lot. In fact, a February 2011 study concluded that buyers who do their shopping online usually spend an average of 8-10 hours or 60% of their shopping time online before making a purchase.

No matter how nice we try to make our Dealerships look for eye appeal, apart from a few late at night tire kickers, I doubt if people today come in just for the joy of hearing a Salesperson give their spiel. Especially, when we so often hear that most people would rather have a dental root canal than go to a car Dealership. When an orderly and first class appearance and a professional sales staff are operating together in an informative, enthusiastic and professional manner, it can be very appealing to the Customer who is really looking for a car; especially when you consider that they have already most likely shopped online before coming to your Dealership. You can assume they are visiting for a good reason.

When a Dealership has eye appeal, with untrained or weak sales personnel, what often happens is the Salespersons eagerness to make a sale runs headlong into the Customers nervousness about dealing with our sales process. Instead of focusing on building a common ground to work from, the Salesperson starts the routine he or she has memorized. Word Tracks are certainly great tools for an effective selling presentation, but they only work when they are in response to a Customers questions or dialogue. Just rolling them off does little for initiating communication.

Taking the time to let the Customer become relaxed and at ease before picking up the conversation too much has proven to be the best approach. Some Customers just want to walk around and look so they can gather their thoughts and emotions before they start bringing you into the picture. As I mentioned in Chapter 14, when you surprise a Customer with a unique response to these kinds of Obstacles you catch them pleasantly off guard and help them become more open than they initially had intended to be.

It's important to understand that most people don't want to be overly tense or matter of fact with a Salesperson. It is just the nature of the car selling environment and the perceived reputation of our business that tends to make them that way.

Don't be afraid to let your inventory speak for itself. Often Customers who are left alone will land on a car that peaks their interest. When that happens, you can be of great assistance to them, while at the same time finding out what it is they like about that particular vehicle. Some of the most profitable deals happen with very little negotiating. When the Customer finds something they like, they will often take ownership without too much effort on your part. From there it's just a matter of negotiations and working things out on paper.

On the other hand, some Customers are very nervous and will start rattling off stuff so fast that you can't make heads or tails of it. If you jump into that too quickly you can find yourself going in a thousand directions without a compass. That's the time to hold your tongue and casually assess their posture and expressions to see what those things are telling you. If you start trying to take control of a Customer who is like that, it will usually go downhill. They may be nervous and a bit scrambled, but that isn't necessarily an invitation for you to take over.

Someone once said the definition of a fool is a person who doesn't know what's going on around them. As a professional Salesperson, you should always be aware of your environment and your Customer's reactions to what they are experiencing. Your time with them must be a combination of listening and observing, as well as presenting stimulating comments or questions that perk their interest.

Remember, it's not what you are excited about that sells the car; it's what inspires your Customer that matters. Learning how to read their mannerisms and behaviors is critical, and can save you a lot of time asking too many harmful questions. Paying attention to their reactions and body language is a key to connecting with your Customer's interest and buying motivators.

Think about how you feel when you are trying to communicate with someone who won't stop talking long enough to hear what you have to say. That's how a Customer feels when they run headlong into the sales pitch before the Salesperson even knows what they want and need. Their natural reaction is to put up defensive walls and look for the first chance to leave and shop elsewhere.

Selling truly is a great profession and without Salespeople, little would get done in the marketplace. In fact, people like being sold. They just don't like being over-sold or pressured.

Your job is to create an environment that makes the Customer feel value in your presentation and in the words you speak concerning you, your product and your Dealership. That is different from creating a whirlwind of words designed to amaze them with your talking skills and savvy presentation.

The more you get to know your Customer, the better the chances are that you can connect with their wants and desires. The best way to achieve this is to Stop – Look – and Listen before going forward with what you have to say. When you do that, the Customer is much more likely to listen and consider what you have to say.

CHAPTER 16
THE SALES PROCESS

All good journeys start with the first step. And so does the sales process. As I mentioned in a previous chapter, many people think that a Salesperson can only be truly successful if they possess the gift of gab. While it is certainly beneficial to be able to make a good verbal presentation, that is definitely not the key to successful selling.

Great Salespeople understand the need for being able to make a good presentation, but also know that a process which focuses on the Customers wants and needs require a balance of listening, observation and speaking, as well as asking the right questions and verifying your understanding with the Customer. When these are in place, the sales process you present has a good chance of accomplishing a sale.

I am sure that most of you have probably heard about Einstein's definition of insanity. He defined insanity as doing the same thing over and over again, yet expecting different results. If that truly represents insanity, we are in real trouble in our business and it's easy to see how we got here.

If you have been in this industry for a while, you can certainly validate that most car Salespeople have been trained with a sales process that produces far less than what is desired. The proof is that most Salespeople utilize a process that is older than they are. A process

that has been taught for decades, in spite of the fact that
none of our Customers appreciate being handled in that
fashion. In fact, it is largely responsible for creating the
reputation that has plagued the car business with a
negative stereotype in the public view.

Along with that, it has also produced a Customer that in
most cases comes to a Dealership riddled with anxiety,
apprehension and hoping just to survive the process
without being totally ripped off. They know they need
a car, but they would rather go to the dentist than go
through the process of buying one at a Dealership.

If that's not insanity, what is it?

We know what the Customer desires and they deserve to
be satisfied. We know that those Dealerships who focus
on Customer Service are the most profitable in our
industry. We know that those Salespeople who focus on
meeting and exceeding the Customer's wants and needs,
have the best careers; yet we still teach a selling process
that produces the opposite result.

Why do we do this? Because most of us have not taken
the time to truly study both the Customer and the
process. We accept mediocrity as the standard for
success. So isn't it time to learn a better way? Of course
it is!

As long as we continue to teach control and pressure as
the key elements to success, while promoting Customer
service and satisfaction in our advertising, the only
thing that is missing is a certificate on the Showroom

wall showing that a psychiatric examination has validated that we are clinically insane.

I will now break down each step in the sales process for you. You will notice that I have actually added a step, moved a step up sooner in the process and taken a step from the delivery process and added it to the sales process.

Within each step you will notice that my process has only one thing in mind, the Customer. Not whether they will be buying today, but it is solely focused on their defensive posture and how to bring it to its lowest possible level. Once that has been accomplished the sale becomes a natural conclusion and not a struggle once at the negotiations.

To do this you need all the steps. There is not one step, or set of steps, that will fully accomplish this goal. It is the combination of all the steps. At no point in time, will I make any statements or ask any questions that will bring that posture up. As a matter of fact, throughout my entire presentation, I will follow my 4 Rules of Sales Success.

Rule #1: Never ask a question that could produce a lie.

Rule #2: Never ask a question that could result in an answer you do not want to hear.

Rule #3: Never ask a question or make a statement that could make the Customer more defensive.

Rule #4: Always try to catch the Customer pleasantly off guard.

By utilizing these Rules as my guide, I will improve my odds of reducing any Customers defensive posture, which in turn will increase my odds of making a sale.

Step #1: The Meet & Greet

Every sales process must have a beginning, and in most it is the Meet & Greet. The Meet & Greet is your initial encounter with the Customer and has 4 goals:

Goal #1: To welcome them to the Dealership.

Goal #2: To get their name.

Goal #3: To give them your name.

Goal #4: To catch them initially off guard.

We all know that upon arrival at the Dealership the Customers are in their most defensive state. We do not want to utilize any gimmicky sales lines that might increase their posture. We want to be kind, courteous and stay focused on achieving our 4 goals, and only our 4 goals.

We have also learned that people enjoy being acknowledged in a formal sense. The formal sense I am talking about is Mr., Mrs. or Ms. It puts them on a pedestal; it makes them feel important and special.

The Meet & Greet is also something you do not want to over complicate. Keep it as simple as possible.

The following is my Meet & Greet:

David: *Hi welcome to ABC Motors, my name is David Lewis and you are Mr.?*

Customer: *Smith*

David: *Mr. Smith it is nice to meet you, and you are Ms.?*

Customer: *I am Mrs. Smith.*

David: *Mr. & Mrs. Smith again welcome to the Dealership. Have you been here before?*

Customer: *No, this is our first time.*

David: *Again, welcome to ABC Motors.*

That is my entire Meet & Greet, it does not get easier than that. I got their last name, and will continue to use it throughout my presentation. You might have noticed that I asked her if she was *Ms.* and not *Mrs.* I did this because I did not know if she was his wife, sister, friend or co-worker. By addressing someone as Ms. you will never offend them, and if they want to be called by something else they will tell you.

I kept it simple, simple, simple.

Step #2: Qualification

This next step is where most Salespeople truly start going in a bad direction. They start asking questions like:

- What are you looking for?
- What is your budget?
- Are you paying cash or financing?
- Do you have a trade?
- What do you think your trade is worth?
- How much do you owe on your trade?
- What is your timeline for buying a car?

All these questions do is make the Customer even more defensive, they produce lies and they make the Salesperson sound just like all the other Salespeople the Customer will encounter during their shopping process. And this is surely something I do not want to do.

Sales rules have been broken, postures raised and when the Customer lies most Salespeople either end up showing them cars they are truly not interested in or fall victim to the most silent sales killer, psychological warfare.

Psychological warfare is when the Customer makes a statement or answers a question that sends the mind of the Salesperson in a bad direction. When a customer states, *"We are not buying a car today,"* that is psychological warfare. The Customer did not do it intentionally to send the Salesperson off track, but it does just that. Most Salespeople will now make a different type of presentation than if the Customer had clearly stated they were buying today.

Our sales process needs a qualification step, but not the old traditional set of questions everyone has asked for years. When most Customers visit the Dealership their sole intent is to only look at cars, not make a purchase. And understanding the Customer is all about understanding and acknowledging their intent.

Customers want to be on the lot, they want to look at cars and they want to be excited about the prospect of eventually making a purchase. Yet our process removes those events.

There are only 3 questions most Salespeople need to ask in order to qualify the Customer, with some only having to ask 2 questions. Those questions are:

1. Are you looking for a new or used car?
2. Which brand of car were you considering?
3. Would you like to look at a Coupe, Sedan, Minivan, Utility Vehicle or Truck?

That is all one needs to know to start the process.

The goal of the qualification is to determine a general direction of where to start on the lot. Are you headed to the new cars or used cars and if you have multiple franchises, which one and what type of body style is desired.

None of these questions are going to produce lies or make the Customer more defensive. And isn't that one of our goals? Who cares what their budget is, you will see in the next step how to figure that out. Who cares at this point in the process if they have a trade, and if so, what they think it is worth or how much they owe on it. And why does it matter when they plan on making a purchase or who else will be involved in the buying decision?

Your only goal, as I have stated many times before, is twofold. First, always be releasing their defensive posture, and second, inspire them with your product, personality and Dealership. Handle this step incorrectly and you are starting down the path of danger.

Step #3: Inventory Walk

Now that we know the Customer wants a new sedan, it is time to do an Inventory Walk. The goal of the Inventory Walk is to select a model or body style and not to select a specific car.

When we study the Customer we have learned that the more they feel that they are in control of the sales process, the quicker their defensive posture comes down. Control is an entity that no one wants to relinquish.

As you start your Inventory Walk, you always want to start the Customer out at the cheapest car in the category they have selected. For example, if you sell Toyota's and the Customer has stated they would like to look at new Toyota sedans, you would start them out at the Yaris, which is the smallest sedan that Toyota makes.

Mr. & Mrs. Smith, this is the Toyota Yaris, it is the base Toyota sedan.

After making this statement, stop talking and watch to see how the Customer responds. If they walk closer to the vehicle and start looking at it closer, they are telling you they like it. If they make a statement of it either being too small or not the style they had in mind, then take them to the next size up and present that model for them to view.

If the Customer walks over to the row of vehicles, most will start by looking at the window sticker, and that, too, is a good sign. You must observe them closely to look for body reactions and listen closely for any verbal comments.

If the Customer continues to walk around the car or starts looking at different ones in the row, then they are telling you that the price initially meets their satisfaction. In essence, that they can afford this particular model.

It is very important that you remain silent. Give them plenty of time to look and admire the car. If they have questions, they will ask them. By volunteering information now you may run the risk of raising their posture or interrupting the viewing opportunity. The last thing you want to do is stop someone from looking at a particular car or row of cars.

This step can take 10 minutes or 30 minutes, but however long it takes, it is worth every minute of time spent.

Step #4: Selection

The next step, the Selection, is very simple, but must be done with ease. The last thing you want to do is rush someone into selecting a car or make them feel that you are leading them to a specific car versus another one.

You must be watching for both verbal comments and body language as to when you think they might have narrowed themselves down to one particular car. Maybe they ask a question about a specific car, or they start to linger around one certain car or maybe they keep going back to the window sticker of a specific car.

Once you think the time is right, the Selection of a particular car is accomplished with one simple, but important question. A question that must incorporate specific verbiage.

The qualification question is: *Mr. & Mrs. Smith, would you folks like to sit inside one of these cars so you can determine if you like the interior?*

You will find overwhelmingly that most will say *Yes.* Why? Because it is not a threatening question, and it makes logical sense. First, it is not threatening because you are not asking them to drive the car or even buy the car. All you want to know is if they would like to sit inside the car to determine if they like the interior. Second, it is a logical question, because as I told you earlier most have ventured to the Dealership to look at cars, and looking at the interior of a car would be considered a part of that process.

Once they say *Yes*, simply ask them, *"Is there a particular color or one with particular options you would like to sit inside of?"* Once they pick one, the Customer has indirectly landed themselves on a car, without you telling them which one best fits their budget or criteria, but one that they like. It was their decision, not yours.

Once they tell you which one they like, go get the keys, start the car up, pull it 10 feet out of the spot to isolate it and then offer to have them sit inside of it.

If possible, you want to get the primary driver to sit behind the wheel. Sometimes, it is difficult to determine who that may be, and if you remember, we did not ask that question. Why? Because that question may raise their posture a bit and it is really not that important. Many times you will be able to determine who the primary driver is by their comments and actions, but if you cannot, don't worry.

It is also important that everyone present gets in the car, just start opening doors and offering each person the opportunity to sit in the car. Once in the car be sure to try and close the doors, as to give them some privacy.

Once they are in the car this is your time to be like a ghost and disappear. Not to leave the area, but maybe stand behind the car where they cannot see you, or perhaps walk 10 feet away. The idea behind this is to give them a minute or two to get acquainted with the car, but more importantly to give them an opportunity to speak freely about their thoughts of the car.

You see, if you are present, they may not want to talk openly, to show too much emotion or display any form of physical excitement about the car. If they don't like the car, you want them to figure that out now, not in an hour from now by just telling you they want to go home and think about it.

Should they decide this model is not for them, then take them to the next model up in size. This is a good sign, not a bad sign. In essence, this is still all about them being in control, and not you. The ironic thing is, you are actually the one who is in control, all you are doing is giving them the presumption that they are in control. Never forget that perception equals reality. If they presume to be in control, then they will believe they are in control. I told you earlier, if they think they are in control, their defensive posture will come down.

After about a minute if they are still in the car this is your sign to now join them and to move on to the next step.

Step #5: Internal Presentation

The Internal Presentation is going to be a new step for most of you. This step has two goals, the first is to continue the presentation process, but this time solely on the interior features of the car. Most of us present the interior features of the car either on the Demonstration Drive or at the time of delivery. And neither one of these times is optimal.

First, if doing it while on the Demonstration Drive, it

means the Customer cannot focus on the task at hand, which is driving the car. You would never want the Customer to take their eyes off the road, which would be dangerous. How can the Customer focus on what you are demonstrating if they are driving the car?

The second common option for presenting the interior features is during the delivery process. When you think about it, that does not make logical sense. Why would you only want to present and demonstrate these features and options to only those who buy the car? Shouldn't these great benefits be presented as part of your sales presentation?

The second and most important benefit of doing an internal presentation is it acts as a transitional step to the Demonstration Drive, sort of like a buffer. It allows for the Customer to become comfortable with the inside features, to become relaxed with this important environment and when asked if they would like to drive the car it becomes more natural for them to agree.

During the Internal Presentation, you want to present and demonstrate every feature and benefit as if you were actually delivering the car to them.

Start off by showing them how to adjust the seat, tilt wheel and both external mirrors. Then how to turn on both the air conditioning and heating system, how the recirculating air works and how to turn on the rear defogger and front defroster. Be sure to show them how to turn on the radio, tune it to a station and how to program that station. How to use any type of GPS or

Navigation system. Invest time and show them how all the functions on the steering wheel work and their benefits. And don't leave out the simple things like how to turn on the lights, windshield wipers and sun roof, if one is present.

This does not have to be a long presentation, just long enough so that they acknowledge and understand how all of these features work.

Once this has been completed, the next question is easy and a natural one, *"Would you like to take the car for a drive."*

If you have done all of these steps properly up to this point, have not utilized any of the common trial closes, and have not made any statements, or asked any questions that would have made them more defensive, your odds of them taking a Demonstration Drive are in the high 90 percentile range. Isn't that an important goal, to get as many people as possible to drive the car?

You have to always keep in mind that most people are very hesitant to drive the car. Their reasoning is mostly out of fear. Fear that they will fall in love with the car, become an easy target for an aggressive Salesperson, buy the car and then regret their decision. Thus, it is easier to just say NO when asked.

So let's make that NO hard to state. Let's add this step, which will lower their defensive posture and increase our ratio of Demonstration Drives.

Step #6: Demonstration Drive

There is only one main goal of the Demonstration Drive and that is for the Customer to develop the ultimate level of Mental Ownership possible, and the only way for that to happen is for them to drive the car. Ironically, most Salespeople have been trained with methods that are not conducive to that happening.

First, let me discuss with you the length of the Demonstration Drive, and to get right to the point, a 10 minute lap around the block is not sufficient. How can anyone fall in love with a car that they only drive for a short period of time? It is impossible.

The length of your Demonstration Drive will clearly determine the ease of effort needed to close the deal. As I have mentioned continuously, the lower their posture, the better our position is. The more they love the car, the lower their posture will become.

I am also 100% against planned demonstration routes. First, the Customer clearly tells us that they do not like them. That they feel out of control and I can understand why. When I am at the mercy of someone telling me where to turn, when to turn and how long I can drive, I too would feel that I have given up some control.

Second, if I were to actually have a planned demonstration route, I would plan that route to be at least a 30 minute route. Again, the longer they drive the car, the more likely they are to fall in love with it. The more they love it, the easier it is to close them.

Let me also give you another example of why a short drive is not beneficial and do so with a scenario that happened to me. Now some of you will not be able to relate directly to this situation based on your location and climate, but I think you will get the point.

The other day I flew into Philadelphia, PA. It was the middle of winter, so it was very cold. I think the temperature was around 20 degrees. I was fortunate enough at the rental car counter to be upgraded to a luxury SUV at no charge. I was very excited.

Once in this very expensive car I started to realize that I really did not like it. After only driving it for about 5 minutes I realized I did not like the seats, they were very hard and uncomfortable. I prefer more of a softer, cushiony type seat. I even noted in my mind that if in the future they offered me such an upgrade, I would turn it down.

After about 20 minutes it dawned on me that the seats were actually getting more comfortable. They were starting to feel softer and more to my liking. After about 30 minutes I even commented to myself that I was wrong, and I would take this car again if offered to me.

You see, when I got in the car, the seats, which were leather, were hard as a rock, because it was so cold outside. The more I drove the car, the more the car warmed up in the inside. As the car warmed up the seats started to soften up and the true comfort of the leather became evident.

If I had been in the market for this type of vehicle, had visited the Dealership in the middle of the winter, had then taken a 10 minute test drive in this car, I would not have enjoyed it. That short ride would not have been sufficient for the seats to warm up and for me to feel comfortable with the car. I would have just left, continued my shopping and purchased a different car elsewhere.

Some of you have also allowed certain Customers to take cars home overnight as an extended demonstration drive, which I think is a great idea. Why? Because the closing ratio on these extended drives is extremely high, with some Dealerships reporting rates of greater than 75%. The reason this closing ratio is so high is because the Customer has an extended period of time to fall in love with the car, again, making the point for longer drives.

The best way to insure a longer drive is to select a destination in advance that most of your Customers will be familiar with. This destination must be at least a 15 minute drive from your Dealership, and not round trip, 15 minutes there and then 15 minutes back.

Salesperson: *Ms. Smith, are you familiar with where the Galleria Mall is?*

Customer: *Yes, of course.*

Salesperson: *Why don't we head out to the mall as that will give you an opportunity to drive the car under a few different conditions, and then if Mr. Smith would like to drive the car too, the mall will be a safe place to switch.*

We have also learned that talking during the drive is not in our best interest, unless we are spoken to. Asking questions like; *how does it drive, how is the visibility, are the seats comfortable,* etc. are only going to make the Customer more defensive. They are smart; they realize these are forms of trial closes.

Many times, once a Salesperson runs out of questions to ask that pertain to the car, they start to ask the Customer personal questions; *Where do you live? Where do you work? Do your kids go to the local schools?* Many people do not feel comfortable sharing that information with a Salesperson.

As Salespeople, we have to always realize what the Customer's perception is of us. They know we are Salespeople, that our job is to sell them a car today and they have been conditioned to be very careful and cautious when communicating with us. Don't give them reasons to put their defensive posture back up.

If the Customer wants a dialogue during the Demonstration Drive, they will initiate one. Then it is proper to respond and communicate. Many will ask questions about specific features and benefits, or about the warranty, and some will even ask you personal questions, like *how long have you been selling cars, how long have you worked at the Dealership* or *do you live in town.* When asked by the Customer, they are telling you that a personal dialogue is acceptable to them.

But again, I caution you to let them initiate the conversation, not you.

When returning to the Dealership many Salespeople have been taught to instruct the Customer to park the car in the Sold Line or next to their trade. I grossly disagree with both of those places.

By telling the Customer to park the car in the Sold Line you are indirectly dropping an "Atom Bomb" of pressure on their lap. You are warning them that here comes the sales pitch and pressure. After making this statement I have never heard a Customer state, *that is a wonderful idea, since I would not want anyone looking at this car that we want to buy.* Most will just follow that request, but I can guarantee their defenses just went way up.

When it comes to having the Customer park the car next to their trade, I can be swayed a bit, but for the most part I am against it. I realize the benefit of them seeing this shiny new car next to their old and dirty car, but I also know there could be some possible residuals that could affect the odds of closing a deal today.

I have seen on a number of occasions the Salesperson has asked the driver to park the car next to their trade, to only have the wife get out of the car and while getting into their car state to their husband, *I am going to wait in our car while you get the prices.* This happens quite a bit if they have young kids with them, and they are getting bored and loud.

Thus, my conclusion has been to not take that chance. To simply have them park the car wherever it is convenient. If they happen to park the car next to their trade, so be it, I wouldn't worry about it.

The final place I would never have them park the car is back in the spot that it came out of. In essence that is putting the car away, not to be seen again. You want the car up front. Where they can see it through the window and especially when they leave, that is, if they did not make a purchase.

I want to share one more idea with you that will tremendously increase the level of mental ownership during the Demonstration Drive. There is nothing more exciting and exhilarating than seeing yourself behind the wheel of a new car. Nothing beats the value of seeing how good the car looks and especially how good you look in that car.

Be sure that on the way back from your predetermined destination you find a building that has a glass front. It can be on a main street or an office building. The goal is to get them to slow down or drive in front of that reflective glass. Why? So they can see themselves in the car. Who would not want to actually visualize how great the car looks and especially how great it looks with them behind the wheel?

Some people will sit up in the seat, some will roll down the window and rest their arm on the door, some might put on their sunglasses and all will slow down to carefully look the car over from front to back. You can't get a better selling environment. Now please be careful, you want to make sure this is done in a safe environment. If driving it on a main street, you could have them stop the car or wait until a traffic light turns green. I always found a commercial building with a parking lot. The last thing you want to do is to advise your Customer to drive while not watching the road.

The Demonstration Drive is by far the most important step in the sales process. This is where most will make the decision whether this is the car for them or not. You must never shortcut this step.

Step #7: External Walk Around

Now that you have completed the Demonstration Drive, it is time to do your External Walk Around presentation. The concern I have with this step is the common redundancy that occurs for Customers who have already been to other Dealerships. In essence, they have already been exposed to a Walk Around presentation.

Some of you might disagree, but unfortunately, I know that all Walk Around presentations are literally identical. How do I know this? Because over the years I have judged hundreds of them from all the different manufacturers, and for the most part, they are all the same.

I am not suggesting you skip this step, I just want you to be aware that most people have heard your presentation before. What I am going to suggest is that you actually do two Walk Around presentations. The one that your manufacturer wants you to do and then one that you will want to do. The one that you will want to do will be the one that will truly show your knowledge of the product, your inspirational side and the importance of your Customer's safety every time they are in this particular car.

Your second Walk Around presentation will be a Safety Walk presentation, but not the same safety features that everyone else will present. Sure you will mention airbags, 5 mile per hour bumpers and crumple zones in the hood, but only with a "matter of fact" attitude. As to state, *just like everyone else, we have those features too*.

Tell your Customer about all the safety features that are required by the government, you know, the ones that are in all cars, but no one else will mention. This second Walk Around will be performed at the conclusion of the first Walk Around and will begin with a question.

Salesperson: *Mr. & Mrs. Smith, how important is safety to you in an automobile?*

Customer: *Very important.*

Salesperson: *I am glad you agree as this manufacturer is very committed to your safety every time you are in their car. Let me share with you some of the safety features of this car.*

This is when it is now time to shine and inspire. Take a few minutes and talk about every safety feature, the ones they may be aware of, and the ones they may not. The following are the safety features that most Salespeople talk about:

1. Air Bags
2. 5 Mile Per Hour Bumpers
3. Crumple Zones in the Hood

4. ABS Brakes

5. Halogen Headlights

Now this next list is the safety items that most Salespeople FAIL to talk about, but you should.

1. Safety Tempered Glass – *The manufacturer has learned that most people get injured in automobile accidents from the shattering of glass. In the event of an accident should your head strike the window the glass will shatter, enter the vehicle and could cause you bodily harm and then there is the possibility of you being ejected from the car through the front opening. Not in our car. In our car we have a special kind of glass that is designed not to shatter, but to actually cushion the blow to protect you. Plus, it has been created to now stay within the frame of the car keeping you inside the vehicle, safe and secure.*

2. Maintains Body Weight - *This car is also designed to maintain a minimum of three times the vehicles body weight in case of a roll over. In essence, these pillars that hold up the roof can hold up the entire car so that in the case of a roll over the roof will not cave in causing additional harm to the occupants.*

3. Daytime Running Lights – *Daytime running lights is an automotive lighting device on the front of a car that is installed in pairs which automatically switch on when the vehicle is moving forward, emitting white, yellow, or amber light to increase the conspicuity of the vehicle during daylight conditions.*

4. Anti-Intrusion Bars – *An anti-intrusion bar is a passive safety device, which protects passengers from side impact collisions.   Side impacts are particularly dangerous for two reasons: a) the location of impact is very close to the passenger, who can immediately be reached by the impacting vehicle; b) in many side-impact accidents, the impacting vehicle may be larger, taller, heavier, or structurally more solid than the struck vehicle. The role of an anti-intrusion bar is to absorb the kinetic energy of the colliding vehicles to reduce the intrusion of the impact upon the vehicle being struck.*

5. Electronic Stability Control – A *computerized technology that improves the safety of a vehicle's stability by detecting and reducing loss of traction (skidding). When ESC detects loss of steering control, it automatically applies the brakes to help "steer" the vehicle where the driver intends to go. Braking is automatically applied to the wheels individually, such as the outer front wheel to counter over steer or the inner rear wheel to counter under steer.*

6. 3rd Brake Light – *The lighting system of a motor vehicle consists of lighting and signaling devices mounted or integrated to the front, sides, rear, and in some cases, the top of the motor vehicle. The purpose of this 3rd light is to provide illumination for the driver to operate the vehicle safely after dark, and to increase the conspicuity of the vehicle to others when braking.*

7. Emergency Interior Trunk Release – *A manually operated system that allows for the trunk door to be open in the event that someone is inside of the trunk*

compartment.

8. Tire Pressure Monitoring Systems – *An electronic system designed to monitor the air pressure inside the pneumatic tires. TPMS reports real-time tire-pressure information to the driver of the vehicle, either via a gauge, a pictogram display, or a simple low-pressure warning light.*

This very important safety presentation lets the Customer realize that you understand what is important to them, that their safety should be monumental in their decision process. Many will respect your interest in them as a caring gesture, a gesture that will pay huge rewards when it comes time to make a decision and negotiate a price.

When making your Safety Presentation, never lie or mislead the Customer, as it is not ethical or moral. You do not need to tell the Customer that the other cars they have looked at or plan on looking at do not have these features or benefits. You do not need to tell them these safety features are unique to your car, unless they truly are. Just tell them what your car has to offer and let them come to their own conclusion.

The next step for many in the sales process is to now ask a trial closing question and I am sure, by now, you will expect me to totally disagree with that concept, and I do! There is no place in our sales process for trial closes. All they do is make the Customer more defensive and will lessen the odds of selling them a car today.

The two most popular trial closes that I hear are:

1. *If we can come together on terms and numbers are you ready to buy the car today?*

2. *Is there anything that would stop you from moving forward and purchasing this car today?*

What is your goal with these questions? Surely it is for the Customer to say, YES. Most do not, and the ones that do say Yes, you would have closed them anyway once you presented the numbers and asked for the sale at your desk. What happens when they say NO? Now you are going to ask, why? Which will now lead to an Objection that you will feel compelled to overcome.

We all know the best place to negotiate the price and ask for the sale is at our desk, not on the lot. That is exactly what you are doing with a trial close, especially those two trial closes. You are asking the Customer to buy the car and doing so outside on the lot where it may be cold, rainy, windy, hot or humid, and that is not the place, nor the time, to be asking such an important question. Plus, you are not done selling; you have not presented the third element of the process which is to sell the Dealership.

Another trial close I am hearing quite often is: *On a scale from 1 to 10 how would you rank this car?*

First of all, who is establishing the criteria of what determines the difference between a 1 and a 10? What if I get very defensive with this question, thinking you are trying to pin me down and I state a 7? Now what do you do? I guess the obvious question would be to ask: *What is missing that would make it a 10?* Now again, comes the questions and obvious sales pitches that will make the Customer more defensive.

Stop these trial closes, they do not work.

There is only one thing you want to know when you walk away from the car, and that is, do they like it. Not whether they are going to buy it? Do they like it? Asking them that question, if done in a non-pressure manner will not make them more defensive, and it is a logical question.

The way this is done is to simply ask: *Does this vehicle meet all the qualifications and expectations you are looking for in your shopping process?*

I am not asking them to buy the car, all I want to know is do they like the car, because if they don't, there is no sense in moving forward with the next step. Ironically, you will find that greater than 95% will say, Yes, they do like the car. Why? Because you have done a great job up to this point. You have inspired them, you are different from what they were expecting and you never asked any questions or made any statements for them to raise their defensive posture.

I want to repeat my statement one more time, because there are two words that I have inserted into the statement that is designed to still continue the process of lowering their defensive posture: *Does this vehicle meet all the qualifications and expectations you are looking for in your shopping process?*

The two words are *Shopping Process*. These two words will continue the process of lowering that ever present defensive posture. If you have been doing a great job throughout your presentation, the Customer should already be at a very relaxed state, but it never hurts to continue the process.

Ironically, most people will respond with a positive comment. Why? Because you have been doing a great job. You have selected a car they like, you have done a thorough interior and exterior presentation and they have taken a lengthy drive, how could they not love the car. In the few occasions that their response is not positive, in most cases, their reasoning will be based on either a missing feature or benefit, or an item that they do not feel is necessary in their selection.

Step #8: Service Walk

No presentation is complete without a service walk.

As I have stated numerous times, we sell three things. We sell our product, our personality and our Dealership, and there is no better way to sell the Dealership than with a Service Walk.

After getting a positive response to: *Does this vehicle meet all the qualifications and expectations you are looking for in your shopping process?* It is now time for a transitional phrase into the Service Walk.

We all know we never want to ask them if they would like to see our Service Department, as some might say,

No! So why not just assume this step. *Folks, I would like to show you something we are very proud of here at the Dealership.* And once stated, turn and start walking towards your service department, they will follow.

Now let's face facts, the Service Department is not a very exciting place for most people to visit, so don't spend much time back there. I call it the walk and talk, if you keep walking and talking, the Customer will follow you and keep nodding their heads. Be thorough, but if you are long winded, it will get boring for most.

Explain the importance of making an appointment, how to enter the Service Department, tell them how many Service Writers and Technicians are on staff, show them the Customer lounge and tell them if you have a shuttle or loaner car program. If you really want to inspire your Customer, then introduce them to a Service Writer. Develop in advance what you will talk about, and what they will talk about. It should not be a long visit, but long enough to demonstrate to your Customer that everyone at the Dealership will look after their best interest.

The following is a sample presentation that I teach Service Writers to present:

Salesperson: *Mr. & Mrs. Smith, this is Bob, one of our Service Writers. Bob, this is Mr. & Mrs. Smith. The Smith's are looking at a new Nissan Altima.*

Service Writer: *Mr. & Mrs. Smith it is very nice to*

	meet you. The Altima is a wonderful car, isn't it?
Customer:	*Yes, we liked it very much.*
Service Writer:	*I am sure that David has told you a little bit about our Service Department. I would like to share a few more things with you. First of all, our Service Department is open Monday thru Friday from 7:30AM to 6:00PM and we do have Saturday hours from 8:00AM to 1:00PM.*
	We do recommend an appointment for any maintenance or service work, but if you have an emergency please do not hesitate to bring it in right away, we will fit you in. When you do come in if our garage doors are shut just beep your horn and we will open them up so you can drive in and get out from the elements. While waiting, we have a Customer Lounge with coffee, soft drinks, magazines and a TV. But, if you would like a ride home, to work or even the mall, we will gladly give you a ride and even return to pick you up once the car has been completed.

Now, who is going to be the primary driver of the car?

Customer: *She is. The car is for her.*

Service Writer: *Mrs. Smith there are two things about this car you need to know. First, make sure you check the oil during the first 45 to 60 days of ownership. Sometimes a new car will burn a quick quart of oil, don't be alarmed just add the quart and you will be fine.*

Second, if you want this car to run forever, then all you need to do is an oil change every 5 months or 5,000 miles. We do them here at the Dealership for $29.95 and the local oil change shops do them for $29.95. We do not care where you take the car to have it done, just as long as it is done on a regular basis.
Mr. & Mrs. Smith, it was very nice to meet you, enjoy the new car and if you need me for anything here is my card, please do not hesitate to call me.

Customer: *Thank you, we will.*

Now consider what has just happened?   The Service

Writer added to the value of selling the Dealership. It was a non-threatening presentation providing more information to the Customer about the Service Department. But it was more than just a presentation, it actually presented two separate trial closing statements.

The first trial close was when the Service Writer stated; *The Altima is a wonderful car, isn't it?* As most will, the Customer responded with a: *Yes, we liked it very much.* In my opinion that was clearly an indirect buying response.

The second trial close was at the end when the Service Writer stated: *Mr. & Mrs. Smith, it was very nice to meet you, enjoy the new car and if you need me for anything here is my card. Please do not hesitate to call me.*

Again, the Customer responded with a very common reply of: *Thank you, we will.*

The unique part is the Customers defensive posture was never increased during this entire presentation by the Service Writer. It was very caring, responsible and logical. Nothing stated was unexpected or would have made the Customer more defensive.

I cannot emphasize enough the importance of both a Service Walk and an introduction to the Service Writer as part of your sales presentation. If you are going to deliver the best presentation you can, then including a Service Walk is essential.

The Sales Process

I have now shared with you a set of sales steps that have been carefully designed with the Customer in mind. A set of steps that will never increase anyone's defensive posture, only lower them.

From the time the Customer enters the Dealership, always keep in mind their posture and work it to your advantage. Utilize effective responses to the initial obstacles you hear and then respond with word tracks that lower their posture, and catch them pleasantly off guard. The lower their posture gets, the easier it will be to close a deal now. Remember, they know our processes and procedures, so they come to the Dealership prepared and ready to do battle. Eliminate their fears and you will throw their entire game plan into a tail spin.

Selling a car, just like buying a car, can be a fun experience. We just have to create an environment of ease and enjoyment.

CHAPTER 17
THE FOUR STEP OBJECTION
PROCESS

As you have hopefully already discovered, much of what I am sharing with you is a new and improved way to be more productive and profitable in our business. The old way is outdated and our Customer's are smarter. It is not my intent to criticize what was done in the past, but, as in all things, the world changes and we must change with it if we are to keep up.

Because people have become more educated and knowledgeable about what we do, it is imperative that we also become more in tune with our Customers in order to earn their business and win in today's marketplace. Hence, the title of this book 'Understanding Your Customer.' When you learn to understand what the Customer wants, you can better serve them and potentially earn their business for life.

Today's Customer already knows what to expect when they come to a Dealership to shop. They know that they are vulnerable and do not want to be taken advantage of, therefore they come loaded with anxiety and defensiveness. This causes them to bring Objections that cause most Salespeople to react in a way that makes the Customer even more anxious and defensive. This turns the car buying experience into a negative one, instead of something that should be exciting and fun.

In the old school methods we were taught a 3 step process to deal with Customer Objections:

1. Repeat the Objection
2. Isolate the Objection
3. Overcome the Objection

All of these were meant to give a structure to your response to common Objections. The problem is, they never worked. Structure is good, but only if that structure comes with a viable solution.

Take this first response as an example. If the Customer gave an Objection we were to repeat the Objection back to them. For example, a Customer might state, *we want to go home and think about it.* To repeat that back to the Customer makes no sense at all. In fact, it sounds silly when you think about it.

The only logical response would be, *So.... You want to go home and think about it?* Well, they just said that.

Next, we were taught to isolate the Objection. How much more can you isolate a statement like, *we want to go home and think about it.* The only thing you could say is, *what is it you want to think about?* But all that does is create more objections and possibly something you do not really want to hear.

Finally, we were told to overcome the Objection. If that were possible, it would at least include an explanation of how to structure your response, but they don't tell you how to do that. So where can we go from there?

What I would like to teach you are 4 steps that are easy to follow, make logical sense and work effectively. They are:

1. Acknowledge
2. Counter
3. Seek Acknowledgment
4. Close

Before I deal with each objection response let me first say that the Customer already expects you to respond in a certain way and that is why they are prepared to object and fully expect a pressure response in return to their Objections. That is why it is so important to be unique and creative when you structure your response. This is what I like to refer to as 'Catching the Customer Pleasantly Off-Guard.'

Once the Customer objects, their defenses go straight up, because they expect you to respond back with a pressure statement and attack their Objections. It is a natural defensive mechanism and is meant to protect them from your response. Instead, the acknowledgment step is designed to do exactly the opposite of what the Customer is expecting and that is to agree with them and to empathize with their Objection. When this happens, the Customers defensive mechanisms will immediately begin to come down.

Their defenses drop because they recognize you are not going to attack their Objection and in fact you are saying that you agree with it.

This may sound familiar if you have been taught the old 'feel, felt, found' concept. In other words, *"I know how you feel – many people have felt the same way – until they found out for themselves."*

No doubt this worked better than to directly attack their Objections out right, and it had a basis in a workable process. But like all things over time, this needed to be improved, if for no other reason than just to be new and fresh. Remember, the worst reason to do anything is because that's the way it's always been done.

Let's look at a typical Acknowledgement to an Objection to demonstrate how this would work. Let's use the Objection, *"That payment is too high!"* The old feel, felt, found response would be something like this:

I know exactly how you feel. Many people have felt the same way. Until they found that they needed to go above their expected payment range to get the vehicle they wanted.

The trouble is that this in fact was attacking the Customer all over again, putting them back on the defensive and causing them to respond again. This would not likely bring a positive response from the Customer under most circumstances. And this is the opposite of what you want. Your goal is to make them less defensive, not cause them to be more defensive.

Instead, the Acknowledgment must be sincere and must show the Customer that you understand and can personally relate to their issue before you begin to give them another view to consider.

Here is an example of how this kind of Acknowledgment can be stated:

Step#1 – The Acknowledgment

The Customer states, *that payment is too high.*

You Acknowledge with, *"I understand how you feel. When I decide to purchase a high ticket item like a car I always try to establish a budget to and try very hard to stay within that budget and sometimes it's difficult, isn't it?"*

That's all there is to it! You Acknowledged their Objection in a manner that was not confrontational and showed them that you sincerely heard and understood what they were stating. You Acknowledged it in a manner agreeing that what they said made sense.

Did you also notice that I utilized a tie down phrase *(isn't it)*. The goal of a tie down phrase is to insure the Customer will return the Acknowledgement with a comment, body motion or visual acceptance. In essence, they understood what you were stating and they now agree with you.

If done properly, you will get a return Acknowledgement every time.

This is the first step to effectively handling Customer Objections.

Step #2 – The Counter

It is important to remember that the reason Customers object are a refusal to follow our process, outright defensive statements, or a refusal to make the purchase by delaying the decision. Understand that all of these Objections are triggered by defensive mechanisms and/or a fear of making a mistake and being taken advantage of by the Salesperson.

Once you have lowered the Customer's defenses with a sincere Acknowledgment, you must be careful not to raise them again with an argumentative Counter statement. A good response must be logical, intelligent and must not sound as if you are trying to pressure the Customer. You are only trying to give good, logical and intelligent information for them to consider. To make them indirectly change their thinking patterns without them realizing it.

Let me give you an example that many of you can relate to: The other day my son came and told me he was going out for the evening with some friends. I told him to be home by 10:00PM. He asked me why so early. And my response was, *"Because I said so."* For the next 30 seconds he begged, pleaded and whined requesting to stay out later.

Why? All my friends can stay out til 11:00PM, why can't I? Please! Come on!

The more he begged and whined, the easier it was for me to say No.

Ten minutes later his sister told me she was going out for the evening to. I made the same response, be home by 10:00PM. She then stated that last weekend I let her stay out til 11:00PM knowing that she was at Becky's house, and I did so because Becky's parents were both home and that at 10:45PM Becky's dad was going to drive all the girls home, with the last girl being home at 11:00PM.

That tonight she was going to be at Mary's house, and just like last weekend both of Mary's parents were home and Mary's dad was going to drive all the girls home starting at 10:45PM, with the last girl getting home no later than 11:00PM.

Like most of you, I said OK. Why did I say OK to her? Because she gave me a logical reason to change my mind. All my son did was beg, plead and whine, with no logical reason to change my mind.

The goal of the Counter step is the same principle. To give the Customer a logical reason to change their mind.

An effective Counter is to make a statement, tell a story or provide a scenario that will allow the Customer to have a second thought as to why they were objecting. The following is a Counter response to the same Customer Objection, *that payment is too high:*

Mr. & Mrs. Customer, let me share with you something that I think you will find very interesting. A couple of weeks ago I was in our Service Department and bumped into a Customer whom I sold a car to about six-months ago. I asked him how he was doing and he stated that he was doing fine. Then I asked him how the car was and wow, did I get a response that I wasn't expecting!

He stated that he was very unhappy with his purchase; not with me, the car or with the Dealership, but with himself. He said that he could actually be the Poster Child for that old saying, 'Don't be penny wise and pound foolish.'

He reminded me that he saved $40 in his monthly payment by not getting the model that had the sunroof and the leather seats, and that every day when he gets in the car he kicks himself for that decision. He stated that today he would gladly pay an extra $40 a month for those options and that he found it hard to believe that he made such a poor decision over such a small amount of money; that sure, $40 seemed like a lot at the time, but to save a few bucks on such a large purchase was a big mistake.

And that the worst part of all, is that he still has 54 more payments on this car.

That's the completion of my Counter Statement. The goal is to give the Customer a situation, story, or scenario they can relate to. Your Counter must be short, sweet and to the point. This particular counter story is designed to help the Customer have second thoughts as to whether to spend the additional money in order to get what they want.

Step #3 – Seek Acknowledgment

Before you can proceed to the final step, which is the Close, you must first verify that the Customer has accepted your Counter response and acknowledges it as a valid reply to their Objection. If you don't have that, you will need to return to step #2 for another Counter response to the Objection.

Again, in my Seek Acknowledgement, I like to use tie down phrases to confirm they have accepted my statement. The following is my Seek Acknowledgement to, *That payment is too high:*

Obviously, just like me, you have to feel bad for this guy in this situation, don't you?

If the Customers response is positive this automatically sets you up to move to the next step and go for a Close, which is your ultimate goal.

Step #4 – The Close

In automobile sales, just as in all other selling situations, it is absolutely critical that you ask for the sale. No matter what steps you go through in your sales process, if you don't ask the Customer to make the purchase, it is very likely they will not make the decision to do so. But choosing when to ask for the sale is just as important towards a successful closing. There are 3 important steps that you must confirm before asking for the sale:

1. Are they sold on the car?

2. Are they sold on you?

3. Is your Dealership where they want to do business?

When these are confirmed, you have earned the right to ask for the sale, and then, and only then, should the sale be asked for. Remember, asking the Customer, *"what do they think?"* or sitting silently and waiting for them to respond is not the same as asking for the sale.

When you have:

➢ Acknowledged their Objection
➢ Offered a Counter Response
➢ Received the Customers Acknowledgment and acceptance of your Counter Response

Only then can you, with credibility, ask for the sale. Why? Because you have earned the right to do so.

When asking for the sale, do so with confidence. Again, the number one reason most of us don't close a deal is because we fail to ask for the sale.

There are seven simple words that will increase your rate of sales immediately, and they are:

Would you like to buy the car?

If you have done a good job with your sales presentation and if you have successfully handled their Objections using the structured process I have just shown you, you have earned the right to ask for the sale. So just do it!

Ask once! Ask twice! Keep asking as long as you keep earning the right to do so.

I cannot tell you how many times I have seen Salespeople make the most amazing presentations and then fail to ask for the sale. I know most of you are saying to yourself, *"I always ask for the sale."* But do you really, and do you do it in a manner that truly asks for the business or in a roundabout way just hoping to get a positive response?

The old school style of just being silent, is extremely ineffective. The concept of, *'he who speaks first loses'* does not apply in this situation. The amazing part is that in some cases once asked, the Customer may just say YES! And that happens more often than you think it will.

So don't be fearful, don't be bashful or offer innuendo's expecting the Customer to close the sale for you. Just ask for the order and you'll probably get it. Why? Because you have earned the right to have their business.

CHAPTER 18
SOLD CUSTOMER FOLLOW-UP

Have you ever wondered why Salespeople continually sell the same amount of cars year after year? How 10 car per month Salespeople tend to sell 10 cars per month their first year in the automobile business, their fifth year, their tenth year and even their twentieth year? Logically, you would think that to be impossible. One would have to sell more cars each year. The laws of physics would dictate a client base would have to grow.

Not in our industry. Not with our Salespeople. We are the only industry that Salespeople fail to get better each and every year.

This problem is actually the root of other more serious problems. Our failure to improve has caused the industry to lose talented people; it has created an atmosphere of poor acceptable performance levels and even worse, to attract new talented individuals. In essence, it may just be the root of so many of our industry problems.

Most people want a career, and not just a job. A career is something you look forward to doing every day, something that offers you a constant challenge, with room for increased income, stability and promotions. Yet most Automobile Salespeople consider what they do as just a job. A job that does not challenge them daily provides minimal stability and includes a weekly work schedule that most would consider ridiculous. What kind of family life does one have when they work 60 plus hours a week?

So how would one turn a position in automobile sales from a job to a career? They build a book of business that grows each and every year. A client base that provides them with long term stability, a great income potential and the ability to work a schedule that others in our business would only dream of having.

The solution is to treat every person who buys a car from you as a long term prospect and opportunity. During the sales process most Salespeople state that one of the reasons why they should buy a car from them is because they will take care of them after the sale. That their long term happiness with this car is one of their utmost goals.

The best way to accomplish this goal is to become the Customer's Automotive Liaison after the sale. To take care of their car in a manner that no one else will, to a level the Customer does not expect and to do so with care and pride.

Every car has a scheduled maintenance program recommended by the manufacturer. As the Salesperson, why not contact the Customer each and every time a scheduled maintenance is required. Call the Customer every 5 months informing them that their oil must be changed. Every 10 months to remind them to again, change the oil, but this time to also rotate their tires. Make sure they do their scheduled yearly safety check-ups that all manufacturers recommend. If there is a major recall, then be the one to contact them to inform them of what needs to be done.

Consider this, the average person will buy 12 – 15 cars in their lifetime, and will also influence 30 other buyers every 10 – 15 years. That's a lot of people that can be sent your way. And as a Salesperson I want every opportunity I can get.

Imagine this, in year one of a Salesperson's career they average 10 cars per month. They prescribe to the theory of being every Customer's Automotive Liaison. If any one of those Customers over the next couple of years is around anyone that mentions the thought of looking for a new car, who do you think they will remember? You, of course, and now an additional opportunity is created.

It is a proven fact that even the best Salespeople can only sell so many cars per month based on walk-in traffic, and that amount is around 15 cars per month. Under the Liaison program every 3 years they should be selling an additional 3 cars per month from be-back Customers and referrals from their sold Customer data base. So by year 10 that Salesperson is now selling 24 cars per month.

We all know that one of the worst aspects of being in our industry as a Salesperson is the hours. We work nights, weekends and even holidays. We give up time with our family, missing sporting events, school events and just sitting around the dinner table talking.

What do you say to your son who asks you to coach his

little league team or to your daughter who wants you to be a chaperon on the school field trip? You say, I am sorry I can't. I have to work. But not if you are a 25 plus per month car Salesperson. As a 25 plus per month car Salesperson you are not depending on walk-in traffic to make a living, you are selling from a client base, and that client base is only developed if you become a Liaison for your Customer.

When making your routine maintenance calls be sure to only call once. If they are not available then leave them a message, they will get it. Just remind them of the services that need to be done, that you are happy to help them with scheduling an appointment or if they would like to take care of it on their own that your call was just a friendly reminder.

If you do happen to make personal contact with them it is very important at the end of the conversation to NOT, and I repeat, NOT, make any comments in regards to them buying a new car or providing any names to you of their friends that may be in the market for a new car. By doing this you have changed your role from a Liaison, or person who truly cares, to a Salesperson. Once the Customer thinks that your contact with them has an alternative motive, they will shut you out and many will refuse to take your calls in the future.

Your only goal is to take care of their car, just like you promised them during the sales process.

This concept is not designed to be hard, timely or miniscule. It is simply making a 60 second call every 120 days or so, to keep your name in front of them in a manner that benefits both of you. There is no better way to build a long and lasting relationship with your Customers than this.

I have also seen many Salespeople take this concept to an even higher level. We all know that we cannot sell everyone a car. That some people find different cars they like, whether it be the style, comfort or performance. Sure, we want to sell everyone our product, but we know that is just not going to happen.

Some Salespeople have actually utilized the Liaison concept even with those Customers who make their purchase elsewhere. Why not? It is still a contact, the development of a relationship and an opportunity to show the Customer you care. In many cases you can still perform their scheduled maintenance at your Dealership.

By doing this, you will insure that on any future purchases most will feel compelled to contact you first, and most will definitely send any friends, family members or co-workers to you if the need for a car comes up in conversation. Remember, a Customer is a long term opportunity. An opportunity to develop a long relationship that in most cases should never end.

What do you have to lose? An investment that only takes 60 seconds every 4 – 6 months. I would gladly make that investment knowing the potential rewards.

So don't be one of those Salespeople who 10 years from

now is still selling 8 – 10 cars per month. Someone who looks at what they do as a job, and not a career. I do not make many promises, but this one I will make, commit to this concept and you will be very glad you did.

CHAPTER 19
CUSTOMERS FOR LIFE

Every serious career minded Salesperson dreams of building a Customer base that will grow over the years to produce a consistent and prosperous living, and a stream of residual business for their future. If that were not possible, selling cars would not really be a career, it would be just a job.

Throughout this book, I have shown you what it takes to understand your Customer, the values of taking the time to get to know them and how to help them accomplish their goals, thereby accomplishing your own in the process. I have taught you the value of calming their fears and defensiveness, and how to understand what they are telling you with their words and their actions, so you can learn how best to serve them and earn their business.

Throughout every sentence, paragraph and chapter I have had only one thing in mind: helping you to become the best that you can be so that your career in automobile sales can be fulfilling, successful and enduring.

You cannot truly build a lifetime career in this business without building Customers for Life. If your success depends upon finding and selling brand new Customers every day, day in and day out, your job will become like a treadmill that wears you out, and offers little joy and pleasure from a career perspective.

Though some who start in sales will go on to become Department Managers or even Dealers, many who are excellent at selling choose to remain Salespeople throughout their career. Those who do so and have learned how to nurture their Customers for long term business loyalty can expect to have a growing and successful career that eventually requires little selling and more time spent taking care of their regular Customers.

This type of career professional views their Customer base as their business family. In turn, their Customers come to them whenever they have transportation needs and they refer their family and friends to them as well.

Considering the fact that the average American in their lifetime will own 12-15 cars, and the average household today has 2-3 cars in their driveway or garage, earning someone's business for life can grow your Customer base exponentially. When you add to this the trade-ins that come to the Dealership when your Customers buy a new car, you have a substantial amount of potential vehicle sales taking place from just one Customer.

Of course it's nice to get Dad's business, but what about Mom? What about the car for the daughter or son who just graduated and is headed off to college? Don't you want their business too? Who's going to sell them a car? . . . or all the cars they buy in their lifetime? Why not you?

Then there are the relatives and friends, or the neighbor who sees them pull in the driveway in their shiny new car? Who's going to take care of them when they decide it's time to change vehicles? Again I ask, *why not you?*

I assure you it can be done, and it is being done by those Leaders in our trade who know the value of winning a Customer for Life. They have a long term vision for their career and they are working smart to bring that vision to pass.

Of course there's always the Salesperson who just likes the thrill of the kill. They want to win every time at all cost. Their thoughts rarely stray beyond the Customer that is standing in front of them at any given moment. Their long term view for their career ends every month and starts over again on the next deal. If they see a previous Customer again it won't really make a difference unless they came to get another car. They rarely remember the last Customer, because they are so busy working on the next one.

If they do see a former Customer in the Service Department they avoid them so they don't have to hear about any problems they may be experiencing. They are not interested in helping them if it doesn't mean money in their pocket today.

If that's the way you see this business, you might want to step back and take a long look down the road to your future. Why would you want to chase down new "Ups" every day when you could be sitting at your desk writing deals for your faithful Customers and the people they keep sending your way who also need cars?

How do you make that happen? You find out what a buyer truly wants and needs, and do your best to help them get it.

After you have served your Customer in the sale, you keep in touch with them regularly as their Automotive Liaison. Always reminding them of when scheduled routine maintenance is due.

You care for them as though they were family. Why? Because they are! They are your business family; a part of your growing and appreciative Customer base.

From the minute a potential Customer steps onto your Dealership lot, how do you see them in your mind? Do you view them in relation to your monthly sales goal or do you see them in relation to your professional career? Are they the potential answer to getting this month's bonus or someone who represents an extended family of vehicle owners who will buy only from you, because you do your best to treat them the way you would want to be treated if you were buying a car?

If you're not sure, you may need to ask yourself this question: *Do I really care what the Customer wants, or do I only care about making the sale today?*

Though that may sound like a ridiculous question, it is often the latter mindset that drives many Salespeople to use pressure tactics and manipulation to get another deal on the sales board. It is what those in our business have been teaching for decades and it has contributed to the negative reputation our business has in the public mind.

Does that mean you don't want to do everything you can to sell them a car today? Of course not! You want to sell them a car today if you can. But not if it isn't what they want and need, but is just the result of your slick or pressure sales tactics. That has short term value for you, but is a negative in the long term value of gaining a Customer for Life.

Instead, what if you could sell to them and all of their extended relationships today, tomorrow, next month and over the next twenty years? Isn't that worth your best effort? Of course it is. Isn't that worth planning for a long career rather than a month's end bonus? I think so. Ironically, if you follow these concepts that I have described in this book you will have huge month end bonuses every month.

Being the best at anything requires dedication, learning, consistency, change and growth. Being the best in automobile sales demands not only these, but it calls for a level of Customer care that is not usually required of the sales clerk at the department store or the Salesperson who sells vacuums door to door. It requires an interaction and relationship with the Customer that always looks out for their best interest and benefit.

Creating Customers for Life is an art form that is first unique and inspiring, and then relational and genuinely helpful. It's not something that you have to fake. It is the result of real integrity and a sincere desire to help those who come to you with their transportation needs and desires. Whether it is for them, their loved ones or their friends and business relationships, when someone needs a vehicle they will tell them about you and how you served them during and after the sale.

The resulting benefit of such professionalism in our business is a growing stream of Customers who will place their trust in you when it comes to buying and servicing their vehicles. And this is what it means to build a business based upon quality Customer care and professional knowledge of retail Automobile sales.

Remember, anything learned can be unlearned. Start today to plan your career in this business and set long term goals for developing a 'Customers for Life' mentality. Before you know it, you will be servicing regular Customers who entrust you with their transportation needs and look to you for your expert assistance when it is time to replace their vehicle.

When this happens you can chart a solid career in this business and expect the rewards that come to those who dedicate themselves to quality and Customer Care in the retail automotive industry. You can expect to be that person who sits at their desk writing deals and calling your Customer base, rather than spending your days walking the lot looking for the next new opportunity.

CHAPTER 20
SECOND PLACE IS LAST PLACE

As we now come near the end of the book, it should be clear to see that understanding your Customer often begins with understanding yourself. What are your goals in life? How do you plan to achieve them? Do you look at your current employment as a job or as a career? What are your personal values? Do you perform in your profession in such a way that your Customers and co-workers receive benefit from their relationship with you?

These may seem like unusual questions in a book about selling, but the truth is, all of life is selling. Everything we do in life is in fact influencing others and selling ourselves, our beliefs and our views, as well as the products we sell to earn our living. Whether we win or lose in life, is in some way connected to all of these things. We choose how we want to live and if we are wise, we plan our life with some long term goals, and take orderly steps along the way to help us achieve those goals.

In reality we know that not everyone wins. There are endless stories of Salespeople with minimal achievements that have never experienced success in this business. And there are those who have wonderful careers in retail automotive sales and have risen to the top of our industry. It is up to you to decide which of these you will be.

Though you cannot ultimately control what and from whom your Customers choose to buy, the techniques and processes that I have shared with you in this book will help you take advantage of those things that you can control. They will teach you to work hard and smart, with an expectation of success, as well as a plan of how best to achieve it.

The title of this chapter, 'Second Place is Last Place' is not meant to suggest that you should turn your life into a competition with everyone around you to make sure you always come out on top. Winning is not about always beating others across the goal line to take the prize. It is far more than that. It is about making sure that you are maximizing every opportunity you have to achieve your best and to have a life that has meaning and purpose; achieving your goals for success, having earned the right to do so by learning, changing, and growing to your full potential.

As an Automobile Salesperson, the rewards of your dedication and commitment to your craft are abundant. None more so than when you have developed a loyal clientele that returns to you whenever they have transportation needs to be filled. They also refer family, friends and business associates to you who are looking to buy a vehicle. These too can become your loyal Customers who will do the same, which will help your business grow exponentially with endless possibilities.

The joy of knowing that you are doing your best to meet your Customers' needs and the financial blessing that comes from this can be quite substantial. Your career potential is only limited by the level of commitment you make to your personal growth and your professional development. When these things are in line, the sky truly is the limit.

When you choose to aim for the top you will face many things that will challenge you. You must commit to your success no matter what it takes. Those who allow themselves to settle for mediocrity will never know the true joy of winning the race.

The tools that I have given you in this book will serve you well if you implement them into your practice of selling, and devote yourself to learning how best to understand and serve your Customers. They have proven themselves in the careers of many people over the years that have attended my seminars and practiced the principles I learned through my years in the industry.

Nothing is more important to you as a Salesperson than developing a thorough understanding of those who come to you looking to purchase a vehicle. Find out what makes them tick and what inspires them to buy. Learn how to present yourself in a way that gives them confidence in you as their go-to person in every aspect of the retail automobile business. This is what will set you apart from your competition and give you a reputation as an honest, ethical and professional representative of your company and your trade. It is the key to your success in this business.

Those who continuously come in second place with their competition, come in last place with themselves and their potential Customers. No matter what you think of yourself, your product or your Dealership, if you do not convince your Customers of the value of buying from you, they will go elsewhere and someone else will win their business. This is not only bad for you, but it can be the same for those who should have become your Customers, but bought elsewhere.

Too many Salespeople in our business focus on their own agenda. When a Customer comes to their Dealership, they devote themselves to one thing and one thing only: selling them a car today regardless of what they must do to accomplish that. They have no desire to understand the Customers' needs and their process is a battle of wits or a flashy game of persuasion and control. This often leaves the buyer sorry they made the purchase and vowing never to return there again when they need another vehicle.

In too many cases this is in fact the method of your competition. If you fail to do your best to understand and serve your Customers, they may ultimately end up in the hands of those who sell this way. When this happens, second place becomes last place. When it happens a lot, you will walk away from all the potential that could be yours in this business and find another career.

What I have given you in this book comes from many years of selling and management in the retail automotive business, and even more years of traveling throughout North America training Dealers, Managers, and Salespeople in the things I have written about in this book. I know they work and I know they can bring you to a successful career that will be both personally and professionally fulfilling, and that will allow you the kind of lifestyle that often accompanies success.

Winning is a habit. It is a habit that is formed from having the right perspective and practicing the right methods and principles in your life and in your business.

Losing is also a habit and can be habit forming. Once you start down the path of taking the easy road and begin to take for granted those things that lead to success, you will experience the down side and may find yourself unable to regain your lost ground. Don't let that happen to you.

At the heart of this is learning how to understand your Customer. Every person is different and therefore every Customer is different from the next. Because of this you cannot let your guard down and operate from a memorized program that only worked to a level of mediocrity in the past.

Each time that you step out onto the lot to 'Meet & Greet' your next potential Customer, you must start all over again the process of earnestly listening to what they want to tell you about why they have come to your Dealership; learning how to read their actions and their words to correctly understand what they want and need, and how you can best help them find it.

You must make every effort to help them shed their natural defensive mechanisms and become comfortable with you as their Salesperson. When you can do this, your potential for an inspiring and effective presentation is unlimited.

With each new Customer you must commit to the time required to learn what it will take to earn their business. Every new Customer is your first Customer. The one that can take you toward achieving your personal sales and career goals, because you are seriously committed to helping them achieve their buying goals, by meeting and exceeding their expectations. You are not just selling a car! You are selling yourself, your Dealership and potentially earning a Customer for life.

Don't forget the value that you bring to your Dealership as a successful, career minded Salesperson with a great future ahead of you. In my experience the doors open wide for this type of professional when they have a proven track record that consistently brings in new business as well as return Customers from sales they have made in the past.

Why not? That's what makes a successful Dealership: the people who work there day in and day out producing results that make for a growing and increasingly profitable business.

Second place is last place! Set your sights on success and you will never know the discouraging reality of bringing up the rear. There may be times when things are challenging and difficult, as life has a tendency to be like that no matter who we are. But in the big picture you will be able to look back with satisfaction knowing that you made the right choices along the way and chose a career that had great potential for you and your family.

Always remember that I will be there cheering you on from the bleachers. Those who practice the principles that I teach in my seminars, training programs and in my books and videos are in some way a member of my family. You are my Customers and my friends! Hopefully, we will both continue to benefit from the relationship we now have.

I encourage you to make a genuine effort to understand your Customers and find out what it takes to make them yours for life. Never give up the pursuit of learning how best to do this business and genuinely serve them, and you will find that they will be there when you need to make the next sale to accomplish your goals and achieve the next step toward your success.

If you do these things I assure you that you will never have to settle for last place or see your Customers going anywhere else to have their transportation needs met. As long as there are people needing to purchase vehicles for their busy lives, you will be able to make a great living.

CHAPTER 21
CONCLUSION

I hope you have enjoyed reading this book, as much as I have enjoyed writing it. I feel like I have been preparing my entire career for this book. My travels, speaking engagements, time visiting Dealerships and meeting Salespeople all over the world truly has made my career in this industry a wonderful experience.

I truly cannot think of a better industry than the Automobile Industry. Everyone takes different a path in life; some enjoy the steady environment of a 9 to 5 job, while others, like me, thrive on the excitement of a new adventure each and every day. I learned a long time ago that my drive is learning and training. There is nothing better than seeing the look on someone's face when you teach them something new, something that they can take back with them and put to immediate use, and see benefits from that idea right away.

I have always stated that once someone thinks they know it all in a particular industry, then it is time to move on, to do something else. Think about it, how fun can it be once you have reached the top, once you have learned everything there is about a line of work and that you have mastered the craft. I would think the challenge of new heights is what would drive most people.

As for me, I am far from knowing it all. Every day I strive to learn something new, something exciting, something that will make me better at what I do, and will take me to the next level in my career. I want to be challenged every day.

My first book, 'The Secrets of Inspirational Selling' received a great response from people in our industry and has become a staple of an item in Dealerships all over the world. A book that many Dealers insist their new hires read before taking their first 'UP' and one that veteran Salespeople read over and over again to further their thoughts of how the sales process should be conducted.

My second book, 'The Leadership Factor' has become a symbol of how Dealers and Managers must think if they are to succeed in this very competitive industry. How the recruitment, development and motivation of their team is the foundation of structure that ultimately determines their revenue and growth as an organization.

Now with this, my third book, 'Understanding Your Customer', my goal was to prepare our industry for the change that is taking place on our showroom floors. A change that has been long overdue and will have to be accepted if most of us are going to stay competitive in this industry. The Customer clearly has the edge over us. It is a buyer's market, and they know that.

As I am putting the finishing touches on this book, I am already making notes for my next book. As long as I keep learning, I will keep sharing with you those ideas and concepts that I believe will continually improve our ability to succeed.

I'd like to hear from you as you progress through the process of applying the things you have learned in this book. If I can help you in any way, or if your Dealership would like to sponsor a training session at your Dealership, please contact me or visit our company website for additional information. Our web address is: www.davidlewis.com

Thanks again for taking the time to read my book and for making the commitment to become the kind of Salesperson we need today in our industry.

David Lewis
dlewis@davidlewis.com

NOTES

he could see now, quite drunk. "Don't believe a word he says," she told Dave. "We wanted to get to you while the halo was still hot."

Constance, who had begun to feel her drinks a little too, giggled. "Miriam always does have to catch the opening nights. The run is for the common folks."

"You're darn loving right! First cabin or no cabin at all. Nothing I hate worse than warmed-over heroes. Listen, Dave, I've been dying to ask you all night, but Lester warned me to keep my big mouth shut."

"Ask me what?" He felt himself go tense.

"What you *did* over there. How it happened. Is it all right to ask, or will it send you into a traumatic shock from which you may never recover? I try to keep track of these things but the headshrinkers who write magazine articles about it change their minds from one war to another."

"Miriam," Lester warned her. "Leave the man alone. It's his first night back."

"Lester reads the leave-him-alone men."

From her chair alongside the couch, Constance came in, smug and possessive. "Dave will talk about it when he's ready, Miriam."

Miriam lay back on the couch, her shoes kicked off, her long legs asprawl. Walsh turned his eyes away. Not without regret. Nor without a faint sense of guilt. *Yes, indeed. There was that about those short skirts.*

"Okay," she said, "I can take a hint. I've got no tact. All right, so don't tell me!" She wrinkled her nose at him. "I'll make it up. Probably be a better story anyway."

"You're damned right it will," Walsh said, more forcefully than he had intended. He gulped his sparkling champagne. "Believe me, it wasn't all the way you read it in the papers."

Amos Walsh slapped both hands down hard on his thighs. "Noooooo. . . . Just ran over a couple of thousand

of them Vietcongs, that's all. Davy always was like that. I never seen a boy so shy about being praised. You tell him he did something good, and he could always deliver you eight reasons to show how he hadn't done nothing at all."

"Never you mind, Dave," Miriam chided him, "ten years from now, we won't be able to shut you up. They'll all say, 'Oh, God, here comes Dave Walsh with that awful story about how he wiped out all them Commies.' You'll be a bigger bore than Lester with how he got the partnership."

"Thanks a load!" Lester said. "Thanks a ton."

"I'm perfectly willing to talk about it," Walsh said, deliberately. "I just want to warn you that you're going to be disappointed."

Miriam held up her glass to the light to see the fine bubbles rise to the surface of the wine. "Modesty becomes a hero," she said dreamily. "Of course, it becomes a little sickening after a while. But at first it's nice."

"I'm not being modest." He was trying very hard to conceal his annoyance. "I'm just telling you that Adam March went overboard on a routine little thing, the kind of thing that was happening all over the sector."

The quick exchange of glances between Lester and Amos Walsh made it very clear that Lester agreed with him completely about Dave's inability to accept praise.

"No. I just don't want credit where no credit is due."

"Knock it off, Dave," Miriam told him. "We have come halfway 'round the world to worship at your feet. Like it or not, you're going to be lionized." She threw him a bawdy wink. "Like Confucius say, 'Lie back and enjoy it!' No, that wasn't Confucius, that was my Chinese laundry man. Lester, I keep telling you, you have to do something about my allowance."

"Yes," Lester said. He spoke quietly enough, but his eyes had gone hard. "Or about your mouth."

"Promises, promises." Husband and wife grinned at

each other. "You!" Miriam said, in a subdued, teasing way. "All you ever do is make money."

"Don't knock it, baby. *You* of all people." Lester turned his attention back to Walsh. "By the way, Dave, have you thought about what you're going to do? I mean after you're discharged and rested up and ready to give a thought to making a buck yourself?"

Their refusal to believe him, or even to listen to what he was saying, had completely thrown Dave. And now they had somehow got detoured to a completely different subject. It took a moment for him to readjust his thinking. "Well . . . uh . . . no. I haven't, Les. I mean, not seriously. I suppose I'll finish up at Columbia Teacher's College, get my New York State certificate."

"That's ridiculous, Dave! You're talking nonsense." With a flick of the hand he pushed all that nonsense aside. For the first time that night, Dave was seeing the Lester Sampson he had always known. The confident, authoritative, take-charge executive. The man who had always known where he was going. "Dave, I don't want to push you. You get a better deal somewhere else, I'd want you to take it. I'd *urge* you to take it. I mean that. I just want to lay our proposition on the line."

"Proposition?" Walsh had no idea what he was getting at.

"Bestor, Sampson and Adams, we want you on our team, Dave."

On our team. What do you know, they really did say that. Dave wanted to laugh, but Lester was being so goddamned sincere.

"What in the world do I know about public relations, Les?" He tried not to sound too ungracious. "I mean that PR job in the Army, that was nothing but press releases to hometown newspapers. And even that was fifteen years ago." He didn't have to tell him about the VA. That, as

Lester knew damn well, hadn't been public relations in the real sense at all. He had simply steered the veterans to the proper counselor.

"You don't have to know a damned thing about it to be in public relations today," Lester said. Before Miriam could make the obvious comment on that, he assured Dave that what he really meant was that anything he had to know, he could very easily learn. "Well, brother-in-law, what do you say?"

Walsh placed his glass on the table beside his chair and chose his words precisely. It was a generous offer, and he did not want to dismiss it ungenerously.

"Now, Lester, you've known me for something like ten years, haven't you? I'm not a high-powered guy. I like to do things slow, relaxed, and comfortable. . . ."

"Oh, sure. Like when you fought your way up old Mt. Goliath." He looked around at the others, and laughed.

"Will you cut it out and listen to me please!" He lowered his voice, but bit each word off distinctly. "No offense to any players present, but the rat race is not for me. I want to get into a line that's nice and secure and noncompetitive, like teaching."

He could feel Connie go cold. "You can listen to him, Dave. He just flew across the country to be here. You don't have to be impolite."

"No, no!" Lester waved it away. "He's still keyed up from all he's been through. Give him a little time to settle down, get back to normal. He'll be all right." He reached over and patted Walsh's knee. "You're headed for the big time, Dave. You can't miss. Believe me I know what I'm talking about. Now, I'm not asking any special favors because you and I are family. I just want to lay our proposition before you so you can weigh it against the others."

"*What* others? Doesn't anybody *listen* to me around here? What in hell are these other offers you think I'm sup-

posed to have, Les? Other offers haven't a thing to do with this."

Lester had not lost his superior smile. "You'll get other offers. A hero, a Medal of Honor winner, a man close to Adam March, is not exactly a leper along Madison Avenue. I started to tell you before. When Clem Bestor heard we were coming back to New York he got hold of me and said, 'Now why don't we figure out some way to charge this trip off on the company. Why don't I order you to get back to New York on the double and go into conference with that brother-in-law of yours about bringing him into the firm.' " He became completely serious. "I know Bestor, Sampson and Adams isn't MCA, but we billed four million last year and we're growing."

He leaned forward, his hands folded down between his legs. "There's a whole new market for the black athlete just beginning to open up." Intensely, never taking his eyes off Dave, Lester explained to him that the agencies and their clients had been reluctant to sign even the biggest of the Negro stars to endorse their products because they had some kind of a fear that too many consumers would be driven off by the sight of a black face. "That's going now. We've got facts and figures to show that in every sport, there's a rising ratio of Negro athletes. It hasn't hurt. We tell them they've been shying from shadows. We've got them—some real big ones—just at the point where they're taking a chance here and there." He shook his fist at him like a cheerleader, "It's cracking, Dave; all it needs is one . . . more . . . little . . . push."

He jumped up and began to pace back and forth, with nervous energy. "That's a big, lucrative market and we're going to cut ourselves a piece. And once we show them that they'll be helped, not hurt, by using Negroes, every-thing is gonna crack wide open. After the athletes, the entertainers. Everything." He wheeled around to Walsh.

"You can give it the final push, Dave. You can make it very difficult for them to sit there and tell you, 'No, we won't even give it a chance.'" A harsh, wounded look came over him. "'It isn't me,'" he mimicked, "'I don't have a prejudiced bone in my body. And, I hope you believe me, Sampson, this agency isn't as bad as some people say. We got a nigra gal sitting right there in the reception room where everybody can see her. I'd really like to help, Sampson. Those figures are mighty impressive; they sure give us something to think about it. But those advertisers, Sampson. You know how those advertisers are.'"

It was the first time in his life Dave had ever seen Lester anything less than purely objective or more than totally cynical about his work.

"You can help, Dave. You can do a job." Lester sat back down, a little shaken himself. He drained his glass. "We're prepared to offer you a full partnership. You could do an awful lot worse than that."

It took a while to digest. Miriam had rolled over on her side so that she was staring at him, a little smile on her face, waiting, it seemed, for him to faint with joy. From Constance, he had the sense of held breath.

From his seat at the far end of the table, Amos Walsh said, "That would be a very fine thing for you to do, Davey. That would make me very proud."

"A full partnership," Walsh said finally. "You've talked this over with Bestor and Adams?"

"Man, I told you. I've been with Clem Bestor all afternoon. It was their idea, not mine." He winked at him wisely. "But, as you may well imagine, they didn't have to try that hard to sell me." He chuckled. "Miriam was waiting there at the hotel, and you know how that woman hates to be kept waiting."

"I'm shocked, Les. I don't know what to say."

"Try yes," Miriam said. "Y-e-s, yes. I have been urged to

say that word many a time and I can tell you, David, I never regretted it."

"Bestor, Walsh, Sampson and Adams," Lester intoned. "Has a nice ring to it, doesn't it?"

Bestor, *Walsh,* Sampson and Adams! It kept piling on top of him, burying him. He had a flash image of a little man stenciling the new title on the office door in gilt letters. *Bestor, Walsh, Sampson and Adams.* He hadn't had time to consider the job offer, and already he was getting second billing to the president.

"Lester, this is crazy." He bent over, his face resting on his hands and began to laugh, softly, within himself. "I'm sorry, Les." He pulled himself back upright and wiped his eyes. "But you must see the humor in this too. Here I've always worked hard, lived clean, and written readable, respectable press releases for the Army and the VA. Now, after all these years, my true worth and ability have finally been recognized." He flung his arms up into the air. "The Great American Dream Lives Again!"

Out of the corner of his eye, he caught the sight of his father, watching him with sad, bewildered eyes.

Lester was peering at him too. He was not amused. He was—what did Dave see there—concerned. "What's eating you, Dave?"

"Nothing's eating me. I just have to get used to the idea that I write better copy with an M-16 rifle than with a typewriter."

"You tell 'em, Davey Crockett!" Miriam cheered. "You tell 'em what they can do with their filthy lucre!" She clasped her hands dramatically to her bosom. "Keep yourself pure for the woman you will one day marry."

"Oh, for Christ sake, Miriam," Lester said in disgust.

"I'm sorry, Dave," she said. "I really am. But you should hear yourself." Her eyes shifted quickly to Lester, but before he could say anything else, she said, "All *right!* So I

got no tact."

"And you're so proud of it, aren't you?" Constance snapped.

For once, Miriam was startled. She stared at her sister's cold profile as if to say, *I thought I was on your side;* then, lifting her palms in surrender, she settled back into the cushions, tucked her head down into her shoulders and, drawing her front leg up, began to contemplate her empty glass. From where Dave sat, the whole rounded bottom of her buttock was exposed.

Lester, having had some time to regroup his forces, began again: "Dave, we're all big boys here. Neither of us came with the morning milk. You know we don't want you to come into the firm to write copy. We can pick bright, imaginative kids off any campus for a hundred bucks a week to write press releases. What you can give us, Dave, is executive ability." He looked over at Constance. "Honey, what do you think? Does what I've been saying make sense?"

Constance said primly, "I'm not going to say a word. It's up to Dave. I want Dave to do whatever will make him happy."

Miriam couldn't resist it. "You ever need a witness, Dave. I heard her say it."

"It's a proposition, Dave," Lester said. He was, thank God, going to let it rest. "Think it over. That's all I ask."

"I'll think it over," Walsh promised. He grinned. "I've got three months to pull yet, so I'll have plenty of time to think it over."

"Ahhhhh!" Lester came forward in the chair, waving his cigar at him as if he had one final little magic trick to pull out of his hat. "A Medal of Honor winner can get a discharge upon request."

Walsh felt the bands of muscle tighten around his chest. It was as if Lester had leaned over, wrapped his arms

around him and squeezed. For a long, long moment he had to struggle to catch his breath. "Let me try this once more, Les," he said, when at last his breath came back to him. "That's the second time you've mentioned the Medal of Honor. Well, if you're offering me this partnership on any mistaken idea that I'm getting that medal, or *any* medal— Jesus Christ, are you crazy? The Medal of *Honor?* . . . Well, I just better start thinking about all those other offers of employment that also won't be coming my way."

"Of course it wasn't, Dave." Although the tone was placating, Lester's expression conveyed the pride of a bearer of good news, a man with a happy secret to tell. "You'll get it, though. Adam March is bearing down on it, and March is not completely without influence in the Pentagon. And," he said, significantly, "the White House."

He would not have thought that Lester could say anything else to shock him.

"That isn't how you get the Medal of Honor, Les," Walsh explained quietly. "It may be how you get a ringside table at the Copa. Or an Emmy Award. Or whatever. But it is not, thank God, how you get a Medal of Honor."

"So young, so innocent," Miriam murmured. She caught her husband's warning glare. "Sorry. Sorry about that, Chief."

"You may know public relations, Les," Walsh went on, "but you do not know the United States Army."

Lester's smile was indulgent. "I guess you haven't been reading the David-Slew-the-Red-Goliath theme March has been pushing. Of *course* he can't *get* anybody the Medal of Honor. All he can do is oil the gears a little. Once they start taking testimony from your command, the medal is as good as yours."

Walsh stared at him, dumbfounded. The man was serious! Lester Sampson!

"Yeah," he said drily, "let's not knock it." He stood up

What do you talk like that for?"

" 'I'd want you to take a better offer,' " she said, in a high, mincing voice. " 'Not just because I'm family.' Well, I was glad to see you stall him, Dave. With a really big company, the way he talked, I'll bet you can get. . . ." She stabbed for a figure. "Twenty-five thousand easy."

Walsh had to smile, remembering her pretty speech about wanting him to make up his own mind. "Connie, do you know what a full partner would take out of an outfit that has four million dollars worth of billing?" She should have been able to guess that Lester would have made sure that Dave knew what was at stake before the night was over. "Fifty thousand dollars. Bare minimum. If that's crawling, don't knock it. Don't knock it."

Constance swung around on the hassock to face him, her eyes open wide. "That much? Oh, Dave!"

"That much."

"Oh, Dave!"

He cut his eyes to the ashtray on the bed beside him, grinding out the half-smoked cigarette. He did not want to see the naked avarice he could hear in her voice. He shouldn't have dangled it in front of her, the way Lester had dangled it in front of him.

"Fifty thousand dollars. Oh, Dave. Dave, you're going to take it. You'd be a fool to turn down that kind of money. You're going to call him right now. . . . First thing in the morning and tell him that. . . ."

He forced himself to look at her as, her forehead wrinkling, her mind clicking, she dictated what he was going to tell Lester, as if he were a small child being told what to tell the teacher. "After giving it due thought overnight, having slept on it. . . ." (She liked that phrase, he could see.) " . . . I have decided to accept your kind and generous offer."

"Connie, I am going to do no such thing. Forget it."

"You're going to take it!" She sprang up off the hassock and went to him, hugging him against her. The feel of his cheek against the bare flesh of her waist made her weak with desire for him. Holding him tightly she rolled over, so that she was on top of him.

"Oh, Dave!" Her voice trembled as she rubbed her hips back and forth. She pressed her breasts against his naked chest, the signal for him to reach up and rip off her bra.

He took hold of her arms and, pushing her back gently, swung off the bed and onto his feet. "Sit down, Connie, I want to tell you something," he said.

"Not now, honey," she gasped. She put one arm around his neck, drawing him back, her mouth reaching for his mouth. Her hand was on his belly, the soft fingers working down inside his shorts. He gripped the hand, restrained it, removed her arm from around his neck.

"It's going to be now, Connie," he said firmly.

"Goddamn it!" If he had struck her with his fist, he could not have hurt her more than this brutal rejection. Humiliated, she slumped down on the hassock again, head lowered, her fists clenched tight on her thighs. It required all of her will and effort not to cry.

Walsh took another cigarette from the pack and lit it. He rubbed his knuckles across a persistent itch above his eye. He waited until she had finally contained herself and opened her eyes.

"All right, so tell me something," she snapped. "It's late, and I'm tired. And cold." She reached for a negligee draped over the top of the vanity and pulled it around her shoulders, covering as much of her body as she could.

Walsh went to the closet where his uniform was on a hanger hooked over the top of the open door. He touched the captain's bar pinned on one shoulder.

"Now, Connie, I want you to do me a favor. This isn't going to be easy for me, so, please, give me a break and

don't interrupt."

He rubbed his jaw thoughtfully with the back of his hand. How to begin? How to tell her how this fairy tale had begun when he wasn't sure of all the facts himself. Constance listened in stony, unblinking silence as, laboriously, he reconstructed the unlucky chain of events that had brought Adam March crashing into their lives. What March had told him, and what he had learned from the official Defense Department version. It was like putting together the isolated fragments of a jigsaw puzzle.

Major-General Randolph (Stonewall) Ritter was losing his grip. He had sensed the onset of something intangible, irrevocable, dire over the course of the past eight weeks. When he had received his command nine months earlier, he had come to his office at 6 A.M. each morning with a sense of expectancy and excitement, a feeling that great things were in the air. There was an aura of festiveness about the rooms he and his staff occupied at the divisional headquarters. The wooden walls were decorated with bright, multihued charts and maps, all festooned with red, white, and blue pins. The soft cannel coal crackling in the pot-bellied stove spewed forth rainbow jets of flame and brought forth nostalgic remembrances of a boyhood spent with toy soldiers in a cozy attic room under the eaves on blustery New England winter mornings.

This early winter of 1968 had turned out to be the low point of his career. Of his whole life. In the beginning it had been like a game. Outguessing and outmaneuvering the elusive will-o'-the-wisp enemy, anticipating where the

Vietcong would strike, flushing them out of their jungle hideouts and underground warrens, destroying the little men in black pajamas wherever they were to be found. Reptiles, rodents, something less than human was how General Ritter regarded his North Vietnamese and Vietcong adversaries. He cared scarcely more for the United States' South Vietnamese allies if the truth were known. They were his wards; backward children for whom he had to make allowances. Randolph Ritter had been a respectable athlete at West Point, and he had retained an ardent interest in American sports all of his fifty-eight years. Baseball was his special passion. In his private thoughts he often fancied himself as a "manager" piloting a "team." He pictured himself as Casey Stengel in those invincible years with the Yankees. You accepted small setbacks; there were always those bad breaks that cost you a game here and there. You can't win 'em all. But you won the games that counted.

The change had come about slowly and inexorably. Ho Chi Minh was pouring men and guns into South Vietnam. These new enemy troops, tough professional fighting men tempered by almost twenty years of unremitting wars, did not hit and run like the VC. They stood and fought, giving back as good as they got. They didn't seem to know that America didn't lose wars. *They thought they were as good as us.*

They *were* good. They were *as* good. Before Ritter knew quite what had happened, "Charley" had become a word to be spoken with respect instead of contempt. It had upset something more than his military calculations! It had upset something deep-seated, something in the marrow of his bones. What had been so violently upset was the certainty —so certain that he had never consciously had to articulate it—that he, as a white man, was a superior branch of the species and he, as an American, was the highest flower

of that superior branch. The best of the breed!

He blamed the strategy that had been imposed on him. His hands were tied. You went out and killed and came back where you had started. What the hell kind of a way was that to fight a war? Where the hell was the sense in that? Even when you took ground, you took it temporarily, waiting for the order which you knew would eventually come to pull back. Ritter's casualty lists were spiraling up and up; his reputation was going down and down. And he knew, in his heart, that it wasn't his fault.

The protest and dissension over the war back in the States echoed halfway around the world to threaten the spirit and morale of his troops. The allied military brass received especially harsh treatment from the correspondents in the battle zones. Some of these so-called war correspondents were nothing more than kids, hardly out of college. They knew nothing about military affairs, nothing about his problems. All they knew was that they could make themselves a reputation by criticizing their own side, by showing that they could stand up to the generals. Ritter himself was constantly ducking their barbs and slings of late. There were times when he wanted to shout out, "Whose side are you on, theirs or ours?" Thank God, he had been able to hold his tongue. He knew how that pack of wolves would tear him apart for something like that. All Commie bastards, he thought. Or smart-ass intellectuals. Or traitors. With one or two possible exceptions, most notably Adam March.

It was March who had originally begun to call him "Stonewall" Ritter in his dispatches, creating the first faintly favorable "image" for him. The general was still not aware that his troops used the nickname in terms of ridicule. Or that, as often or not, they changed it to "Stonehead."

Now, seated at his desk, a stout but erect figure, balding

on top, with an increasingly cherubic face, Randy Ritter felt overwhelmed by his years. Adam March's follow-up story on Captain David Walsh was spread out on his green desk blotter. As he read, the general tugged at his dewlap with one hand. A pencil in his other hand beat a tattoo on the metal desk top. Across from him, Adam March lounged on a leather couch one long leg slung over the back of the couch. He looked complacent, blowing perfect smoke rings into the air. Adam March, God damn him to hell, had not a trouble in the world.

When he had finished reading the last page, Ritter sat staring at it in numb concentration. He had serious reservations about the whole damn thing. His military instincts, honed sharp by thirty-six years of Army service, warned him to go very slow on this one. He had already made one very bad mistake. He should never have permitted March to send out the original story that morning without clearing it first through censorship.

"Well? What do you think, Randy?" March asked.

General Ritter cleared his throat, rubbed his nose throughtfully, and did his level best not to meet the reporter's insistent gaze. Somehow or other, he had permitted their positions to become reversed. Instead of the lowly civilian reporter having to defend his story to the eminent general—the commander—the general felt obliged to defend his actions to the reporter. There was no doubt about it; the world had been turned upside down.

But no, that didn't apply here. Adam March was not just another reporter. Adam March was Adam March.

Before March had come to Vietnam as special war correspondent for his New York newspaper (and national syndicate) he was a widely read, influential columnist. Ritter could remember when March was host of a highly rated television interview show. The leading politicians courted him. The President called him "Adam." He had been re-

ceived with open arms by all the important world leaders.
No man could rise to become a general in the Army without developing an impeccable sense of protocol. General
Ritter knew very well that the two silver stars on his collar
merited small regard from March.

It would, then, be well to proceed with caution. "Aren't
you laying it on pretty heavy, though, Adam? It sounds
like something out of a war novel. . . ." Seeing March stif-
fen, he added quickly, "Beautifully written, of course. I
had some thoughts of doing some writing myself, you
know. My memoirs perhaps; things like that. I always did
have a flair. . . ." He could see that March was becoming
impatient. "This reference to Mt. Goliath now. This com-
paring Walsh to David." He sent a pained, gentle smile
across to him, as one writer to another. "I *mean*, Adam!"

"Everybody's an editor these days," March said indulgently. "Just endorse it, Randy, so the censor will shoot
it through, huh?" It was not a question. "What about this
guy Walsh?" he said, moving himself, with considerable
groaning, back to a sitting position. "Have your PR boys
come up with his dossier yet?"

The general leaned forward, clasping his fingers. "That's
what I mean, Adam. This Walsh. I've done some checking
on this for you myself. Personally. This Walsh, he's a captain. Attached to the South Vietnamese unit as a communications officer. A radio interpreter. He seems to have an
unusual talent for Asian languages. Taught himself
Korean and Japanese during the Korean War. That's a remarkable feat, Adam. Really remarkable. I think I'd be safe
in saying that it was the reason—the only reason—he was
recalled to active duty last year. We always have a short-
age of good interpreters here, you know." His face turned
grim. "Among other things. Our men, that is."

"That's great, Randy!" March brought both hands down
heavily against his thighs. "This story is getting better all

the time. No run-of-the-mill hero here. Our boy, he's got brains. On top," he said, virtuously, "of being colored."

Ritter winced, pulling his head down between his shoulder blades like a turtle. He took a deep breath and tried again. "Adam, I'm afraid I have to tell you that Captain Walsh has had a most undistinguished military career." Reaching into the top drawer, he came out with a well-worn file folder and opened it up on top of March's story. "Married. A son, Joshua, age fifteen now. In World War II he served in an all-black port battalion. Two years loading liberty ships at Hoboken pier. Got a job with the Veterans' Administration after the war and went to college at night."

"Ambitious," March nodded approvingly. "Some of 'em are, you know."

Ritter grunted. Could March really have been over here all this time without knowing that the Negro troops were among the very best combat troops he had? Could March, the one correspondent he had come to trust, be baiting a trap for him? He had better move very cautiously with this one. He had better keep his flanks guarded at all times.

"Anyway," General Ritter said, "he got caught on the flypaper with a lot of other vets who stayed on the active reserve list to collect their monthly handout. Ended up in Tokyo doing public relations for the Army." He looked up sharply. "Never saw any action in that one either."

He turned a couple of sheets over, couldn't seem to find what he was looking for, and retraced his steps. "Here," he said, finding it. "He's a bright one, all right." He shook his head in admiration. "This flair for picking up languages makes him a valuable property. Recommended for OCS in Tokyo, approved by the commanding general, and he comes out of the service after Korea as a first lieutenant."

March was so delighted that he seemed to glow. "A battlefield commission," he said.

"No . . . no," General Ritter explained patiently. "I've just got through telling you. OCS. He never got out of Tokyo."

"That's right. They never did get to fighting in Tokyo, did they? Well," he said, making do with what he had, "he rose from the ranks of enlisted men. That ain't so bad either."

March dropped his cigarette to the floor and smeared it with the heel of his combat boot. "Poor bugger, then they hook him again for Vietnam. He's been due for this kind of a break."

Ritter flipped through the rest of Walsh's file, with a visible lack of enthusiasm. "He was close to the bottom of his class in military grades. His academic grades were good enough, but in everything else he was a bust. Just did qualify on the rifle range. Never evidenced the slightest qualities of leadership." He lifted his eyes back to Adam March. "A book man. I know the type."

"Until *now!*" March roared bouncing off the couch in sheer glee. He began to pace up and down in front of the general's desk. "Imagine, three wars. In the first one, he's breaking his back like a. . . ." As he realized what he was about to say, he stopped to chuckle to himself briefly. "In the next one, they chain him to a desk. And now . . . ," he snapped his fingers sharply, "just like that, he's David Walsh, a hero all black fighting men can point to with pride. All the blacks back home too. No handouts for David Walsh, huh? No whining and rioting. The opportunity of America was there, and he took it, an object lesson for his people, and," he said, piously, "for those Americans who think they're all the same." Catching Ritter's guarded but nonetheless suspicious gaze, he quickly amended, "White Americans, that is. The members of the White Establishment."

Ritter was still regarding him rather suspiciously. "You

won't find any of that kind of thinking in this command, Adam."

"Dammit, Randy," March said, pounding his fist into his hand, "the color of his skin is just part of it; the icing, you might say, on the cake. Every GI who ever sat out a war in a rear echelon, dreaming of a chance to rise to the great occasion, will identify with David Walsh. Every veteran of the Battle of the Bulge. Identification! That's what makes a story great."

General Ritter put on the sour expression of an old soldier who knows all there is to know about the ambitions of rear-echelon troops: to stay out of sight, out of trouble and, most of all, out of combat.

"But we don't even know if the story is true," he said. "What I'm trying to tell you, Adam, is that until we get some kind of verification from Intelligence I'm going to have to ask you to hold the story. A day or two, that's all it should take."

March planted both hands against the front edge of the desk and leaned forward until his face was just as close to Ritter's as he could get it. His voice was restrained, though. He was willing to be reasonable about this, you could see, as long as he got his way. "General, I can smell a good story. This is a good one. A legitimate one. It's *my* story, dammit, and I am going to stay ahead of the pack on it, and that means I cannot afford to wait any day or two. As soon as I file this copy, I am going to requisition one of your Hueys and go up to Mt. Goliath to see how Walsh and his boys are making out."

For the first time during the entire interview Ritter rallied behind his rank. "No! Absolutely not! I am responsible for the safety of the correspondents in this sector."

"Swell. Now that you've shown me you know all the chicken regulations, you can pick up the phone and tell the airfield to warm up a helicopter for me."

"The answer is *no!*" The general sat puffed up like an angry toad. "That's out!"

"Now, now, General. Let's not both be getting our balls in an uproar. I'm quite willing to sign a waiver releasing you from all responsibility."

Ritter was holding onto his temper with effort. "Adam, if it was just your own neck you were risking, I might make an exception. But there're the lives of the crewmen to be considered too. Not to mention the safety of a helicopter that cost the government a quarter of a million dollars."

March pulled himself up to his full height, his arms folded across his chest. "I guess we've got a problem here." He gave the general a crooked grin. "In my profession, when we have a problem, we have ourselves a little snort." He scowled toward the window. "This damn weather's beginning to creep into my bones anyway. Mine and everybody else's."

Opening his bottom drawer, the general came out with a bottle of bourbon and two Dixie cups.

March took his cup, filled about halfway to the top, and, smacking his lips, raised the cup in a toast: "Here's to the State Department or whoever the hell is supposed to be running this fuckin' war!"

Ritter sipped unhappily at his own drink for a few moments. "Adam," he said, sighing heavily, "just look at the weather out there." The rain was still drumming relentlessly on the roof. As if it were already night outside, the glass reflected their images. "We haven't sent a Huey or anything else up in this soup in five days."

"I know," March said, injecting just the proper dose of sarcasm into it. "And it makes the flyboys sore as hell. I hate to tell you this, but you're becoming very well known down at flight headquarters as Nervous Nelly. They're saying you're afraid of getting Uncle Sam's flying machines all wet and rusty." He took his first little sip, and gave a bark of

laughter. "*Stonewall,*" he said, as if he were echoing their derision. He shook his head sadly. "I don't know, Randy, there's only so much I can do."

Ritter, flushing heavily, reached for the rest of the drink. "That's not my directive, and they know it. It's handed down from Saigon."

"Sure they know it. They also know what a field commander can do with chicken directives that reduce the operational efficiency of his command!"

"No one has ever challenged the efficiency of my command," Ritter said, bridling.

"No one's been praising it very much lately either," March said. "Think about this, General. Less than fifteen miles away from where we're sitting, five thousand American Marines are fighting for their lives. And here you are, sitting tight on your dry and rosy duff, sipping bourbon, and keeping all your Hueys nice and clean. The wives, mothers, and sweethearts . . . the loved ones of all those fine young American boys might not understand about things like directives from Saigon."

The cherubic face was suddenly drained of blood. That, March could see, had been the unkindest cut of all. He had really hated to do it. "That's a pretty lousy thing to say." General Ritter found his voice at last. "Even," he added bitterly, "for an American newspaperman."

Adam March was shocked to see how completely the general had misunderstood him. It was true enough that he had to file his follow-up story very shortly, he said, and if the general couldn't find it in his heart to clear the piece that Adam had already written, then Adam would quite obviously have to make do with whatever else came most quickly to hand. But that wasn't what Adam March wanted to do at all. Adam March was trying, with a minimum of goddamn cooperation, to let the American people know what a jewel of a commander they had in General

Randolph "Stonewall" Ritter.

"It is not very easy," March told him, "to make national heroes out of generals who play it close to the vest. You know what happens to military commanders who play it safe, Randy? Nobody . . . knows . . . their . . . names. Except," he said, affecting a clipped British accent, "good old Monty. And good old Monty had Churchill and the whole damn British Empire, or whatever remnants were left, playing PR man for him, because they were in desperate need of a general in the grand tradition of the Duke of Wellington or, lacking that, for chrissake, who could win a battle sometimes."

March had a sudden inspiration. "Was Wellington any good, Randy, or did they build him up too?"

"He was good enough. Solid. Not brilliant, but solid. Hell," he said, making that sour face again. "He won the last battle, and that's the one that counts. It doesn't matter that much what you do as long as you win the last one."

"All right," Adam March said. "Now you see my problem. I'm going to lay it right on the line for you, Randy." Backing off from the desk just a little, he jabbed a finger at him. "Why did I pick you to build up, Stonewall?" He answered his own question. "Because you were there. Luckiest day of your life when I was assigned to your sector. I'll protect you wherever I can. I got to protect you now to protect myself. Except you foul up real bad and then I've got to be the one to destroy you. Nothing personal, General. Nothing personal one way or the other. This is a lousy war for generals. A no-win war means no-win generals. And that makes it a lousy war for us newspapermen too."

A curious look had come over General Ritter's features. A curious, quizzical look. "You know," Ritter said, more to himself than to March, "I never thought of it that way before."

"Well, think about it. If you can't do it one way, Randy,

you've got to do it another. If you and I can play this Walsh thing right, Captain Walsh's glory can be used to reflect a golden light on your whole division. On you personally. I want to give this thing the whole *schmeer*. Lots of photographs, you and David, plastered over every newspaper in the United States. I promise you I'll get your name in my dispatches at least once in each installment. Let's see, how about this for openers: 'General Randolph Ritter told me: *I couldn't be any prouder if David Walsh was my own son!'* You touch a lot of bases with that one."

Almost absently, General Ritter picked up the paper cup, washed the liquor around in it, and placed it back on the desk. "No," he said. "I never thought of it that way before."

"You've got to appreciate how big this thing is," March said, watching him intently. "The way things have been going from bad to worse over here, the American public needs a good shot of morale. The public needs something to restore its faith in the American fighting man. The men need something to restore their faith in themselves and their country. And in their gallant leaders. It won't hurt your standing in Saigon either. Or the Pentagon. Listen, Randy, let's lay it on the line. You're in no position to play footsie with me on this thing."

General Ritter leaned back in his chair, his lips pursed thoughtfully. "That South Vietnamese Ranger who got away, he wouldn't have any reason to be lying about Walsh and those others, would he?"

"No reason at all," March said. "That one is a pretty brave boy himself, we don't want to forget that. I ought to get something on him, too. Hey, there's an angle for you." He had suddenly become excited. "An interview with the gook on how he got back through the lines, with David Walsh acting as my interpreter, *and Walsh himself is hearing the story for the first time*. Front page, every paper in

the country. Personally guaranteed. You can quote me."

"You really want to go up in this stuff, huh?"

For one brief moment, March didn't understand what Ritter was saying. And then, his eyes opened wide. "Try me!"

General Randolph Ritter fingered the stars on his collar, smiled a secret, interior smile and reached for the phone.

What delighted the general as much as anything else was that Adam March would never know what had finally got him his helicopter. Adam March would never doubt for one second that General Ritter had been corrupted by his eagerness for the cheapest kind of publicity. Nor would he be entirely wrong. But not for the reason March thought. What had convinced Ritter in the end was March's line about the no-win war and the no-win generals. Randy Ritter, raised by the Army man's simple creed of honor and patriotism, believed in his heart that his country was dishonoring itself and, believing it, he was tearing himself apart, floundering around, letting himself be chipped away in pieces. All right then. If his country would not let its generals win its battles. . . . It was, he could see, something like a husband walking coldly and deliberately into a cheap affair with a cheap slut so he could stop hating a beloved wife who had been unfaithful to him.

He knew he would never be able to spell it out to himself entirely, but he also knew that he knew, deep in the marrows, what he meant. He knew it, because for the first time in months he felt wholly at peace with himself.

Flatiron, official U. S. Army designation Hill 611, re-christened by Adam March, Mt. Goliath, was a pretentious title for a dumpy hill that had the appearance of a haystack flattened on top. Around its base and crawling up its steep slopes grew matted, near-impenetrable jungle. The growth thinned out higher up the slopes where ancient volcanic

ash had hardened into sterile rock.

On the north side, just below the summit mesa, a tunnel ran back about 30 feet into the mountain to a high-ceilinged vault-like cave hollowed out of solid stone. A sandal covered with green mold, a mound of rusting cans, a broken cot, and other artifacts of human occupation lay scattered about the cavern. A band of Vietcong guerillas had burrowed into the side of the mountain, high up, years before, and the secret, remote stronghold had served them well. But with the increasing build-up of North Vietnamese troops in the area, the VC had been able to leave their jungle and mountain hideouts and sometimes even operate in conventional military fashion.

Before allied air power became so overwhelmingly superior in Vietnam, the VC had labored to construct a secret airstrip on the plateau. The project had been abandoned on orders from Hanoi when it became abundantly clear that it would be futile to try to mount any sort of air offensive against the overwhelming American air power.

In the center of the big cavern two men in dirty fatigue uniforms sat cross-legged before a small fire. One was a T/5 corporal wearing the insignia of the medical corps. The other was a captain whose ebony face shone in the glare of the firelight.

There was a third man by the fire, lying on his back, wrapped in a blanket. His forehead and cheeks were wet with sweat, and from time to time he stirred and moaned in a tortured sleep.

Beyond the fringes of the firelight were a number of South Vietnamese soldiers. Some of them had rolled themselves up in blankets on the hard rock floor. Others were hunched against the rock walls of the cavern. A few puffed on precious cigarette butts, so short they had to be impaled on slivers of wood. Their weary eyes stared unblinkingly into the flames. Their smooth, fragile, finely featured faces

were without expression.

Only the captain and the corporal acknowledged the entrance of two more U. S. soldiers from the tunnel leading to the outside. Both carried M-16 rifles slung over their shoulders.

First-Lieutenant Joseph Delvecchio was slender, dark, and Latin. He would have been handsome but for a smallish, pinched mouth and eyes set too close together.

Master-Sergeant Frank Rinkon, the oldest of the Americans, had the mystique that sets apart professional soldiers from the amateurs. A short man, too thick about the middle, bow-legged, and with a face that wore the bumps and affronts of uncounted battles, he should have been a comic figure. But in the way he walked, handled a weapon, in all of his actions, there was a grace and economy that told of a competence the others lacked.

"Fire feels good," Rinkon grunted. He reached over for the lieutenant's rifle and stacked it with his own alongside a conglomerate of other weapons against one wall.

The captain looked up at Delvecchio. "All clear out there, Joe? The sentries have anything to report?"

Delvecchio took a cigarette from a rumpled pack and jammed it between his lips. "How would I know? You're the only one speaks their language. My own guess is there's not a Commie within ten miles of us. They're all too busy swarming around Khesanh to bother with us." He pulled a burning stick out of the fire and lit his cigarette.

Sergeant Rinkon came back to warm his hands over the flames. "I think maybe you should talk to 'em again, Dave," he said, indicating the South Vietnamese with a motion of his head. "They're beat, hungry."

Delvecchio flipped the stick back into the fire. "Talk to me, Dave, in my native tongue. I'm beat and hungry too. Also wet and cold."

David Walsh bent his head and sighed. "I told them

what the score was. I told them they should try to make
their way back to friendly territory any way they could.
Singles; in pairs; any way they wanted. But they won't
leave until we do."

Delvecchio's dark eyes hardened. "Well?"

Walsh, uncomfortable with the authority that had been
thrust upon him, kept his gaze riveted on the fire. "We're
not moving Bob. It would kill him for sure. And we sure as
hell aren't leaving him here. That's final."

Delvecchio looked down at the wounded man wrapped
in the blanket. "So we sit here until the cavalry comes
charging over the hill, waving their green berets behind
them. Yes, *sir*, Captain."

His tone brushed the raw area of the Negro captain's
sensitivity. Dave Walsh glared at Delvecchio, his throat
tightening.

"What's that suppose to mean, Lieutenant?"

Delvecchio grinned his small, crooked grin and tapped
his fist gently on Walsh's shoulder. "Just what it sounded
like, Dave. You're in charge of this party. We'll do whatever you decide is best." The grin broadened. "Isn't that
big of me?"

Walsh was ashamed of himself for jumping on Delvecchio, of all people. As always, Joe had paid him the
compliment of saying exactly what he damn well thought,
something which Walsh appreciated. In his tours with the
army, Dave's unfavorite kinds of people were the bigots,
who were out to see how tough they could make life for
you, and the kindly liberals, who were always going so far
out of their way to be helpful that they made you feel as if
you had a broken leg or something.

Given any choice—as he'd told Constance, his wife,
after the Korean thing—he'd take the wet-eyed liberal
over a weekend in Mississippi any old time. But that didn't
make him any the less uncomfortable with them. "What it

is," he had told her, "is one of them is coming up and saying 'nigger' to your face and you have to take him as your enemy, and the other is coming up and saying 'why, you poor colored gentleman' with his eyes, and you got to take him as your friend. It's a hell of a lot easier to get rid of an enemy."

Delvecchio was neither. Delvecchio was one of a kind. We're all what we are, Delvecchio seemed to say, and let's have no bullshit about it.

Dave had met him back in the states in the waiting room of the point-of-embarkation hospital, while they were waiting to take their final physical before shipping out. They shouldn't really have met at all, since Delvecchio had been the first name on the shipping orders and Walsh the last. But Joe hadn't answered the roll call when his name was read. By the time he did come strolling into the waiting room, there was nobody there except Mark Textauer and Dave. While Joe was stripping down, he had told Textauer how he had slipped out of base the night before for one final farewell shack job. "What can they do to me? Take my name off the orders? Those kind of odds I like."

When Textauer was called, they had been left alone in the waiting room, a faintly uncomfortable situation for Dave until Delvecchio came over, stuck out his hand and said, "My name is Joe Delvecchio. Delvecchio. Don't let the name throw you. I'm a wop."

When Dave introduced himself in return, a look of great perplexity had come over Delvecchio's face. "Walsh?" he had said. "Walsh?" And then, lowering his voice: "Hey, that's a nigger name, ain't it?" And looking him up and down he had said with his little innocent eyes, "You a nigger?"

It was such a direct hit that Dave had thrown his head back and howled. All his life, he had seen the expression

change on people's faces when, after hearing the name
Walsh, they were confronted with a black face instead of
the anticipated Irish one. And all his life, white men had
gone to almost as ridiculous pains to show that they didn't
really see "any difference."

We're all what we are, Delvecchio's attitude always
said. One as rotten as the other.

Delvecchio would say, "My God, they put together a
wop cardsharp from Steubenville, a nigger memory machine from Harlem, and a WASP English teacher from
Sacramento, and they actually think they're going to win
this war. Not if we have anything to say about it." And it
would pull them all closer together.

By referring to race and nationality so constantly, he
succeeded—conversely—in making nothing of it at all.
Walsh liked him, and Delvecchio knew it.

"You know why you like me," Joe once said to him. "Because I set out to make you like me. The first two things
they teach us in Steubenville are how to deal cards and
how to pour on the con. You're my superior officer, so I got
to suck up to you and pretend like I think you're as good as
I am."

Dave reminded him that the first time they'd met he had
been balls naked.

"That's the third thing they teach us. How to tell rank by
the size of the cock. You'd be surprised how handy that can
be back in civilian life."

Bob Nichols had flown over in that same shipment but,
strangely enough, in view of the friendship that eventually
developed between them, Dave couldn't remember exchanging a single word with him until they were assigned
to translate a Buddha text together, with Dave doing the
word-by-word translation and Bob Nichols working it into
a polished manuscript.

From the little he had seen of Nichols, Walsh had

thought of him as a rather snotty withdrawn type. But he
had learned quickly enough that he was an almost pain-
fully shy man, with an enormous capacity for friendship
and the sweetest nature in the world. It was Walsh and
Nichols who had become the close friends, exchanging
everything except the most intimate details of their personal lives. Delvecchio, whose interests ranged to more
various things—like women, women, and women—made
up the third member of the group only as the spirit moved
him.

They had talked about him a lot, because he absolutely
fascinated Nichols. "The thing about Joe," Nichols finally
decided, "is that he has no social consciousness at all. No, I
mean it. You have to have a social consciousness to be a
bigot. You have to identify very closely with one group before you can even begin to hate another. That's why ortho-
dox religions are the most intolerant. Joe travels alone.
Like skipping out of camp the night before we shipped out.
His whole training class was in that shipment, but he
couldn't have cared less whether he went over with them
or somebody else. That's why he can say all those things
without anybody ever taking offense. He has such an inno-
cence about him that it's impossible to take offense."

The one thing he would never have called Delvecchio,
Dave told him, was innocent. As a matter of fact, he
thought Joe Delvecchio was the most practical man he had
ever known.

Nichols was wearing his patient schoolteacher look.

"Ah, but in this context they're not mutually exclusive.
They're opposite sides of the coin. He's also the most objective man I've ever known because he has no emotional in-
volvement with anybody or anything. Even I can be perfectly objective about somebody I don't care about. It's
only when I become emotionally involved that I begin to
lose perspective. Which is why dumb blondes can make

fools out of the most brilliant men in the world."

Eventually, as with almost everything else, Walsh had come around to agreeing with Nichols. Once, in a discussion about Army friendships, Delvecchio had told them, with characteristic frankness: "I've got no friends in the Army, only acquaintances. There's no percentage in it. Now take you, Dave. Suppose you come to a club where I'm dealing, and the management has a policy against having any black folk around. I got to either look right through you or get ready to throw the deck into the pit boss's face and tell him what he can do with the job. Either way, I'm a loser. There's no odds there. The percentage is zero."

"It's changing," Nichols said.

"In your books, professor! In your imagination! In your dreams!"

"We'll live to see it change," Nichols had insisted. "By the time we get home, you won't recognize it, it will be so changed."

Looking down now at the pale, sweaty, drug-wracked face, Captain Walsh was overcome by a rage of helplessness. Bob Nichols wasn't going to live to see anything change. Bob Nichols wasn't going to get home.

Joe Delvecchio knew it. All of them knew it. That's why Delvecchio, the most practical man he knew, was so anxious to pack him on to a stretcher and get the hell out of there.

Delvecchio had hunched down alongside the medic. "How's he doing, Cummins?"

Corporal Cummins was a blond, sallow youth of nineteen with a long, solemn face. His voice was a constant whine. Captain Walsh couldn't blame him for whining. Cummins had been shipped up to him, as a replacement, only one week earlier. Just in time to catch it.

"Hell, I'm only a pill-pusher, Lieutenant, you know

that." He regarded the unconscious officer glumly and very quickly turned away, as if he felt that studying him too closely would suggest that he might be able to do something. Would *commit* him to do something. "He needs a transfusion in a hurry, I can tell you that."

Sergeant Rinkon had settled his gross behind on a flat rock near the fire. "If Dhu gets through to the Rockpile, the helicopter ambulance boys should have a Huey here any time now."

"In this soup?" Delvecchio, completely unaware that Rinkon had been talking entirely for the benefit of Cummins, was incredulous. "Any chopper pilot crazy enough to fly in this soup would pile himself up on the mountain. Any pilot crazy enough to fly in here is too damn crazy for me to fly out with."

"We could signal him with a couple of volleys," Rinkon said, trying to catch Delvecchio's eye. "And then guide him in with flares."

Delvecchio laughed nastily. "That'd be nice. He'd think Charley was zeroing in on him and take off like that well-known bird."

Cummins cleared his throat to let them know he was about to contribute a thought of his own. "And it'd be a gold-plated invitation for the Commies to come up and get us." It was, they could all see, a question. And it had been put not to the captain but to the sergeant.

Walsh couldn't blame him. He was disgusted at his impotence too; his inability to make any positive decision beyond the purposeless determination to "sit tight" and wait.

"I should have ordered the South Vietnamese out of here days ago," he said, clenching his fists. With sudden resolve, he sprang to his feet. "What am I talking about, *should* have? Am I in command here or ain't I? Joe, I want you and Rinkon to round up these troops first thing in the morning and take them south. That's an order, Lieutenant."

A smile spread slowly across Delvecchio's face, and his eyes were insolent with amusement. "A *direct* order, Captain?"

"A direct order!" Walsh took another step forward so that he was towering over him threateningly.

Delvecchio reclined back on his elbows and said imperturbably, "Well, I ain't going. That's a direct answer. When we get back, you can put me up for a general court martial."

"Joe. . . ." There was more plea than reprimand in Walsh's voice, and damn little threat at all.

"Uh-uh, Dave. Screw the martyr bit; you're not staying here alone. You want to save me for a good *Putan,* you got to come with. You stay, we all stay. They'll immortalize us in face and legend and celebrate us on Brotherhood Week." He lowered his head, reverently. "Let us all pray to be worthy of the honor that is about to fall upon our heads."

Looking up, his stubborn eyes met Walsh's. Neither of them wavered. "The three musketeers," he said, quietly. "Remember?"

Walsh was more moved than he would have thought possible. More moved, for that matter than he wanted to be. To hide his emotions, he kicked at a glowing coal that had rolled out of the fire. What, he wondered, would Bob have to say about that? Where was the man so totally lacking in social consciousness now?

"It's all wrong staying on top of this mountain," Walsh said. "Don't you think I know that? I've got no right to put the safety of one man above the safety of one hundred and fifty men. It's a lousy decision for a commanding officer to make, and, God knows, I've loused you all up enough as it is, going north when I should have gone south." He closed his eyes and massaged the lids. "God knows, I never asked for this job."

"I never even asked to be born," Delvecchio said. He tapped the lighted end off his butt out with a fingernail and very carefully placed the butt back into the nearly empty pack. "Come on, Dave. Nobody's blaming you. If the South Vietnamese couldn't find their way in that fog, why should you? The articles of war to the contrary notwithstanding, those bars don't come equipped with any special powers of divination."

Sergeant Rinkon was a little embarrassed. "Sure, Dave. Nobody's blaming you."

Delvecchio regarded the sergeant wryly. "That's more than I can say about you, you fat slob. Here's a guy been goofing off for fifteen years, giving orientation lectures to recruits, and when he finally gets a chance to pay off the American taxpayers, he can't even orientate north from south. Sergeant, I'm going to have those stripes when we get back. I'm going to have you dishonorably discharged. You know what I'm going to do? I'm going to. . . ."

A sudden movement alongside the fire drew all heads in that direction.

"Captain!" the medic called out. "He's coming out of it."

Walsh sprang over to the wounded man and kneeled down beside him. Lieutenant Nichols' eyes, he saw, were wide open, the pupils dull and dilated. Walsh placed his black hand over the pale, bloodless hand on the blanket.

"How's it going, Bob?" he asked.

Nichols took a deep breath, winced. "It's beginning to hurt. A burning like."

"Morphine's wearing off," Corporal Cummins said. "You want I should give him another shot, Captain?"

"No, it's not bad," Nichols said. "I don't want to go under again." He tried to prop himself up on one elbow.

"Easy, man." Walsh slipped an arm underneath his shoulders and lifted him gingerly while Cummins slid a bedroll underneath his head.

Nichols had never taken his eyes off Walsh. "I'm not going to make it, am I, Dave?"

With an effort of will, Walsh compelled himself to meet the feverish, questioning eyes. "Hey, how you talk, man. How you do ramble." The tone altered, the easy familiar tone of a voice filled with shared jokes, shared secrets below the words. "I'm not going to try to kid you, Bob. I don't know how bad you're hurt. Soon as the weather breaks, Air Rescue will come in and take us home in one of dem dere flying machines."

"Sure," Nichols said. He gave a dry little laugh. The strain of it made him gasp and draw up his legs under the blanket.

"Maybe you better have that shot," Walsh told him.

"No . . . I'm okay now. . . . You know what's really bugging me, Dave? In the back of my head I know I'm going to say something melodramatic." Some reserve of strength did seem to be coming up in him. Delvecchio was leaning over Walsh's shoulder, and for the first time Nichols seemed to recognize his presence. Whether he did or not, it was perfectly clear that he was talking only to Walsh. "Here I am dying, and the fear uppermost in my mind is that I'm going to sound like the death scene in a war movie . . . and embarrass everybody." He closed his eyes, as if he wanted to shut out something too terrible to see. "I got to be afraid of something, don't I?"

"You're talking too much."

"I got to talk, Dave. If I go under again, I'm not coming back." His forehead creased in painful concentration, as he struggled to bring his drugged mind to focus. "Dave . . . when they hit the camp . . . it was . . . such a shock. . . . But I wasn't going to run away . . . I swear . . . on my wife . . . I was going to turn back. I wouldn't say that if it weren't true. . . . Not here, the way things are." Little pools of moisture were gathering at the underlids of his

eyes. *Dear sweet Jesus,* Dave Walsh thought, *he doesn't have the strength to cry.*

Dave managed to smile at him. "What do you think the rest of us were doing? We weren't there to fight. The way we were outnumbered we couldn't have stood for three minutes. All we could do was get the hell out of there."

"But you didn't panic. Only me." Nichols shut his eyes, breathing in heavy asthmatic gasps as he relived those tortured moments. When he began to talk again, his teeth remained tightly clenched. "I had stopped running. I was just about to turn back. I was thinking: 'I got to go back and find the guys.' If it had been just a couple of seconds later, I'd have got it in the front instead of in the back." The growing pool of tears finally began to spill over. "I wouldn't care so much if only it wasn't in the back."

He tried to sit up, but the medic restrained him. "You better stay put, Lieutenant," he said, looking to Captain Walsh for help.

Nichols fell back on the bedroll. "I keep going over and over it. Even in my dreams. I keep trying to make it come out different. We're in that brush on the high ground above the clearing. I'm holding them off with a machine gun while the rest of you get away. Some imagination." He turned his head away. "Some joke!"

Delvecchio had already drawn back a step or two. He turned away now, dug an elbow into Rinkon's well-padded ribs and muttered, "Come on, Rink, let's check to see whether the guards need checking."

Rinkon sent him a look of relief which said, *I'm with you.* They picked up their rifles and ducked into the narrow tunnel, as Walsh's voice faded off behind them: "We were all running, Bob. All of us. There were no heroes and no cowards. . . ."

Outside the cave, Delvecchio fished out his butt and handed the crumpled pack to Rinkon. "Joe," Rinkon said.

"If you could arrange for that dishonorable discharge to take effect immediately, I sure would appreciate it."

"Don't think I can quite manage that, but I'll tell you what I'm prepared to do for you. You have my permission to burn your draft card."

"He's gone if the ceiling don't crack," Rinkon said.

"Or if he don't crack. Why doesn't the poor son of a bitch die and get it over with?"

Rinkon took another couple of drags on the cigarette. "I've seen a lot of men die," he said, in a not too gentle rebuke, "and I've never seen the one I wanted to hurry along. Our side or theirs."

The anger never left Delvecchio's face. "You never seen no schoolteachers die. These thinking men can't die without they want to know how they're looking and how it's done." He gave a short bitter bark of a laugh. "Hell, that's the most useless information he'll ever have."

Another few moments of silence passed. "Well, all I know is that I still don't want to hurry him along."

". . . hurry him along," Delvecchio mimicked. "Hell, he ain't going to go until he gets Dave to tell him how brave he really was."

Rinkon slammed his cigarette to the ground and stamped down hard on it. "Yes, *sir*, Lieutenant."

"Fuck *you*, Sergeant."

Inside the cave, Nichols was still rambling. "I keep going over it like that, making it come out so that I look good. And I begin to believe it really did happen that way." His eyes opened slowly. "Only when I wake up here I am by the fire, dying, and it didn't happen like that at all."

He gripped Walsh's hand with a strength that astonished the big Negro captain. "Dave, I'm scared." A note of surprise had come rushing into his voice. Walsh couldn't tell whether he was surprised he was so scared or surprised that he had revealed it.

Cummins turned the hypodermic needle over in his hand, asking Captain Walsh with his eyes whether he wanted him to put Nichols out again.

With the barest perceptible shake of the head, Walsh indicated to let him be.

"Dave . . . if I do . . . die. You'll write Anne, won't you? It will be more like she was hearing it from a friend. I've told her a lot about you, did you know that?"

Walsh stared down at the waxen, blue-veined fingers entwined around his hand. "No. I didn't know that." An ache thickened in his throat. "You'll write her yourself. You'll tell her all about it."

"Dave," Nichols said. "If you get off this mountain, do what we talked about. Kiss the VA goodbye and do what you want to do. You'll be one helluva good teacher. You've got the touch. You could do a lot of good."

"You got a deal. One of these days, I'll be teaching your kids. Is it a deal?"

"I'm serious, Dave." The thin note of self-mockery was back in his voice. "That was supposed to be intoned as if from the graveside."

"I know it was." *Sweet Jesus, I know it was.*

As if it had been signaled by the word graveside, the flush of fever deepened on Nichols' face. The glaze over his eyes thickened. The voice came unstrung.

"I was a good teacher. . . . Not much with a gun, but good . . . Dave . . . Anne . . . don't let her know . . . make it sound like . . . as if . . . died like good. . . ."

"Captain!" Corporal Cummins had risen up on his knees. He was pointing toward the South Vietnamese.

The South Vietnamese troops, those who were not asleep, were looking up toward the cavern ceiling. Several of them began to talk excitedly.

"What is it?" Walsh asked them in their own language.

The canopy of rock surrounding them was vibrating, a muffled, drumming sound that kept building in volume.

"Captain Walsh!" The medic's voice was trembling. "You think the mountain is going to cave in on us?"

"Not a chance," Walsh said. "It's all solid rock around us." Leaving Nichols in Cummin's care, he raced out through the tunnel. The instant he hit the open air, he saw what it was. The huge churning rotor blades of a helicopter settling down on top of the mountain.

On his hands and his knees, he went scrambling straight up the steep slope that led to the unfinished airstrip on the summit. He reached the plateau just in time to see the Huey make its landing, guided down through the dissolving mist by a circle of flashlight beams pointing skyward. A miracle, he thought, as he offered up a silent prayer of thanks to her skillful and incredibly daring pilot.

Delvecchio came rushing up to Walsh, waving his torch gleefully. "The Marines have landed!" He let out a whoop. "They're Marines. It's a Marine helicopter ambulance." In a fit of exuberance, he went into an Indian war dance, prancing completely around Walsh, and then racing back to the helicopter.

Before the rotor blades had stopped whirling, the side door of the Huey swung out and a figure in full battle dress leaped to the ground. Immediately, he was surrounded by the South Vietnamese sentries, all speaking at once and all reaching out to touch him in enthusiastic welcome.

"Hey! Get your hands off that weapon," Adam March shouted. "I said get your hands off it, dammit!"

The figure turned back toward the helicopter, and Captain Walsh could hear him saying to the crewmen: "Any of you guys speak gook?" Apparently they didn't, for the next words Walsh heard were, *"Take . . . me . . . to . . . the . . . American . . . captain."*

Walsh eased his way through the mob scene, quietly

issuing commands in Vietnamese. "As you were, men. Everybody back to his post. We're going to have to be extra sharp tonight. If the enemy spotted this chopper landing up here, they'll send up a patrol to investigate." Switching to English, he said to Rinkon, "Sergeant, you'd better double up on the sentry posts for the rest of the night. . . . Now, let's everybody douse those lights."

He moved through the last group of Vietnamese soldiers, and Adam March and David Walsh confronted each other in the darkness and swirling mist.

"Am I glad to see you," March said. "I've been trying to get these gooks. . . ."

"They're not gooks!" Walsh said sharply. "Let me set you straight on something here. These are South Vietnamese Rangers, and you're a guest in their country."

March rocked back under the reproof. It had been a long time since anyone had dared to use that tone of voice to him. Not publishers. Not network presidents. Not admirals nor generals. It had taken a two-bit nigger whose life he had come to save, at the risk, goddamit, of his own!

Whose exploits he had—through the goodness of his heart—been flashing around the world.

But he recovered very quickly. With Adam March, the story always came first. It was natural enough, he told himself, that Captain Walsh would be hypersensitive to the derogatory terms white men applied to the colored people's of the world. He wouldn't have been able to do what he had done if he didn't have some spark to him. Besides, Adam March reflected, Walsh didn't have any idea who he was.

Swallowing his gall, he said pleasantly. "No offense intended, Captain. I don't like the word myself. Just one of those bad habits one picks up from the GIs." As he offered his hand, the sense of his historic mission overtook him, "Captain Walsh, I presume."

It was Walsh's turn to be taken aback. He had not expected this apparition to know his name. "Then the messenger did get through?"

"He sure did." March grasped Walsh's hand and shook it vigorously. "This is a great honor, Captain Walsh."

Confusion compounded astonishment. "I'm not sure I know who. . . ." He frowned at March's regalia, the Colt pistol, the grenades. "You're not a doctor, are you?"

March laughed indulgently. "A medic? Lord, no! I'm a war correspondent. Adam March. Maybe," he said, with an attempt at modesty, "you've read my stuff."

"War correspondent," Walsh repeated, really bewildered now.

Delvecchio had come looming up alongside. "Joe," he said, "I thought you told me this was a Marine ambulance?"

"Adam March," Delvecchio told him. "This is Adam March, the columnist." Delvecchio thrust his hand at the correspondent. "First Leftenant Joseph Delvecchio at your service, sir. It's a pleasure to meet you, Mister March." He gave him his most engaging smile. "It was only a fortnight or two ago that I wrote my sister that the two things I miss most from home are steady ass and Adam March's column. She's been sending me your column ever since."

"Glad to hear it." March gave the hand a limp touch and brushed it aside. His hand had gone to Walsh's elbow before Delvecchio's words finally sank in, and he turned back to give Delvecchio a longer look and a squinty appreciative smile. "Well," he said, "you can't have everything." Taking him by the elbow, applying pressure, he attempted to steer him off to the side. "Captain Walsh, you and I have a lot of talking to do. Where can we. . . ."

"Mister March," Walsh said, breaking in on him. "We've got a dying man here." He knew who Adam March

was all right, but at the moment he couldn't have cared less. "The only thing I'm interested in talking about right now is how long it's gonna take to get him back to a hospital."

If the meteorologists were right, March told him, the weather was due to clear rapidly after midnight. "By daylight a squadron of Hueys will be winging over this mountain to pick up you and your men."

"That may be too late," Walsh said grimly. He turned away from March and trotted over to the crewmen disembarking from the helicopter.

"We've got a man we've got to get to a hospital fast," he told the Marine master-sergeant. "Do you have any plasma aboard?"

"Let's have a look at him, sir," the Marine suggested. He nodded to the T/5 corporal standing just behind him. "Kelleher, grab the kit and a stretcher."

Walsh led them single-file down the rocky hillside toward the tunnel, with March scrambling along right behind him, the beam of his flashlight trained on the uneven ground.

"Watch yourself," Dave shouted, as March's feet skidded out from under him on the loose pebbles and dirt. The war correspondent came tumbling into his arms and a small avalanche went crashing down the mountainside.

"Jesus!" March said. He remained in the same hunched position even after Walsh had let him go, his head darting this way and that. "All this noise, we're going to stir up a hornet's nest. You better douse that light, Captain, before somebody gets picked off by an enemy sniper."

"I don't think you have to worry about that," Walsh told him. We haven't seen any Commies since we've been up here."

Slowly, ever so slowly, Adam March straightened up, never taking his eyes off the Negro captain. He opened his

mouth and closed it. He peered into Walsh's face to make
sure he wasn't being put on.

"What did you say, Captain?" he asked in a low, strained
voice.

Walsh was peering back at him curiously. "I said we
haven't seen any VC or North Vietnamese since we moved
up to high ground." Anger sharpened his voice. "We saw a
few before that, though. In case you haven't been listening,
we've got a dying man to prove it."

Delvecchio called to Walsh from the rear of the column
where he had been baiting the Marine medics about the
soft touch they had, just like the flyboys. "What's holding
up the parade, Cap? Get the lead out, huh?"

Lieutenant Nichols died while the Marine medical
corpsmen were preparing to administer blood plasma to
him. Although the weather had not completely cleared, the
Marines took his body back to Calu along with the six
South Vietnamese soldiers who had suffered minor
wounds in the rout by the Communsts.

The Marine pilot, Master-Sergeant McNaughton, assured
March that they could easily make room for him if he
wanted to fly back with them and file his story, but March
insisted on remaining behind "to permit these wounded
allies to return with as much comfort as possible."

Adam March didn't give a damn about the comfort of his
wounded allies, of course. Adam March was hiding out.

For Dave Walsh, there was nothing to worry about now
but to keep the fires going until the rescue helicopters arrived. Sergeant McNaughton had contacted Calu by radio
before taking off and had been informed that the weather
was breaking to the west and north.

"If you can believe Weather," Sergeant McNaughton
told Walsh. "You should be out of here tomorrow morning.
If Weather runs true to form, I'll try to find my way back

here and drop you some supplies."

Captain Walsh understood well enough that in sitting around the fires, telling tales, they were doing what the friends of the dead always do, in war or peace. Still, it troubled him that he had experienced no real sense of grief, no real depth of mourning, for Bob Nichols. He just sat there and poked at the fire, as if his best friend were not lying under a blanket—under a shroud—at the head of the cave.

When the helicopter took off with the body, there was still no grief, only that hollow feeling that comes at the end of any assignment. He realized that he had accommodated himself to Nichols' death much earlier. That he had, in effect, pronounced his own last rites over him during that last painful conversation.

This was war, soldier, and in a battle zone your mind is programmed to accept death. Yes, soldier, this was war, and in a war you bury your dead and go on. As the chopping roar of the helicopter faded into the distance, Dave Walsh headed back to what was left of his command.

Adam March, on the other hand, disappeared into the mists around the mountainside for perhaps an hour. When he finally did return, he settled himself back against the cavern wall, away from the fire, deep in the shadows.

Adam March *was* grieving. Adam March was grieving for Adam March.

In all his illustrious career—and no objective observer, he was sure, could deny that he was a monumental figure on the journalistic scene—he had never been involved in such a fiasco.

Oh, there were some who would deny him his true place in journalism, he knew that; but he never doubted for a moment that any criticism of him was motivated by either jealousy or the routine carping and yapping of the hacks. The vultures! He had always given them the back of his

hand; or a taste of his heel.

The thought of returning to Calu and exposing his fiasco made him physically ill. During the night he had seriously played with the idea of talking the helicopter pilot into taking him to Saigon where he could file a final wrap-up story to the series, backing away from the David-Goliath theme without revealing the whole truth. He had even thought about blaming Ritter or Walsh himself for trying to put across a phony story. It was a technique he had developed to a fine art during his days as a Broadway columnist, when he would vigorously denounce as false rumor an item he had printed himself. If the wind were with him, Adam March could make a retraction sound like a coup of enterprising reporting: "Despite anything you may have read, the only medals Captain David Walsh and his fellow phonies will ever get will be for sprinting *away* from the enemy."

Came the morning and he had seen very clearly that there was no running away from this one. This was no item among a column of items, this was a front-page story he had placed his name and reputation behind. There was no possible way of backing away without making it clear that he was backing away.

To cut and run, leaving his clothes behind him in Calu, would only make it worse. That kind of story would be passed from mouth to gleeful mouth in newspaper offices and bars around the world.

There was nothing for it but to go back to Calu and squirm. Publicly. And oh, how they'd love it, all those two-bit hacks he'd been showing up for years. Oh, they had all been waiting for something like this to happen to Adam March. Praying! Praying for the one slip, the one bad break. All of them sitting back, waiting to pick his bones clean.

The vultures he called them in his column. He had been

recounting his triumphs over the vultures for years.

All his life he had been fighting them off, and now they finally had him. Adam March sat there, his back propped against the hard rock, racking his brain for some saving angle, some brilliant strategy. He racked in vain.

The first two installments were already on the news-stands, and he could visualize the headline just the way it had undoubtedly been printed up in his own New York newspaper:

DAVID AND GOLIATH (By Adam March) *Exclusive*

Adam March, who had supped with kings, had been un-done by a dumb nigger captain and a dumber gook messenger.

His reverie was broken by Captain Walsh himself stand-ing above him, big and black, with a canteen cup of steam-ing coffee.

"Listen," Walsh said, "we still have some soup left if you want."

March glared up at him sullenly. "You should have sent a written message instead of trusting it to that half-wit."

"Written messages can be intercepted," Walsh said coldly. "Now, look. Private Dhu is a good soldier, thor-oughly reliable. I don't see how G-2 could have come out with such a . . . such an incredible distortion of what we sent back, but I told you . . . if you've got any beef, it's with them, not us."

He shoved the canteen cup toward the correspondent's outstretched hands, so that the handle was toward him. Unsuspectingly, immersed still in his own thoughts, March clasped the hot metal sides.

"*Keeee-rist!*" he screeched, letting go of the cup. As the burning coffee splashed down over his trousers and com-bat boots, he leaped up and banged his head against an outcropping in the rock.

One hand went to the back of his head; the other tried to
pull first one pant-leg and then the other away from the
scalded flesh. What resulted was an odd little dance, with
March shaking one leg, then the other, while his head
rocked back and forth and his lips screamed out an interrupted flow of obscenities. It was, to Adam March, the sum
total of all the plots and indignities that had been perpe-
trated against him these last few hours.

"Sorry about that, sir," Walsh said.

He was not sorry at all. It was only with great effort that
he was managing to keep a straight face. He had disliked
March from the moment he saw him shove the Vietnamese
hands away from him and snap out the word *gook*. He
wouldn't have bothered to offer him coffee at all, if it had
not occurred to him that March just might possibly be of
use to him. Adam March seemed to be in desperate need of
a hero for this operation. Bob Nichols wanted his wife to
think well of him. Why not?

He picked up the canteen cup and waited for March to
settle down. "I really am awfully sorry," he said. "Can I get
you a refill?"

"What the hell do you want to do this time," March
groaned. "Throw it in my face? Goddamit, I didn't *want*
any coffee in the first place. What I need is a drink."

"I guess we all do, sir," Walsh said, trying to save whatever might be left. "But I'm afraid we can't oblige you
there."

"That's right, Adam," Delvecchio said, "the bars close
early here in Flatiron City. Tough local ordinances in all
the best caves around here. Rigid curfew."

Delvecchio had been coming over from the fire when the
coffee hit, and he had been forced to turn his back on
March until he had wiped the smile off his face.

March's grimace of disapproval at the gratuitous use of
his first name didn't phase Joe a bit.

"I've been thinking about this, Adam," he said, "and I don't think we can fault either G-2 or Dhu on this thing. What we have here, as Bob Nichols used to say, is a failure in communication."

"Oh, hell!"

"No, think about it. We *did* get attacked by an overwhelming Commie force. We *did* fight our way clear." He met Walsh's objection before it could be made. "Well, we did *get* clear and we *were* firing our weapons to cover our . . . uh, withdrawal. I'm asking you to put yourself in place of G-2, remember. We *did* come up here to the top of this mountain. And the Reds were building an airfield up here *once.* . . ."

While Delvecchio was talking, March had stopped brushing at his wet trousers. The gook's version of the escape had been pretty much as Delvecchio had described it. If that idiot interpreter could be believed, anyway. Which at the moment, he doubted. But that was neither here nor there. He regarded Delvecchio with sudden interest. His eyes narrowed and a hint of slyness brightened his face.

"I guess you're right, Joe," he said. "It was just one of those unavoidable things. An accident of war."

"That's very generous of you, Mr. March," Walsh found himself saying. Well, he thought to himself, it was. The man may have been unreasonable but he was admitting now that he had been wrong. He felt rather guilty now about the surge of pleasure he had experienced when the coffee hit.

He felt, in short, the warmth toward Adam March one feels toward someone whom one senses is in precisely the right frame of mind to do you a favor. The words came rushing out of him.

"Mr. March, I'd be grateful, all of us would, if you could do one thing. If you could give Lieutenant Nichols a small write-up. Just that he was a brave man who was mortally

wounded while covering our escape. Just for his wife, you know."

"Be glad to, Captain," March said. "It will be my pleasure." Adam March was beaming at Walsh. He was positively expansive. "That's what the whole thing is about, isn't it, to see that our fighting men get the credit they so richly deserve?"

"An obituary by Adam March himself," Delvecchio murmured. "Bob would have liked that."

Walsh sent him a sharp, warning look, but it was clear that Adam March was not a man to look for sarcasm in any praise of himself. Far from being offended, he took it as his due.

Unzipping the upper pocket on his combat jacket, March came out with a small flat metal packet of cigars. "Sorry I don't have a peace pipe, fellows," he said. He chuckled slyly. "But you know how the local ordinances are on those things, Joe. Tough local fire ordinances, huh?"

Out of his big side pocket, he took a gold cigarette case, embossed with an impressive crest. "Why don't you pass these around to the troops," he said, holding it out to Captain Walsh. "Poor fellows deserve the best we can give them."

He most certainly had misjudged Adam March, Walsh thought as he hurried over to pass out the cigarettes. Once the man saw the error of his ways, he was all out to make up for it.

Adam March was lighting Delvecchio's cigar for him. "Lieutenant, did you or Sergeant Rinkon say anything to those Marines about how you came to be on this mountain?"

Delvecchio's eyes narrowed shrewdly on March. "No, sir. The medics were too busy trying to save Bob Nichols' life to make small talk. And the big, brave driver was too busy making his own small talk to care." Having taken a

couple of puffs, he removed the cigar from his mouth so that he could gaze at it appreciatively. "Any special reason you want to know?"

March smiled. "No special reason, Joe. Like you say, just small talk," he pointed to the cigar. "Cuban. It's still possible to get anything you want in this old world of ours if you know the right people."

Dave left it there. He was just too physically and mentally exhausted to talk any more about it. He sat hunched over on the side of the bed, his underwear drenched with perspiration, his eyes closed . . . waiting. Waiting for his wife's reaction. Constance was silent. Finally, he looked up at her. Her face was strange to him. It was wearing a cold, bony, artificial smile, like a mannikin in a store window. When she spoke, her voice was strained and bony too.

"All right, Dave, have it your own way. It never happened." She stood up, clutching the robe very tightly about her. "You know, I think I'll take a hot shower. It will relax me, so I can get to sleep."

"Don't walk away from me!" he yelled at her. "For God's sake, Connie. . . ."

She looked back at him, with a slow turning of the head, and, although her face was still all but expressionless, she was plainly saying, *You can say that to me after the way you walked away from me?*

"For God's sake, Connie," he implored, "don't close your ears to what I'm saying."

She had turned away like a sleepwalker, but with two great, bursting leaps he beat her to the door, blocked off

the entrance, and pushed her back, almost carrying her really, onto the hassock. "What do I have to do to convince you people that it never happened? There's no sense just telling you, because you won't listen to me. I say it never happened, and you just keep saying it did happen like a bunch of goddamn parrots! *What* do I have to *do* to *convince* you it *never happened?*"

He was bending over her, his face so close to her face that their noses almost touched. Her face registered nothing. A blank. Only the lacquered mannikin smile.

He let go of her shoulders. What else was there for him to say? He felt weak, vulnerable. Drained. A weird idea flashed through his mind. This woman, seated here in his bedroom, was not his wife, Constance, at all. She was a creature from another planet who had somehow taken possession of Constance's body. A usurper from outer space or, more likely, out of a television science fiction show. The Invasion of the Mannikins, he thought idly. There was not the slightest doubt about it, he was going out of his mind.

"You don't have to convince me, David," she said casually. Her eyes were steady on his eyes. "You know, I never really believed it. That's an awful thing to have to say to you, but it's the truth." An almost imperceptible note of triumph had crept into her voice. Hurt, she was hurting. "And you won't settle for anything less, will you, David. You do have that thing about the truth."

She reached for her brush, lifted it to her hair, but he could see that she had no intention of brushing. ". . . at first I thought it was some kind of . . . like those stories where the wife gets a telegram saying her husband has been killed and the next night she gets a telephone call from him." She placed the brush back neatly in the corner of the table where she always kept it. "Mix-up of identities," she said, the phrase coming back to her. "It wasn't until I saw it in the paper, you know, with your picture that

it seemed like it might be true. And even then, back in my mind, I knew it wasn't."

As she spoke, Walsh kept drawing away from her. Shying away from what she was saying. The back of his legs bumped the bed, and he sat down heavily. *Hurt for hurt.* The moral ascendancy he had felt in telling her the truth, what was it worth now? *Truth for truth.* Her truth had left his totally deflated. Her truth bit deeper than his. To the bone. To the heart!

The awful truth was that the person who knew him best in the world believed him incapable of a single act of bravery. In the face of all evidence, *she* had known.

Her voice went on monotonously, relentlessly. "They sent a reporter over to get some other pictures of you. Of Josh and me too. The only one I could find of you was that one you sent from Tokyo in the Korean War. . . . You really should get some pictures taken of yourself, David. You never know when. . . ." Her voice choked off into a whisper, ". . . when you might need one." They sat in naked, unbearable silence, Constance hunched over her table, David hunched over the bed.

At last, he said, "Well, you knew your man all right. I'm not a hero, and there'll be no Medal of Honor and no fifty-thousand dollar partnership."

"And you're so proud of it, aren't you?" she said with contempt. "Why?" She lifted her eyes to the mirror. "Why? How many times have you told me that everything's a fake. That given a certain amount of money to work with, you can scientifically predict how many people are going to be talked into believing whatever you want them to believe. Was that just talking to show me how smart you are? Isn't that how they *do* it in public relations? Isn't that what advertising *is?*"

"You don't really believe this is the same thing?"

"Yes! The same thing! Yes! If Adam March wants to be

your press agent, who are you—little David Walsh—who
are you to tell him that he can't? Who are you to be so high
and mighty? Do you think that Lester would hesitate for
one minute? Why do you think you have to be so much better than everybody else?"

It was not a comment this time. It was not a rhetorical
question. It was an accusation. She had turned around to
face him, demanding an answer. The air was charged between them. He could feel it prickling along the back of his
hands and the nape of his neck, like static electricity before
a gathering thunderstorm. His first night home, he
thought. And if she said the wrong words—right now—it
could all end. He had to stay cool, he told himself, keep
everything under control, everything reasonable.

"I don't want to be better or worse than anybody else,
Connie," he said quietly. "Lester or anybody else. I just
want to be me, Dave Walsh. What I am. What*ever* I am. So
I can live with myself."

"And what are you? When they take away those bars
from you, you'll be a hack in the back office of the VA
again." She saw the hurt in his face, and savored it. "Lester
always looked at you like he could buy you for a buck and a
half and a pat on the back. Until tonight. Didn't you see the
difference, Dave? Oh, David, if you turn your back on this
opportunity, if you throw all this away, you'll never be
anything but a hack in somebody's back office." She spat it
out: "Lester Sampson's hired boy."

"Now wait a minute!"

"Hired boy! He got your job with the Veterans, or did
you forget that?" Her thoughts turned inward, her mouth
clamped down. "Believe me, *I* didn't forget!"

"You can never get over that, can you? That I had to go
to Lester for . . . that *you* had to go to your sister for a job
for me." *All right, hurt for hurt.* "She married better and
you can't get over that. Your kid sister. She married first

and she married better. Big talk and phony charm, huh? You'd sell your soul to be the wife of Lester Sampson."

"That's not true! How *could* you, Dave!"

Her face seemed to be coming apart. She turned her head away so that he would not see that she was on the verge of tears. She clutched the robe even more tightly around her shaking body.

Walsh got up and turned away from her. He did not want to feel anything for her. *Truth for truth.*

"Miriam, she forgot it eight minutes after she spoke to Lester," he said gruffly. "She was glad to do you a favor. That's all it was, a little favor she was glad to do. It's only you who can't forget it."

"He owed it to you!" Constance said, like the voice of vengeance. "You were in a war . . . you've been in three wars now . . . while he sat back and made money."

"Lester owed me nothing. And let me tell you something, Lester *gave* me nothing. I did the VA a job. And if I go back there, I'll do them a job again. And when I get my certificate I'll do them a job too."

"Sure you will, Dave," she said, clutching at it. "And if you take Lester's partnership, you'll do them a job too! Isn't that what really matters, doing a good job?"

"A good job!" Walsh snorted. "All they want is a handshaker."

"Then you'll shake hands for them. Fifty thousand dollars' worth. Never mind whether Lester owes you anything. You've got a family. Never mind me. You've got a son. You owe him something. You don't know what's happening here, Dave. You don't know how they talk. They've got guns. They talk blood; they talk murder. Little boys," she said, as if she couldn't quite believe it. "Dave, if you let him down on this, I don't know what he'll do. It's this damn neighborhood. This neighborhood isn't like it was when we moved in here. We've got to get him out of here."

"Yeah," he said, "those niggers sure do ruin a neighbor-hood." He knew that wasn't fair. It had been a mixed neighborhood when they moved in. It had been becoming increasingly black by the time he left. He himself had noted carefully driving in from the airport that there were no white faces to be seen on the streets.

"Don't tell me about niggers," she said.

"And just what's that supposed to mean?" It was coming, was it?

"Don't tell me about niggers, that's all. It means what it means."

"No, tell me."

"You know."

"Tell me."

Their eyes locked. There was only the sound of heavy breathing in the room.

Very deliberately, she said, "What's this country ever done for you that you think you owe it so much?"

"You can do better than that."

"All right," she said, "I'll do better. Did you ever hear a white man ever say he don't deserve anything he can get? Buy, borrow, or steal!" She pinched up her face, her nose in the air. "Lawsy me, Mistress Scarlett," she said in a high reedy tremolo, "this poor darky gwanna take somethin' he didn't earn from The Great White Father. Lawsy me, Mistress Scarlett, what they gwanna do to dat poor darky, whup him?"

"Okay, you finally said it. Happy?" Now that it was out in the open and done with, it wasn't as bad as he had thought. He had been ready for it. He had brought it on so that he would be ready to handle it.

"Don't you look at me as if I'm a bitch pushing you. You asked me to do better. Maybe *you* can do better. Maybe you better do better. You've got a wife. Let's *not* never mind about me, huh? I waited out this war too, you know.

You think it's easy being the mother and father to a 15-year-old boy? You think it was easy working in that office, surrounded by women straight from their men; big with their men; talking about their men? And never knowing whether I'd ever see my man again? What the hell do you think I had to come home to for ten months and fourteen days?" She pounded the flat of her fist against her chest. "What about me? I'm owed! I want! I need!" It came racking out of her body, overwhelming any resistance of her mind. It was torn out of her, low and throbbing. "And when did I ever push you away? When did I ever turn my back on you?"

They came to each other; they fell into each other's arms. "You bastard," she sobbed. He carried her to the bed, and slipped off her panties, and then he ripped off her bra and flung it away as far as he could. She lay there, against her satin robe, one arm already free.

"You bastard," she sighed. She grunted when he penetrated; she was tight with ten months and fourteen days. So tight that even Dave was surprised. And then it was as it had always been.

"Sweet bastard," she sighed. . . . "Oh, you dear sweet honorable bastard."

She nuzzled against him afterward. Momentarily, she dozed off, she even gave off a couple of deep contented snores. Dave lay back, one arm around her. He had come at her, once it had got started, as strongly as she had come at him. But now that it was over, his mind was right back on his problem.

Constance's mind had come right back to it too. "They don't care whether you really earned that medal or not," she said, drowzily. "They'd think you were crazy for telling them. All they care about is that those hands you're going to shake know you have it."

He tried to get it through her head that he wasn't being stubborn or, for heaven's sake, spiteful. Did she think he was so crazy that he didn't *want* that money? Didn't she think he wanted to give his family the kind of life that money could buy? He had only been trying to let her know that he wasn't going to get the partnership because, whatever Lester had said, they both knew that the whole thing was based on the medal.

"Adam March can write what he wants, but once they start taking testimony, they're bound to find out what really happened. There are three other guys in this country right now who know the true story."

She kissed his arm and his shoulder and his neck. "And what do you think those three other guys were doing tonight? Wiring their congressmen that they're not really heroes?" She chuckled deep down in her throat. "I'll bet." She kissed his ear in a succession of little humorous petting kisses. "They're home getting the hero treatment and loving it." She lay her head back on the pillow and drew his head down to her. "They're in bed with their wives or sweetheart and letting them know how lucky they are to be getting laid by a real live hero."

"I don't know," he said. After that first day in Calu things had been different between the four of them. Relations among them had remained cordial, but there had developed a certain reserve. They were all a little too polite to each other. They walked softly. They did not avoid each other, but they didn't seek each other out either. Only Delvecchio had asked him, quite casually, how it had gone with the interrogating officers in Ritter's office. And, just as casually, Walsh had replied, "You sure had the right scoop, Joe. You don't have to tell them a thing! They tell you."

Was that—all bullshit aside—why they had all signed the statement? So they could bask in the reflection of the

glory they had bestowed on Bob Nichols? *Getting the hero treatment,* she had said, *and loving it.*

And, ah, how much greater the glory reflected from the Medal of Honor.

"Connie," he said, "I want to tell you about someone." Propping himself up on his elbow, he told her the whole story about his relationship with Bob Nichols, on to the attack, the retreat, the mistake, the almost thoughtless decision to ask March to give Nichols a write-up and the discovery, only that very night, that March was not only holding tight to his original story but out to give it a final credence by bulling through a Medal of Honor for him. "My God, Connie," he asked, "do you have any idea what men have done to earn that medal?"

"I don't want to know. Don't tell me. All I know is that if you keep your mouth shut, we've got a whole new life, and if you don't you'll be deliberately setting out to bring disgrace on yourself and your son. Do you have any idea what this means to him? He's been like a new boy. Dave, you let this story come into our home, and now you've got to protect us. If a man's not anything else, he'll protect his home and family."

"If a man's anything at all, he's not a fake. Can't you see that what I was telling you was that it's like I'm giving that medal to myself?"

She propped herself up on one elbow and stared down at him. "I just want to know one thing," she said finally. "How come if you're so high and mighty you didn't mind giving it to your friend, the white man who cut and run? You could have been killed too, Dave—and don't tell me any more about that either, I don't want to know. You didn't run; you got what men you could out of there." She turned away from him and groaned, "I wouldn't mind so much, God save me, if you hadn't done it for a white man. Just explain to me, because I'm such a bitch, why what

you'd do for a white coward you won't do for your own son?"

Involuntarily, he grunted. She had scored heavily there, and she knew it. "What am I asking that's so bad? All I'm asking is that you keep your mouth shut. You said yourself they'd find out anyway. Do you think they're going to make a public announcement? The way things are, they'd do their best to keep it as quiet as possible and just let the whole thing fade away. You never told Lester you were getting any medal. Lester," she said, remembering, "told *you*. You didn't even know about it. You didn't ask him for a partnership. You told him you didn't even want it, that you wanted to be a teacher, and he sat there and begged you. He begged you. Nobody can fault you, Dave. You didn't do anything except try to do a favor for your white friend. You'd be crazy, can't you see, to. . . ."

"All right," he shouted. "All right, I'll keep my mouth shut. I'll take that partnership. Anything that will shut you up and let me get some sleep. But if it comes to it in the end, Connie, and hear me good, I swear on my mother's grave that I won't take that medal under false pretenses. I am not going to live the rest of my life as a fake and a fraud."

Contented, she went off to sleep.

Dave lay there, fully awake. He was not only tired to the bone, he was overtired. He knew that it would be a long while before he got any sleep.

His stomach felt raw. He could feel the wine, the coffee, and the cake fermenting in his stomach. And then he could taste it, as it all seemed to rise into his throat. The nausea hit him in waves. He staggered to the bathroom and threw up everything, and for a while he was afraid he was going to have the dry heaves.

To get the acrid, acid taste out of his mouth, he began to brush his teeth. He was looking right into the mirror, and he saw himself, bent over, shaken and sweaty.

"Welcome home, soldier," he managed to say to the tortured face in the mirror. And then, for no reason at all, "the whole world loves a lover."

The Army had scheduled a news conference for Captain David Walsh in the Manhattan Public Information Office at 663 Fifth Avenue. He was booked for a private audience with Adam March earlier the same day. An official limousine picked him up at his St. Albans apartment at 11 A.M. and drove him into New York City.

March Enterprises occupied a luxurious four-room suite at the top of the Time–Life Building. By prearrangement, Walsh was greeted by four pretty young girls in miniskirts —one of them a chic Negro—and the office boy. All of them carried pads and pens for the purpose of getting his autograph.

It was an unsettling experience for Walsh, especially when the receptionist, a stunning blonde, gave him the message with her eyes.

The prospect of coming face to face with Adam March had left Walsh somewhat unsettled anyway. He welcomed it and yet he dreaded it too. He welcomed it because it would give him the opportunity to make one last attempt to get March to drop this thing before they both got hurt. He dreaded it because if he failed, as he secretly suspected that he would, there was nobody left to stop it short of a Military Board.

Constance had left him at the limousine with a look that was both a question and a plea. Neither of them had made so much as an oblique allusion to their argument of that first night: David because there was nothing further to be said, and Constance, he suspected, because she felt she was binding him to their agreement by her silence.

March's secretary, a brunette, led him into the plush inner sanctum where sat Adam March looking rather small

and nondescript behind his big desk.

The office was something, all sunshine and drapery and thick pile carpeting. The glass-block walls were broken by a rich mahoghany paneling, well covered with impressive paintings, undoubtedly originals.

March himself was tieless. His shirt sleeves were rolled up just below the elbows. As soon as he understood that Dave wasn't going along quietly, he settled back in his reclining chair and heard him out, never interrupting once, his feet propped up on the desk, which was cluttered with letters, manuscript sheets, newspaper clippings, and other scattered miscellaneous items. One of his hands toyed with a deactivated hand grenade which he was using as a paperweight.

For Adam March, it was the best of all possible worlds. If he prided himself on his affluence and position, he prided himself on being a working reporter too.

When Walsh had finished, March dropped the grenade back on the desk and walked around so that he could rest his hip on the corner closest to Walsh's chair.

"You know something," he said. "You're an ungrateful son of a bitch. How can anyone be that ungrateful after everything I've done for you? There isn't a man over there in Vietnam who wouldn't give his right arm for the Medal of Honor."

"You're beginning to get the idea," Walsh said, glaring at him. "The ones who earn it mostly do. They give their arms and their legs, and sometimes a lot more."

March shook his head at such ingratitude. Dave might as well have saved his breath. "You know what the President's going to say to you in the rose garden at the presentation? He's going to say, 'I would rather have this medal than be President.' And he'll mean it."

"Exactly. And how can you square that with what you're doing. What's the biggest award in the newspaper busi-

ness? The Pulitzer Prize? If you were given a Pulitzer Prize for a story that wasn't really yours, would you accept it?"

March gave a short, abrupt laugh. "You just go bet the family jewels I would. That's what it's all about, Captain, to go for the prizes. Listen, if you knew how many no-talent slobs I've plugged into fifteen thousand a week, you wouldn't be so sensitive."

"I'm not one of your no-talent slobs," Walsh said coldly. "And I'm not looking to be plugged."

"Now let me tell you something. . . ." March was shaking a finger at him like a teacher reprimanding a pupil.

"No, you let me tell you something," Walsh shouted. "You're going to call off this farce. Now. Right now while you still have the chance to get there first. Because if you don't, I'm going to blow your whole story right out of the tub at that press meeting this afternoon." Walsh gestured impatiently at the paperweight on the desk. "Bounce that half-assed grenade of yours off that, Mister!"

"Now, Captain Walsh. . . ." The tone was smooth and conciliatory. ". . . just what is it that you're asking me to do? Call my friend, the Chief of Staff, and say, 'Forget about the whole thing, will you, we were just having our little joke.' Do you honestly expect me to do that?"

Walsh, honestly, did not know what he expected March to do. Or what he was going to do. He wasn't even sure he'd have the courage to blow the whistle on March and himself if he could. Not after what he had promised Constance.

"Just let it die," he said, avoiding March's intense, probing gaze. "Just drop all this David and Goliath crap and let it die a quiet, natural death."

"Just let it die, huh? Just like that." March made a little grimace to show what a pitiful suggestion that was. "For a man who's going into public relations, Captain, you've got a lot to learn about the uses of publicity."

Walsh looked up, startled. "Who says I'm going into

public relations?"

"Oh, word gets around." March taunted him with a thin, knowing smile. "I don't reveal my sources to everyone but, just between us girls, I was talking to Clem Bestor a little while ago. I hope I'm the first to congratulate you, Captain. Full partnership . . . my, my. You have a real rosy future ahead of you." His voice went flat and dry. "Any time I can be of help, don't hesitate. . . ."

It was so clear what March thought of him, coming in here screaming when all the time he had set himself up with a fancy partnership, that he felt constrained to make an explanation. "I haven't agreed to anything. If it hangs on what they think about that medal, I'm not going to take it."

March did have to laugh. "Whatever gave you that kind of an idea? They offer partnerships to captains coming out of the Army every day. It's called patriotic fervor. Christ, Walsh, don't be disgusting."

He picked up the grenade and stroked it lovingly. "I'm afraid it's out of our hands now. You can't rub the magic lamp, then change your mind and order the genie to climb back in. Nothing's going to stop this thing now. I couldn't drop this thing now, even if I wanted to. We're riding a tiger, you and I, Walsh, and there's nothing to do but hold on tight and enjoy the scenery." He slid off the corner of the desk, as if to show that the pleasantries were at an end. "The only thing would happen would be that a lot of people I could name would want to know why Adam March was all of a sudden letting go of a good thing. They'd find out, too. No. I drop you now, Walsh, and we're both dead."

"I'm willing to take that chance," Walsh snapped. But underneath he was thinking that, by the time the truth came out, he'd have signed the contract with Bestor, Sampson and Adams. And if the truth never did come out. . . .

"Well, I'm *not!*" March slammed the grenade down hard on the desk. "What do you think this is, a coffee klatch? A daisy ring? This is conflict! This is life!" His eyes were bright and manic. "Every day, you've got to beat 'em, beat 'em, beat 'em." He pointed suddenly toward the ceiling. "What do you see up there, Captain?"

Dave, reacting automatically, squinted up toward the empty air.

"There are vultures circling up there, Captain. I've got enemies in this business, Captain. I went over to Vietnam, and they were laughing at me." He snorted contemptuously. "Those smart-ass foreign correspondents!" He snorted even more contemptuously, "The pool boys! Well, they don't worry me, none of them, because, in the end, Adam March always rubs their noses in it. Adam March walked out of that steaming jungle with the biggest story of the war. *You!* And I'm not losing it."

Dave wasn't going to let him get away with that. "You didn't walk out with any big story. Not a real story. Adam March pulled the prize boner of the war, that's what Adam March did!"

March scrambled back a couple of steps and pointed a finger up at him. Behind the finger was a grim, glowering man. "Let's get one thing straight right now! When Adam March tells fifteen million readers something happened, it happened!"

Walsh could only stare at him, astonished, not only by the ego behind that kind of a statement, but by the burning intensity of it. This, it was clear, was something central to him. His personal philosophy. His private justification. When he began to talk again, he was talking as much to himself as to David Walsh.

"All right, suppose you had done everything I said you did, and nobody had seen you? That would make it just as if you had never done it at all, wouldn't it?"

"No! I'd know, March. I'd know."

March, considering it, nodded. He was willing to concede that he had a point there. A good point. An excellent point. He pulled at his nose, thinking. "All right," he said finally. "Suppose you had been killed. Nobody would know then, and it would be as if it had never happened. That's why the popular chronicler is the most important person of his times. It isn't what is done. It's how many people *believe* that it's been done. Truth is acceptance. Anything fifteen million people believe has to be true."

"That's what Hitler said, 'Hit 'em with the Big Lie.' That's fascism."

"No, Walsh, that's democracy. The rule of the people. What the majority believes will be." The perfect harmony of the theory left him glowing with pleasure. "Is; has been; will be. It has an independent existence of its own."

Walsh's undisguised skepticism seemed to upset him. He pulled on his nose again, looking for a way to convince him.

"All right," he said, finding it. "David and Goliath." He grinned at Walsh. "In the original. A slingshot? Absurd! David probably pushed a boulder down the mountain and killed him. But some popular chronicler—the Adam March of his day—understood that the Jews needed a morale booster, a great hero. So he gave them this beautiful story of the little unarmed man—a boy really—against the panoplied giant. Wonderful little story. Wonderful." There was a note of genuine professional admiration in his voice. "Did it happen? Of course it happened."

The finger stabbed at Walsh again. "It happened, because every literate person in the world believes it happened. And some," he said, as if it carried a special significance, "who can't even read."

He came back to the corner and desk and sat back down, his hands clasped around one knee. He studied him care-

fully for a moment. "Do you know something, Captain, you're a lucky man. You came along at just the right time. Why do you think I picked you out for the full treatment? Because I like you?" His expression of distaste answered that. "I picked you, Captain, because I know what's news! Those other slobs out there guess. I know. This country is ready for a hero just like you. A living, breathing, black hero, who also happens to be an officer and a gentleman. I happen to know the U. S. Army has been looking for *you* for a long time."

March picked up a sheet of paper from a desk secretary and frowned at it. "Are you aware, Captain, that *twenty-three* per cent of the American combat forces in Vietnam are black? That *fourteen* per cent of American casualties are black soldiers." He flipped the paper back on the desk. "Yet the Negro makes up only *eleven* per cent of the population in the United States. Get the picture, Walsh?"

"I don't know," Dave mumbled. "The Army may be looking for black heroes, but I'm not their boy."

March stretched himself lazily and comfortably. "You worry too much, Captain. Did you imagine for one second that I would have gone ahead with this thing without figuring all the angles?" His head bent back so that he could regard anybody that crazy in clearer focus. "I thought this out very carefully. I computed all the benefits against all the risks."

He bent to him again, coming almost all the way off the desk. "There are no risks. Even if they found out, the risk is negligible. The way things are, they wouldn't dare take a Medal of Honor away from a Negro. Not after all the publicity Adam March has given it." A look of anger had come into his eyes, as if in warning to anybody so foolish as to try. "Not the way Adam March would hammer away at them!"

The buzzer sounded on his desk.

"If they found out, Captain," he said, with a businesslike air that put the matter to rest. "They'd be more anxious to cover it up than we would." He reached over to the intercom unit on his desk and flipped a switch. "Yes, Jean. What is it?"

"Bobby Coleman is here," his secretary informed him.

Bobby Coleman, March told him, was the executive director of the National Society for Black Equality. "He's been eager to get together with you, Walsh, since the story broke, so I told him he could come on up."

Walsh didn't have to be told. Coleman had called the house twice the previous day, and Dave had deliberately ducked him.

He turned out to be a tall, slim Negro, in his late twenties, with blue-black skin, a neat mustache, and a sharp nose. He wore a tweed jacket and glasses with dark, heavy rims. Walsh took an instant dislike to him. Disliking him almost as much as he disliked March. Disliking him *because* he was associated with March.

After ordering his girl to send in coffee, March sat them down on one side of his office, around a low table.

"You," Coleman said for openers, "may be one of the biggest things that's happened to the black community in the United States since Martin Luther King." He was regarding him with a personal, possessive pride that recalled, for Dave, that first night with Miriam and Lester.

"Oh, hell," Walsh told him. "Let's not get sacrilegious."

"I warned you about his modesty, Bobby," March said quickly. "I must say, though, that in my long experience self-effacement is the one identifying quality they all share, the *real* heroes. You can quote me on that."

"Indeed it is," Coleman agreed, flashing an indulgent smile at Walsh. "But you had better start accustoming yourself to being in the public eye, Captain."

"Shyer men than David have managed to live with it,"

March said. "Look at Lindbergh."

"Lindbergh?" Coleman said. He hesitated for just a second, and then he said, "From all I've read about Lindbergh, he couldn't live with it at all. Didn't want to. From all I've heard about Lucky Lindy, he wasn't exactly a press agent's dream."

March didn't scowl at him, but he did make a motion, rather impatiently, for him to get on with it. "Same thing," he grumbled. "You know what I mean."

Liking Coleman just a bit more now, Dave glowered past him to March. "I have no intention of letting myself be pushed into the public's eye. I've already told you that."

The smile faded from Coleman's face. "You don't know what you're saying, Captain. Like it or not, you happen to be the Black Man of the Year."

"Not just black, Bobby." March was annoyed this time at having such limitations placed on his story. "*The* Man of the Year."

He'd have had to go a long way, though, to be as annoyed as Walsh. "That's a lot of horseshit, March. And nobody knows it better than you." He turned to Coleman. "Listen, before you go any further, Mr. Coleman, there's something that just between us brothers you better know . . . damn. . . . ."

The untimely entrance of March's secretary with the tray of coffee cups and pastry had cut him off.

While she was passing the coffee around, March explained that Captain Walsh was still edgy from everything he'd been through. "Right now, all he wants to do is go off and shut himself away from this screwed-up old world, and who are we civilians to tell him nay." The secretary, leaning over the table with the platter of pastry, favored Dave with a sympathetic smile.

So for that matter did Bobby Coleman. "Well, let me assure you, Mister Walsh—I mean Captain Walsh—the

NSBE doesn't want to exploit you on a stage like a performing bear. Nor do we want to act in the role of press agent." He smiled in March's direction. "You already have the top man in the business working for you on a purely volunteer basis."

And that, Dave thought, was the understatement of the Twentieth Century.

"There's dignity and deep pride—pride of race, personal pride—when you're up on the podium talking to your own people, letting them talk to you. Letting them see you, you'll be providing inspiration and hope and pride to countless Negroes. I would not call that, Captain, an inconsiderable thing."

Walsh protested that he couldn't see where he could really do that. "I'm not a good speaker. I'm not a speaker at all. I've never given a speech in my life. I wouldn't know how to begin."

That was no problem, Coleman assured him. The NSBE was quite equipped to provide a speech-writer. They had, in fact, expected to all along.

Walsh could see how disappointed Coleman was in him. "It's not that I don't appreciate the opportunity," he said. "Or that I don't appreciate what your organization does. It's just that I think you've got the wrong man."

What was the inspiration in a soldier, he wanted to know, a one-shot celebrity, as against men of real accomplishment? He would have thought they'd have wanted musicians, artists, statesmen, ministers. "The kind of men who could really lead and inspire." By the time he was finished he felt he had made a very good case against himself.

"Captain Walsh," Coleman said. "You are, at this moment, the most unique black man in this country."

Dave cocked an eye at him in a sort of amused wince, to let him know how ridiculous he was getting. He was rather glad Coleman was getting so ridiculous because it would

make it easier for Dave to turn him down.

"Adam," Coleman said. "How many black soldiers have won the Medal of Honor in this century?"

"Just four to date," March said, coming in on cue. "There may be a few more pending, I don't know."

"A few more pending?" Dave asked curiously. "I don't understand."

March explained that nominations for the medal were kept very confidential until final approval came from a board of review. It was not uncommon for a year and a half or two years to pass before recommendations were approved and made public.

March winked at Coleman. "It's not every candidate who has a fairy godfather to cut through red tape for him, Captain."

Dave glared at him. He wanted to say something, but Coleman brushed the subject aside.

"We're talking about *now*. Today. Just four black men. In two world wars, Korea, and now Vietnam."

"And three of them got their awards posthumously," March said. "All enlisted men, too."

"Which will make you," Coleman said, spelling out for him what March had been suggesting to him before, "the only living black commissioned officer to win a Medal of Honor in the history of the country." He was smiling across at Dave triumphantly, challenging him to tell him who was crazy now.

They were hitting him from both sides. Walsh had the giddy sensation that he was back in Vietnam, with the Congs attacking savagely on both flanks.

"You're a landmark, Walsh," March said. "You represent the living courage, gallantry and fighting spirit of the black race. You're the symbol of resurgent black America."

"I know that this sounds very . . . uncooperative of me," Dave told him, "but I'm going to have to say 'no' for

the time being. Like March says, I've been planning to take a trip. In addition to which I have to remind you that I haven't been awarded any Medal of Honor. So far as I know, it's nothing but talk."

"Just to put your mind at ease then, Captain," March said, "you'll get it."

Without really looking at Coleman, Dave said, "Well, if I do, we can talk about it some more."

The man from the NSBE couldn't really believe what he had heard. Walsh didn't even want to imagine what he must be thinking. Coleman walked a couple of tight circles around the middle of the floor, rubbing his forehead, glancing over at Adam March, wondering, it was clear, what he could possibly say to change Walsh's mind.

"Captain," he said, coming to a stop. "I want to tell you a story. A very personal story." He paused and stared at the ceiling. "How shall I begin . . . ?

"When I was 8 years old, my mother got me all dressed up, as best she could, and told me we were going to Cincinnati. To me—well, you have to understand that I had never heard of Cincinnati. We were living, my mother and me, with my grandfather on a scrawny Kentucky farm. You can imagine. How she got the money, I'll never know. I would suppose she scraped together every penny she had saved from working all her life."

His voice had cracked, and he had to stop for just a moment to collect himself. "To me, Cincinnati might have been on the other side of the world. We made the trip on a night coach, one of those old, slow, milk-run coaches. A nigger coach was what it was, and you don't get anything older or dirtier than a nigger night coach coming out of Kentucky. If I haven't already told you, my mother didn't have very much money.

"I don't know how long it took us, Dave—can I call you Dave?—except that it couldn't have been as long as it

seemed to me because to me it seemed like days. Whenever I'd ask her where we were going and whether we'd ever get to see grandpa again, she'd say, 'You'll see. I want you to look on a man, and then we'll turn around and go back.' That's all.

"Well, we finally got to Cincinnati, and went into, I guess, the stationmaster's office—I want you to believe that I've never told this story to anybody before—and she said a famous name to the man, and wondered whether he might be good enough to tell her where they stayed when they were in Cincinnati.

"Well, he was a good enough man. He was good enough to make a phone call to find out, and he told her the name of a hotel, and he even told her what bus would take us the closest to it.

"'That's very kind of you, sir,' she said, 'but if you'd kindly tell us how we could get there walking, I believe the fresh air would do the boy some good. He's been rather poorly later.' Did I tell you that my mother didn't have much money? He was a good enough man, you see, to make a phone call that didn't cost him anything, but he never had a thought to ask a tired black lady with swollen legs if twenty cents might help. Why should he have, though? Why should he have?

"I can remember, Walsh, walking through those strange streets and past those huge, looming buildings, holding onto my mother's hand and picturing that we were going into some mansion to see some great man. Some king.

"And it did seem like a mansion to me. Yes, it did. It was only a hotel lobby, not even a very impressive one probably, but to an 8-year-old black boy off a Kentucky tenant farm it surely did look like a palace.

"We were no sooner in the lobby when my mother said, 'There he is. Oh, I knew the good Lord wouldn't desert me.' Her knees were trembling, Captain, and if I didn't

know why, I still knew it would be an excellent idea for me to be afraid too."

He wiped his hands across his eyes, smiling just a little at the bittersweet memory of it. "She took me tight by the hand, my trembling hand in hers, and walked me across toward a big black man sitting there among all the white men. 'Mr. Robinson,' she said. 'I hope you won't think I'm acting too forward, but I done fetched my boy all the way from Kentucky because I wanted him to touch you. Would it be asking too much of you to let him touch you. You see, I figgered it out that he'll always remember that he took this trip to touch you and, in the remembering, he'll know that he can become a man too.

"And so," Bobby Coleman said, "I touched Jackie Robinson, not even knowing who he was, and then hid in my mother's skirt." He shrugged, as if to apologize for wasting everybody's time with such a trivial story. "And then we walked out of the hotel and back to the railroad station and took the night coach home. . . ."

He had Dave's eye now, and there was no way for him to turn away. "It was a much quicker trip going home, it was a very exciting trip. My mother told me all about the man I'd touched and she put the dream in me. Do you understand what I'm saying, Dave, she put the dream in me. I never doubted that I'd get off that scrawny Kentucky farm after that, and I never doubted what work I'd do.

"Because, you see. . . ." He stopped and wiped his eyes and flashed a big, toothy smile at Walsh. "Because, you see, I had gone to Cincinnati and touched Jackie Robinson."

Walsh had heard him out in growing distress. Not the least of his distress was the knowledge that he had taken it upon himself to dislike this man on sight. He had seen a man in a tweed jacket, and he had dared to fill in his full biography. Part of it, though, was the distress he felt for Coleman himself; Walsh knew what it must be doing to

him to have to tell this story in front of Adam March.

But most of all, it was because he knew very well, as the story came to an end, that there was no possible way he could continue to say no to Bobby Coleman.

"When we were born, you and I, Mr. Walsh, black men were not allowed to play in organized baseball. They were looked on as a contaminant. Five years ago, it took an army to get one black student into the University of Mississippi. This isn't ancient history. This is our country and our time. It's us I'm talking about, you and me. We are starting in this country almost from scratch. We are lifting ourselves up from the bootstraps while we're still trying to learn how to make the boots." He grimaced self-consciously. "Don't worry, I'm not going to give you the whole commercial. What would I be telling you that you don't already know.

"But you asked me, you see, about culture. You're just back from Vietnam so there's no reason for you to be up on these things. There's a whole movement about our African heritage and our black culture much of which does not, in fact, exist. There is not that much there. I'd deny that in public. If Adam March here quoted me on that I'd stand up and say that he's a liar. Otherwise my usefulness in the movement would be at an end, that's how strong that feeling is."

As Coleman looked at him, it suddenly occurred to Walsh that while he now liked Coleman very much, Coleman didn't think very much of him. Why should he?

He wanted to shout out, "And what if they find out that I don't exist either, Bobby? That I'm a fake. That Adam March made me up!"

"Yes," Coleman was saying, "that's pretty pitiful, isn't it? That yearning for roots, that hungering for identification when so many of us don't know who our own fathers are. Including me, Mr. Walsh, including me. I don't much think you missed that while I was telling you my story."

Yes, David Walsh knew what it was doing to Bobby
Coleman to be saying this in front of Adam March.

"You can make a contribution, Captain Walsh. You're a
living black hero. Integration isn't working. The militant
has the field. The militant has the field because he offers
the young black man the chance to assert his manhood. I'd
deny I said that too, Adam. You can give him that pride by
letting him look at you. By talking to him. And, not to be
too corny about this, by letting him touch you. And for our
purposes you can do more than that. You can show him
that he can aspire to the highest honors his country can be-
stow. Yes, Captain Walsh, you can make a contribution. If
I were you, I'd thank God that I was in that position."

There was absolutely nothing David Walsh could do except assure Bobby Coleman that he did, indeed, consider it
an honor to do what he could, within his obvious limitations. There was absolutely nothing for David Walsh to
say except that he was placing himself at the NSBE's
disposal.

With Adam March grinning alongside him, Coleman
told him that he would get in touch with him as soon as
they had put together an itinerary.

"I didn't mean to take up so much of your time," he said
apologetically. "I know you two old friends have a lot to
talk about. I appreciate it, Adam, that you let me cut in on
it."

"Not at all, Bobby," March said. He walked Coleman to
the door, one arm across his shoulders. "Who," he said
generously, "has a better right?" He gave him the knowing
March wink. "I wanted you to talk to him first. Before the
commercial vultures start tearing away."

The door closed behind Bobby Coleman. March leaned
back against it, his arms folded across his chest. Smug, tri-
umphant, challenging. "You let your people down now,
Walsh, it will be the same as if David had slung that rock at

Goliath and missed. Or, worse, defected to the Philistines."

"You dirty white bastard!" Walsh was trembling with rage. He brought both fists down on the table with such a fury that all three coffee containers went skidding off to the floor. "I've never said that before in my life, but you are a dirty white bastard!"

March let it roll right off him. "Don't bitch to me, Captain," he said, strolling back from the door. "You had your chance. All you had to do was tell him. Nothing I could have done to stop you."

"I just may kill you!"

March had come directly opposite him. "Only you don't have the guts. People who 'just may' never do."

March had no doubt whatsoever that he was in complete control now, and he was a man who moved quickly to nail his victories down. His eyebrows raised slightly, his lips curled in mild amusement, he said, "You see that sort of light tan thing sitting on my desk. Know what it is? It's a telephone. An integral part of our far-flung communications industry. Use it, why don't you? Call the President, he's a good friend of mine. Tell him you're going to decline his kind offer of the Medal of Honor. Tell him that you and that joker Delvecchio and the fat sergeant and the little medic all marched into Stonewall Ritter's office and signed false affidavits attesting to your own heroism. Go right ahead!

"No?" His lip curled. His eyes narrowed. "You can't hurt Adam March. All you'll accomplish is the disgrace and downfall of your buddies, of your family, and of yourself. And," he said, brutally, "I don't think there'll be any dancing in the streets of Harlem either."

He started, with a quick, angry step toward his desk, but immediately turned back. "One other thing." A slow smile came to his face. Apparently, this one had just hit him. "You'll hurt every man who ever won the Medal of Honor,

including *those four Negroes!* You'll cast suspicion over
every hallowed grave in Arlington Cemetery."

Walsh felt as if he were going to throw up. "You like to
use dead men, don't you, March? First it was Nichols, and
now it's these. You're not a writer, you're a goddamn
ghoul!" Infuriated as much by his own impotence as he
was by March, he leaped up and headed for the door.

"And who do you use, Walsh?" March called after him.
"If you want to kid yourself, go right ahead, but don't think
you're kidding me. I know you, Walsh!"

Walsh's hand dropped off the doorknob. Almost against
his will, he turned back. "You heard me, Walsh. Oh, I've
seen your kind all my life. Black or white, you're all the
same. The whiners. The snivelers. You want yours like
everybody else, only you've got to have it both ways, don't
you? You've got to have me push you into it against your
better instincts so you can say, 'He did it, not me. Adam
March did it.' Well, I'm not interested in your interior
struggles. You work things out any way that will make you
happy. But you *will* take that medal. You'll take it because
away down deep you really want to take it. You want that
medal so bad you can taste it. Now isn't that right, Walsh?"

Whatever he saw on Walsh's face made him smile.
"You've *got* to have it now, Walsh. These last couple of
weeks you've come to realize what that medal will mean to
you. To your family. It's your ticket out of St. Albans:
printed, delivered, and punched by Adam March. Instant
equality! Instant freedom! Instant money. Instant quiff.
. . . And I believe you signed the testimony?"

Walsh went out of the room and slammed the door. He
could still make out March's muffled voice shouting behind him, "Oh, yes, Captain Walsh, you signed . . . you'll
take it," followed—or did he only imagine it—by
laughter.

On the way back to St. Albans in the official Army

limousine, Dave slouched in the back seat watching a helicopter hover low over the Triboro Bridge. One of those
radio network jobs that gave traffic bulletins to homeward
bound motorists.

The sight of the big rotor blades flashing in the slanting
late afternoon sun took him back to the day the choppers
had airlifted them off Flatiron Mountain.

It was the first time they had seen the sun in six days.
And just as March had promised, a fleet of Army and
Marine helicopters came cruising over the jungle horizon
in the early morning to airlift Captain Walsh and what
remained of his ragtag command back to the base.

Adam March looked out the window, as the Huey
reached cruising altitude and began to peel away. "So
long, Mt. Goliath," he said to the receding mountaintop.
"To quote an intimate friend of mine, now gone, 'We shall
return.'"

"Not if I have anything to say about it," Walsh told him.
Leaving the place where his friend had died was somehow
confirming the irrevocable fact of his death. Heading back
toward the base, he knew that the rest of his tour was going
to be much more barren; much more difficult.

"Never say never," Adam March was saying. "The one
thing I have discovered about life is that you never know
what it has in store for you."

A cordon of military police encircled the helicopter carrying Adam March and the American soldiers as soon as it
landed at Calu. A waiting staff car, sporting a two-star flag,
pulled right alongside them—General Randolph Ritter's
personal car. As the Americans were debarking there was a
burst of applause, and Walsh saw that there was an aston-
ishingly large turnout of soldiers and correspondents lined
up all along the apron.

The applause depressed Dave Walsh. It seemed to him that they were being applauded because they were survivors. American survivors. As commanding officer, it brought home to him, once again, that he had, in a way, left behind 342 of his men—342 South Vietnamese troops —to die or be captured. As a captain, he wondered whether he shouldn't have gone down with his ship? A false analogy here, he knew, because he would have had to row back to the sinking ship in order to go down with it. What he really wondered was, would they have been applauding if it had been 342 Americans who had been lost?

The surviving South Vietnamese who had been airlifted back on the earlier Hueys had already been whisked away. He wondered what they thought of him, the American captain—*say it, the American black man*—who had cut and run. Not fair, not fair. They had been with him, out on the perimeter. They were the most practical of men.

The others in the car were suffering no such pangs of conscience. Just alongside him Cummins was flushed with surprise and excitement. "I feel like a returning hero."

"That's funny," Delvecchio said, from the other side, "I feel like hell."

March, jammed in between Rinkon and the driver, twisted his head around. "As far as I'm concerned, Ernie, speaking as one civilian, you are." His eyes went to Walsh. "And I intend to mention your name when I write about the late Lieutenant Nichols." He placed a hand on Rinkon's shoulder without looking at him. "You too, Rink."

Walsh could just make out Delvecchio's little snort alongside him.

"It's capital D, small v," Joe said. "And no space in between, huh?"

"All right, fellows," Walsh said wearily. "Enough is enough. Mister March is only going to. . . ."

March stopped him with a warning, sidelong swing of

the eyes in the direction of the driver. "I hate to keep reminding you, fellow. But . . . you remember what the big man said. Keep your lips buttoned until you've been debriefed by G-2."

March had spoken to General Ritter over the helicopter's radio before they took off from Flatiron, and relayed the word to the Americans that they were to consider themselves under tight security.

Suddenly, Dave Walsh was very tired. A debriefing session was just what he didn't need right now.

Captain David A. Walsh stood at the window in the small officers' barracks watching, with a minimum of interest, a construction detail repairing a gaping hole in the base fence. He was wearing a clean dress uniform hastily requisitioned by the friendly command. He went back to the table to crunch his cigarette out in the ashtray; the cigarette had not been smoked even half down. Neither had the other dozen or so butts already in the ashtray.

Captain Walsh was the last man to be interrogated by Army Intelligence. The enlisted men, Master-Sergeant Frank (NMI) Rinkon and Corporal Ernest E. Cummins had been taken to G-2 immediately after they had been fed. Captain Walsh and Lieutenant Joseph V. Delvecchio had been driven to the small wooden barracks, in the officers' quarters, and were advised that they would be picked up again in two hours. A big, burly master-sergeant with a growth of bristling, wheat-colored hair had driven up an hour or so earlier.

"Loo-tenant Del-vetch-io," he drawled, "they want you first."

Walsh had seen the man's eyes catch on him in that first moment, and understood perfectly the look that drifted over his face. The broad Mississippi accent came as no surprise to him.

Walsh walked back to the window and, after a minute or two, took out still another cigarette. He was about to light it when he heard the car pull up to the front door.

Plumping the rather raunchy officer's cap onto his head, anxious to get this over with, he headed for the door. Delvecchio was already coming up the walk. The Mississippi sergeant yelled out, "Ah'll be back for you after chow," and gunned the car. He didn't say "Captain." He didn't say "sir."

"Joe, how did it go?" Walsh asked.

Delvecchio, looking tight and uncomfortable in his clean dress uniform, loosened his tie. "How did it go? It went. The train has went." His hand swooped straight up toward the ceiling as if he were describing the ascent of a plane. "Carrying the body of Bob Nichols straight up the mountain."

"Now you're beginning to sound like Adam March. Let's try it without the wisecracks, huh? What happened?" He looked around the room nervously and said, far too loudly, "If you can tell me."

"Oh, I can tell you." One side of Delvecchio's mouth curled up. "They got Nichols up for the DSM."

Walsh opened his mouth to speak. Nothing came out, though, because he was not sure he quite understood what he had just heard. The Distinguished Service Medal was the second highest military award an American soldier could win. Delvecchio and his goddamn sense of humor.

"No, I am not putting you on, daddy-o," Joe said, reading him very clearly. He reached out and plucked the cigarette from Walsh's lips, took a drag on it, and with a flip of the wrist over the palm of the hand in the manner of a courtier offering his opponent a sword, placed it back in Walsh's mouth.

Walsh couldn't quite gather himself together to decide what he wanted to say.

Delvecchio raised one eyebrow. "You're the one who asked Adam to give your friend a small write-up," he said, in the attitude of a man who was very carefully removing all responsibility from himself. "Adam March, as you may have observed, is not a man to do things halfway."

Walsh shook his head. He could hear the breath coming out, tightly, hissing through his own teeth. "That March, he's something else." That's all he could think to say.

"What the hell." Delvecchio shrugged. "How much does a medal cost the government anyway?"

March had saved some small part of his story by building Nichols up. Walsh wondered why he should have been surprised. He saw a woman—slender, pretty, somewhat weary (she was brushing her hair wearily aside)—reading the story in the paper and being happy. He saw Bob Nichols (seeing her happiness) being happy too. He was not displeased.

"Yeah, well. . . ." He ran his fingers through his own kinky hair. "What the hell, Joe. He's dead. I suppose he deserves it as much as some ox who goes charging into a machine-gun nest because he hasn't got enough brains to be afraid."

"Oh no you don't!" Delvecchio's anger was completely unexpected. "Not with me, daddy-o. Nobody dies easier because he hasn't got a college education. You just get that idea out of your head. If they want to give him a medal it's no skin off my ass, but don't try to sell it to me. I saw that . . . schoolteacher chicken out, and so did you, buddy, so did you."

"Is that what you told them in there?"

"*I* didn't tell them anything. They told *me!*" He was becoming aggressively defensive. "All that was required from me was an occasional nodding of the head, the one military movement I can perform as well as anyone in this man's Army." His voice went low with disbelief. "Jesus

Christ, they got that guy attacking machine-gun nests while we were storming the goddamn mountain."

The full impact of it hit Walsh. This time he really was stunned. Adam March had not been content to simply save his story. If he couldn't have Walsh, he could have himself a dead man.

Delvecchio's voice, when he picked it up again, had quotes around it. " '. . . in the face of withering enemy fire with complete disregard for personal safety.' You know the way it goes."

Walsh saw it so clearly now. "That horseshit story of his, huh? No wonder he wanted us to keep our mouths shut." It was beyond belief. "But Joe, what's the matter with everybody? I mean, Intelligence. . . ."

Delvecchio was studying him carefully, his head cocked to one side, his lips pursed. "Adam March is in there now. He's running the whole show. The whole shebang. The whole kit and kaboodle. And all the brass, Stonewall Ritter, General U.S.A. included, act like first lieutenants being inspected by the Chief of Staff. That's another military position I am very well qualified to comment on."

Walsh whacked his forehead with the heel of his hand. So hard that it hurt. "Well, Goddam . . . it, Joe, why didn't you say something? Why didn't you say it wasn't true? Didn't you say *anything*? You *had* to say something!"

"Now, listen, *Captain*. They hit me with this thing as a package deal. I couldn't say, well yes, I'll take this part here about Nichols, but the rest of it you got to throw away, because although he was busily attacking machine-gun nests to spring us free, nobody bothered to tell us about it, and so we were just climbing up a mountain and hoping to God nobody was climbing after us."

The two men glared at each other.

"You're right," Delvecchio said. "I had to say some-

thing." He gave a wry little laugh. "I know what brainwashing is now. And," he said, "I have a feeling that Rink and Cummins do too. They tell you what happened, March mostly, and you just kind of go along."

"And just kind of add a touch here and there?"

"And just kind of add a touch here and there."

Walsh turned his back on him. "You should have said something, Joe." His voice lacked conviction.

"Maybe I should have. But, like I say, they hit me with this thing, Dave. And I'm in the position where if I say no, I'm—what?—spitting in a dead man's face? I'm in a position where I'm thinking what the hell did Rink and Cummins tell them? If I say no, am I making a liar out of them? Did they sign anything? Could I be putting them up on charges? And all the time there's ten eyes drilling into you, waiting for an answer. Not an answer when you've put the whole thing together, but *right then!*"

The faintest note of wheedling had crept into his voice. "They've got me in a position, Dave, where it's got to be this or that. What did you want me to say? 'No, that's just a story March made up. He wasn't a hero at all, he was a coward.' You said it, the guy is dead. So you tell yourself, where's the harm? Where's the harm?"

His own ears finally picked up that apologetic tone, and it seemed to infuriate him. "Let's see how *you* do, daddy-o," he said, returning to the attack. "They hit me with this thing. But *you* know! You got time to think it over. Let's see what you do when they get you in there." He scooped up his hat and placed it jauntily on his head. "I wasn't the one asked Adam March for any favors. And I wasn't the one who promised Nichols I'd write his wife either. In addition to which," he said, heading for the door, "I really don't give a damn. If you give a damn, daddy-o, all you got to do is blow your little tin whistle."

They sat in a circle around a big table like executives at a board of directors' meeting. There was a Major Bessine of Intelligence and a lieutenant from Intelligence who never opened his mouth and whose name Walsh never caught. The master-sergeant who had escorted Walsh into the room worked a stenotype machine, recording everything that was said. General Randolph Ritter was at the head of the table. And Adam March sat right alongside him.

As soon as Captain Walsh was seated, March suggested that they read the rough citation they had put together from the testimony of Delvecchio, Rinkon, and Cummins.

The G-2 major started to protest this disregard for normal interrogation procedure, in a *pro rata*, resigned way which told Walsh that he was making his objections purely for the record. In case anything happened, Major Bessine was protecting himself.

"I agree with Mr. March," General Ritter grunted. "It's getting late and it will save a lot of repetitious talk. Once he's heard it, the captain can make any corrections, additions, or emendations. He smiled benignly at Walsh. "Captain, as you have undoubtedly observed, Mister March is being accorded the special privilege of sitting in on these proceedings. . . ."

The general went on to explain briskly that Adam March *did* have a proprietary interest in this story—as the captain knew better than anyone else—since he had risked his life to go after it. It was only fair, the general felt, and he believed Intelligence agreed with him (the major and the lieutenant kept their eyes cast down), that Mr. March should be permitted to sit in on these proceedings and hear the live testimony of Captain Walsh and his men. After all, security was really no longer an issue. The battle of Mt. Goliath was a *fait accompli*.

General Ritter took up the yellow sheets before him and

read aloud in a slow, monotonous, toneless voice, as if he were feeding information into a computer. Although Walsh thought he had been prepared by Delvecchio, in fact he hadn't really been. Hearing Delvecchio tell about it was one thing. Hearing it come officially, under the fluorescent lights, and from a general, was something entirely different. Especially since Delvecchio hadn't bothered to tell him about their remarkable escape through a ring of enemy troops or Walsh's own brilliant decision to throw them off the trail by heading north.

But it was when the general came to the familiar story, the storming of the mountain, that Walsh found himself most shattered of all. Being prepared for the story, he found that it didn't ring that false to his ears anymore.

He had heard it from March, he had heard it from Delvecchio, and now he was hearing it from General Ritter. It had that feeling of "rightness," of "authenticity" about it.

What would have really startled him, he realized, was if they had read off the true story, for which he was not at all prepared.

"I know what it is now to be brainwashed . . . ," Joe had said.

". . . when he was close enough to the enemy pillbox, he began hurling grenades, and while doing so, received the wound that proved mortal. Lieutenant Nichols' fearless action not only wiped out another enemy installation, a key installation, but diverted its fire as to permit his small, outnumbered force to press forward and seize its objective."

General Ritter tapped the sheets together on the table, laid them down and looked up at Walsh. "And now, Captain? Is there anything you would care to add to that account? Any additions, corrections, or emendations?"

Walsh could only stare at him in silence. What the hell

was he supposed to say? That Delvecchio and Cummins and Rinkon were liars.

After a while the general frowned. "Captain Walsh, you were listening, weren't you? You are all right, aren't you, Captain?"

There was, he saw, a genuine human concern in the general's eyes. Walsh nodded mutely. ("*All they required from me was an occasional nodding of the head.*")

"Lieutenant Nichols was a close personal friend of the captain's," Adam March said smoothly. "It isn't easy for him to talk about it, to go over the whole hellish ordeal again. . . . I also suspect that Captain Walsh's very commendable modesty makes it awkward for him to describe these events which unavoidably reflect so much honor upon himself."

Yes, the general said. A rest for Captain Walsh was most certainly in order. And the others. Their orders were already being cut.

There seemed to be some question about what the last question had been, and the sergeant went back to the little white roll in his machine and read: "And now, captain? Is there anything you would care to add to that account? Any additions, corrections, or emendations?"

"No, sir," Walsh heard himself saying, seeing them all sitting at the table. "No, sir," he had said. It was so easy. All he had to do was let it happen. Keep himself apart and let it wash over him. "No, sir," he said, removing himself from the proceedings, so that he was nothing more than a spectator to the somewhat amusing drama being carried on by these five white men and that Negro captain.

"That pretty much sums it up, from where I sit," Ritter said. He turned to the major. "Major, I believe you have something?"

The G-2 officer's voice had a parade-grounds bark to it. "Captain, how many enemy troops would you estimate

were at Flatiron?"

Dave Walsh felt a quickening of the heart beat. "Oh, oh! The major smells a rat!" He knew it all along; they weren't kidding the major. The round-faced man with the neat mustache had only had to look at Walsh to see that this wasn't a man who could pull off that kind of a deal.

Captain Walsh told him that he didn't have the least idea.

"It's important to me that I have an estimate," the major said. "That's all I expect, captain, an estimate. Just your best possible guess. We've had estimates of from 1,000 to 2,500." Something inside Dave Walsh smiled. Even the major had fallen into the pattern of feeding him information.

"Captain?" They were waiting. All heads were turned to him. ("... *ten eyes drilling into me.* ...") He had an image of himself as a concert performer on a stage, in that brief moment after the conductor taps his baton and lifts his arms. The moment of the upheld hands, the silent audience, the held breath, and the upturned eyes. He moved himself the final notch, letting it happen, letting it wash all over him. "I'd say a thousand. But it's just a guess. Maybe less." Captain Walsh, seated at the table, knew he had taken the final step in. He had, it was true, given them the lowest possible number, as a sop to his conscience, but, still, he had committed himself. Oh, he had been shrewd about it. He caught the exchange of covert smiles around the table. Had he really been trying to play down his role or had he known how impressed they were going to be with all that modesty?

The major nodded to the general, the general nodded to March, and the lieutenant closed the notebook into which he had been transcribing notes, from time to time, throughout Walsh's testimony. Adam March stood up and stretched his arms.

"Well, that about wraps it up," he said.

"Not quite," Major Bessine objected. He explained to Walsh that decorations and awards, while always interesting, were not really a primary concern of his. He was sitting in on this on G-2 business. For the record G-2 wanted to know whether Captain Walsh had any theory why the enemy had not counterattacked to try to retake the airstrip after the element of surprise was gone. He was regarding Captain Walsh with an expression of shrewd speculation. Or was it downright suspicion?

Good God! Dave thought, he's getting set to rip into me now! What is this poor black boy getting himself into here? All he ever wanted was to get his friend a line or two in March's dispatch. The dispatch had been escalated to a Distinguished Service Medal, and now the DSM was being escalated into a matter of vital security. *G-2 business!* The time had come for the boy to put the brake on this.

"I wondered that too," he heard the witness tell the major. "I mean we didn't put on that much of a show of force, and all of sudden they were gone."

Brake it? *Make* it was more like it. What had happened to all those good intentions? How did they lose so much in the translation between the mind and the tongue? Well, at least the boy could stop worrying. He was up to his knees now.

"Maybe they were pulling out to go to Khesanh, anyway," he said, thoughtfully, "to join forces with the rest of their troops. Something like that. I wondered about that myself truthfully. Maybe they figured they could come back and push us out any time."

"Possibly," the major said. "But not probably. I think perhaps you are being too modest, Captain. If military logic were all that were involved here, then I must tell you that the tactical logic of the situation would have been to push you out while the weather was bad, before reinforcements could be sent in. I mean, the Commies didn't invest all that

time and manpower building an airstrip on top of a mountain just to let a hundred and twenty of our guys take it away from them. What they must have had in mind was a series of hit-and-run air strikes on our big bases in the south. Better yet hit Saigon and other dense population centers. Psychological. To try to make our troops and the civilian population wonder how long are we going to be able to maintain total control of the air."

The major had a quick, flashing smile. "Between us, Captain—and I do mean between us—we didn't know about that airstrip. With the infrastructure the enemy has built up over the years, there's a lot we don't know. They sit in caves by day and work and hunt by night. They went to a hell of a lot of trouble to make sure we didn't find out about this project. A beautiful job of security," he said with the ungrudging admiration of one professional for another.

"But after you stumbled on the site and kicked Charley's ass off the mountain, he must have assumed—and quite logically—that that's what you were there for. The fact that we knew about the airstrip was, from their point of view, enough to destroy its usefulness permanently." He flashed his quick smile at Walsh again. "Beyond which reconnaisance has informed us that you did a *pre-e-ety* good job of wrecking it."

They'd wrecked it now, had they? Dave Walsh thought, mildly amused by this time at the Army's infinite capacity to delude itself. It should have been obvious from 5,000 feet that the damn airstrip had been crumbling for years. He saw the undisguised smirk of self-satisfaction that came to Adam March's face. The fixed, wooden expression on his own face never changed.

"Yes, Captain, you put an end to that little show, and Charley knew he had *had* it." Major Bessine settled back in his chair, contemplating the end of the little show with pleasure.

From all sides of the table, grateful smiles were beaming in on Captain Walsh. Even the Mississippi sergeant looked reasonably pleased with him.

"That's why they didn't counterattack, all right," Dave heard the Negro captain say, playing back the words that the major had just fed into him.

"I'm glad you concur with G-2's determination of the situation, Captain."

The major's flashing smile did not unflash this time; but remained there like a clown's grin to signal that G-2's interest in the battle of Mt. Goliath was coming rapidly to an end.

The general told the Mississippi sergeant that he had better have Captain Walsh sign the original citation, as well as his own testimony. "I think," he said, "we should have the usual number of copies . . . and, of course, have it mimeographed for the press."

"Hold the mimeograph, General," March said. "I'll type up my copy, and after we file it I'll deliver the mimeographs to the press room in person. Some of the boys," he said, "will probably have some questions for me."

Walsh's testimony was, in fact, being fully typed while the major was holding forth. Walsh dutifully signed it and, in a burst of good fellowship, General Ritter himself signed as a witness.

When Walsh left, Adam March was sitting at the outer-office typewriter, banging away at his copy. He turned his lean face to Dave, smiling sardonically. Dave turned away quickly. The message in that grinning face was too painful to bear.

David Walsh sat in the living room watching the 11 P.M. newscast on the 21-inch color television set that had been sent over from the St. Albans' American Legion Post. Constance sat at the dining room table, busy with her shears, clipping items from newspapers and *Time, Look, Life,*

Newsweek, and other publications to bring her scrapbook up to date.

"It's for Josh," she had told him when he asked her if she had gone completely out of her head. "It will be something for him to hand on to his own children."

Josh was attending a basketball rally at the school gym; Josh had been elected manager of the sophomore basketball team.

During the commercial, he headed for the kitchen to refill his beer glass. "I don't know that I like Josh out this late," he said accusingly as he was passing his wife.

"It's supposed to break up at eleven, honey, and, anyway, he's getting a ride back. I don't know what you're complaining about. This is like a godsend to me." She shot a look at him. "He used to be out in the streets to all hours, doing God-only-knows-what. Be thankful for small favors."

"I am. I've already signed every damned autograph book there must be in that damn school. If he brings home another one, I'll. . . ." He threw up his hands, unable to decide what he'd do.

How much effort, she asked idly, did it take to sign his name in a book. And if it made the kids happy. If it made Josh happy. . . .

"Goddamn it, Constance!" He slammed the refrigerator door. "You're beginning to act like you don't know! You and that damn scrapbook of yours, you're acting like you . . . Have you read so many of those damn things that you *believe* it?"

She watched him, deeply troubled, as he pushed back through the swinging doors. "Dave," she said. "Maybe that's the best way."

He looked at her, amazed.

"Maybe it's the best way. To believe it."

He gave her a look of such contempt as he stormed past,

that her own anger came rising up too. "Well, you can't go fussing and sulking around forever, you know."

When there was no answer, she arose angrily and strode to the living room door. "Oh, it's going to be the silent treatment again, huh? That's nice. At home with the Walshes. If you're stuck, you're stuck. Accept it."

He still didn't answer.

"And if you want to know something, I'm getting sick of making excuses for you over the phone too. What am I, an answering service?"

"If you don't want to answer, let it ring."

"Dave," she said. "How many times can I tell Adam March that you're not home, is there any message? I don't know what to say to him the next time he calls."

"How about drop dead."

Although neither of them had really been paying any attention to the television set, some key word or other caught both of them at the same time.

". . . the White House made it official tonight. United States Army Captain David Walsh of St. Albans, Long Island, will receive the nation's highest award for valor, in a special ceremony at the White House this coming July Fourth. Captain Walsh's David-and-Goliath victory over superior North Vietnamese army regulars in the battle for the strategic airstrip on Flatiron Mountain just three weeks ago takes its place beside the biblical epic from which. . . ."

Walsh leaned over and switched it off.

"Hey," Connie said. She reached behind him, to turn it back on. He caught her wrist and flung the arm away.

"I want to hear it!" she protested. She swung her body in from the side to put herself between her husband and made another grab for the knob. "I live here too, you know."

Dave came jumping out of the seat. The whole steaming pressure of the day was exploding. He grabbed her around

the thick flesh portion of the upper arm and pulled her away.

In her own bottled rage, exploding too, she swung her free hand, and with a great roundhouse slap caught him flush on the side of the face. Walsh, reacting almost automatically, hit her a chopping, backhand blow just above the ear that sent her sprawling backward on the floor, flat on her backside. She was able to break the fall a bit with her hands, but as a final indignity she hit and bounced.

The storm spent, they were staring at each other, speechless, when the phone rang. David had not answered a call in two weeks and paid no attention to it. It was Constance who could not allow a phone to go unanswered. She finally lifted herself slowly to her feet, and, with a final furious glare at her husband, went into the foyer.

In a moment, she was back at the door to tell him it was Adam March.

"Tell him I'm not in," he shouted, loud enough, he hoped, for March to hear.

"He says to tell you it's about Mrs. Nichols. That Lieutenant Nichols' wife."

As he walked past her, she made him edge sideways to get past her at the door, so that he could not fail to see the look of utter disdain she gave him for jumping when he heard the name of his white friend's wife.

March was affable, ebullient, full of good cheer. As a matter of fact he sounded a little drunk.

"Though anticlimax is not my style, congratulations anyway. Did you hear the late news?"

"I heard it," Walsh grunted. "What's this about Mrs. Nichols?"

"Ah, there's good news tonight, as one of my ancient colleagues used to say. Next Wednesday night there will be an honorary banquet for you at the Waldorf thrown by the national organization of the Sixteenth Infantry Division."

"The Sixteenth Division?" Walsh had never heard of it.

"The Old Spearhead Division. For Christ sake, Walsh, don't you even know your own outfit? Well I can't say that I blame you. It took me a while to dig it up myself."

The good old Sixteenth, he explained, was a reserve division. It was called up briefly during the Korean War, but only a few specialized units had been sent overseas. "Your Tokyo outfit was one of them. Technically, the advisory group you were with in Vietnam was attached to the Sixteenth. You may not have known it, and they may not have known it, but you were attached to them on paper, and that's good enough for them now."

"Tell them to forget it. And tell me whatever it is you have to tell me about Mrs. Nichols."

"That is exactly what I have been doing, Captain. All your buddies are going to be there. Delvecchio, Rinkon, Cummins. And, as your co-guest of honor, the widow of the late Robert Nichols."

There was a grim pause. "You arranged this, didn't you, March? Remember what I told you in your office? It still goes."

"Don't thank me yet, Captain," he said quickly. "There are still more goodies to be unwrapped. I think that sometime next week I'll have to get you together with my business manager. He's the best in the business."

As great as the temptation was to hang up, Walsh couldn't quite resist asking him what he needed a business manager for.

"If you'd come to your phone," March said, "I'd have told you before. For starters, there's an offer from Drew-Page Publishing Company. 'The True Life Story of David Walsh,' you know the bit. They'll assign you a high-priced pro to write it, naturally. Two book clubs are interested in it, sight unseen. There is no reason whatsoever why it shouldn't bring in tens of thousands before it's over. You

still with me, Captain? You haven't hung up, have you? I hear heavy breathing so I guess that you are. MGM has the first bid in for the motion-picture rights. Two hundred grand, but it will go for a lot more. But we do need your permission before we can negotiate any further. That's the hell of these things, David. Every once in a while you have to nod your head and say, 'Yes.' Like in Stonewall's office.

"David," March said, "if you're nodding, I can't tell from over the phone. You're going to really have to put some effort into making all this money. You're going to have to say 'Yes.' Loud and clear so I can hear."

"You don't kid me, March. This is just another of your tricks."

"Since you didn't say, 'No,' I'll go on. You're wrong, Captain. It is not one of my 'tricks.' This 'white bastard' is about to make you a very rich black ingrate. Don't think that I'm enjoying it. There's more, David." A sigh came over the phone. "Adam March having primed the pump, the flow of gold is all but inexhaustible. You're really going to have to start answering your telephone. The Mattel Toy Company wants to bring out a Captain David Walsh soldier doll. There's a game company got a patent on an item called 'Medal of Honor.' They want you to endorse it. Walsh, you can't handle this big-league stuff without a manager. What we're going to have to do is let LCI handle the licensing end of it. They're the biggest in the business. They handle Batman, James Bond, Superman. . . ."

Walsh had pressed down on the cut-off bar. He remained there, his hand on the bar, the earphone in his hand for a long moment, feeling the pleasure at having hung up on Adam March. And above and beyond that, the power of having cut off all that money.

Constance was sitting on the couch, legs drawn up, smoking a cigarette, when he came back into the living room. "What did Adam March want?" she said, casually. It

was as if nothing had happened between them.

"Honey," he said, "I'm sorry." He turned his hands over, his arms outspread to indicate both that he didn't know what had come over him and that he knew that there were no words that could make up for it.

"It never happened, David," she said. She brushed his protests aside. "It never happened." She looked at him meaningfully, and, very deliberately, she said, "If we say it never happened, then it never happened. It's all in the mind. It's all in the memory."

Oh, hell! thought David, they were back to that again, were they?

"It's just like this business about the medal. . . ."

"I got your message, Connie. You don't have to explain."

She had been sitting there planning what she was going to say, though, and there was no stopping her now. "If you just accept that what's happened *has* happened, and there's *no* way to change it, then it will be easier for you to live with it. Like," she said, significantly, "it's going to be easier between us."

There was no sense trying to explain the difference, and, as guilty as he felt for striking her—even as a reflex action—he didn't really want to argue it with her.

To get her off the subject, he told her about the banquet at the Waldorf. He was not going to tell her about the book offer for his life story or the other offers. Not now anyway. He could not bear to witness what the prospect of getting all that money would do to her. She just might push him over the brink with that extra leverage.

She leaped off the couch in feverish excitement. "I've got to phone Miriam." And, as an afterthought, "She's going to help me go househunting."

"Sure," he said. "You do that." What it really was, he knew, she had to rub it in about that classy banquet.

On the way to the phone, she stopped to nuzzle his

throat.

"That was all my fault with the television. We've been living on springs since you got home. We'll work it out, you'll see."

"Sure," he said. He patted her on the cheek and tried to smile because some small gesture was expected of him.

Househunting, he thought. She couldn't wait to tell her sister.

Josh came in while the sisters were talking, pounding into the living room with his pumpkin grin.

"Guess what, pop? Stan O'Malley was at the bash to-night. He wants me to come on his show next week and introduce some of the new rock numbers. Can you imagine me rapping with 'Solid Stan, the Medicine Man?' " His hands riffled down at his waist like a drummer. "Da-da-de-da-da, de-BOOM."

"Who's Stan O'Malley?"

"Who's Stan O'Malley?" For all his presumed heroism, David Walsh had just gone down considerably in his son's estimation. "You've been away too long, pop. Ooo-ya have een-bay away oo-tay ong-lay."

As he turned away and headed for the kitchen, he slapped his hand to his forehead. "Who's Stan O'Malley?" He heard the kitchen doors swing. He heard his son go "Da-da-de-da-da, de-BOOM."

He could put it off no longer. On a cold, dreary morning Walsh traveled by bus and subway into Manhattan to keep an appointment with Bobby Coleman at the NSBE head-quarters on West Forty-fourth Street.

Bobby had called a week or so earlier to tell him it would be most helpful if their speech-writer, a bright young lady from Howard University, could come to his house and in-terview him. Not only so that she could get some of the basic details of his background and thinking, but so that

she could get the feel of him as a human being. She had turned out to be a not overly attractive young lady—or maybe it was just her big, conspicuous teeth—named Miss Warren. She had a first name, a very plain name, which he could never, to his embarrassment, remember. (And could still not remember now.)

As a result, he had kept calling her Miss Warren, and she had kept calling him Captain Walsh, and he was sure that he gave her the impression that, as a human being, he was stuffy and even pompous.

He wore civilian clothes, and he was careful to keep the collar of his overcoat turned up high around his face and his fedora tilted forward so that the brim would hide part of his face. He had developed a phobia that if he dared to leave his house, somebody was going to recognize him and point him out before the whole world for what he was.

Jammed in among the other standees on the subway (as he had been on the bus) it was clear how silly his fears really were. Not only did everyone look alike on a subway, but, on a subway, nobody even looked at anybody else.

He came out of his reverie, with a start, when he looked up and saw that the train was stopping at Fourteenth Street. He had ridden right past his stop. He pushed through to the door just as it was closing and went up and around to catch a train back. Great! Now he'd be late and would confirm his reputation for being a difficult man for Negroes to deal with!

It was raining when he came up out of the subway station at Times Square. A steady, monotonous downpour that reminded him—a bit nostalgically, curiously enough —of the rain in Vietnam. The carefree days of dodging bullets, he thought, turning it in on himself. *Dodging bullets*, he thought, turning the knife in himself a little more. He was beginning to believe that stuff himself.

Bobby Coleman sat behind his desk in the small, clut-

tered cubicle of an office, smoking a cigarette, while Walsh, seated on the other side, read over the speech he was going to deliver at the First Baptist Church in Harlem. Miss Warren stood in front of the single window in the office. Both of them were monitoring Walsh's face for reactions to the material.

At last, Walsh shuffled the pages back together and looked up. "It sounds pretty good to me," he said. There was a wry twist to his mouth. "Not that I'm any expert on speeches. Particularly when it comes to making them."

Miss Warren was exuding such gratitude that it embarrassed him. "Oh, Captain Walsh, I'm *so* happy you like it!"

Coleman laughed. "You *will* be an expert on speeches when we're through with you, Dave."

". . . *when we're through with you.* . . ." That little man inside him who walked the streets with upturned overcoat plucked out that phrase and found a connotation that deeply disturbed him. *He knows*, the little frightened man said.

The other part of David Walsh, the larger man who laughed at the trembling little man, said, quite cooly, "There's one part I particularly like. That idea for a real GI Bill of Rights for Vietnam, that all the black veterans will get a chance at an education or opening their own small businesses, that's the best idea I've heard yet."

They were beaming at him.

"There's one part that will have to come out, though," he said.

They were no longer beaming.

"Where it says in there I'm supposed to relate in my own words an eyewitness account of the battle for . . . uh . . . Mt. Goliath. . . ." That name always stuck in his throat. "I'm sorry, but I can't do that."

"But, Captain Walsh," Miss Warren protested, "what you did epitomizes everything else we've been talking

tally wounded, he kept going to the top of *that* mountain where he killed or routed the defenders in the last pillbox before a grenade tore him apart.

You had a mountain there, Adam. You could have called it Goliath!

There was Specialist Five Lawrence Joel, a medical aidman of the First Airborne Battalion, 503rd Infantry. On November 8, 1965, aidman Joel, over the course of a vicious twenty-four-hour battle with the Vietcong, exposed himself to direct enemy fire time and time again, while administering treatment to scores of wounded on the battlefield. Wounded twice, Joel bound up his own wounds, shot himself with morphine to deaden his pain, and dragged himself over the rough terrain, continuing to minister to his wounded buddies.

I was sitting in a dry, warm cave making brave talk to my dying, wounded buddy, Adam!

But it was the dossier of Milton L. Olive III, the first black man (only a boy really) to win the Medal of Honor in Vietnam, that did it. When he put that dossier aside, he sat rigid in the chair.

"Captain Walsh." There was concern in Bobby Coleman's voice. "Are you all right?"

Walsh looked up and forced himself to smile.

"Yes," Coleman said, believing that he saw. "Brings back memories, doesn't it?"

The heroic act of Private First Class Milton L. Olive, III, had actually been the least dramatic of them all. While he had been advancing through the jungle in the company of four other U. S. soldiers, a Vietcong grenade had landed in their midst. Without hesitation the young private had thrown himself on top of the grenade an instant before it exploded. He died, and four men were alive thanks to his selflessness.

The last document in Milton L. Olive's thin file was a

copy of the letter which his father, Milton L. Olive, Sr., had written to President Johnson after being notified of his son's heroic sacrifice. Dave had been reading through it absently—he had not, at first, been going to bother reading it at all—when the words came up out of the paper at him—as if they were being lifted out on a tile:

THE MOUNTAINTOP OF HUMAN INTEGRITY

The little man inside him, the carrier of his disease came rising out of his hiding place with it. It was a trap, the little man whispered. They had planted it there so they could watch him and make him give himself away by his reaction. Show nothing, say nothing, do nothing. *Don't let them see. . . . Don't give them the satisfaction. . . .*

David Walsh shook the little man off, and went back to read the letter more carefully:

. . . It is our dream and prayer that someday the Asiatics, the Europeans, the Israelites, the Africans, the Australians, the Latins, and the Americans can all live in One World. It is our hope that in our own country the Klansmen, the Negroes, the Hebrews, and the Catholics will sit down together in the common purpose of good will and dedication; that the moral and creative intelligence of our united people will pick up the chalice of wisdom and place it upon the mountaintop of human integrity; that all mankind, from all the earth, shall resolve "to study war no more." That, Mr. President, is how I feel and that is my eternal hope for our great American Society.

It was only a phrase in a letter. The trouble was that he knew that he would never forget it. And, worse, that he would never remember without a pang of shame.

"I'll speak about Milton Olive in the speech," he said.

The head table was placed on a dais, with Captain David Walsh seated in the chair of honor at the center of the table. Walsh felt like an actor on a stage, looking down on the smaller tables that filled every square foot of available space in the grand ballroom of the Waldorf Astoria Hotel, his audience a sea of smiling, upturned, expectant faces. Strung across the wall behind the dais was a huge banner, its block letters shining forth like neon lights.

THE 16TH INFANTRY DIVISION

At either end of the banner was the division insignia, a spearhead imbedded in a diamond. The Sixteenth had served with honor in World War II. In the intervening years, through the undeclared wars in Korea and Vietnam, the division had seen no further action. How Walsh and his small Army group had come to be attached to the Sixteenth Division was a mystery to Walsh and, quite probably, to everyone else there—including the representatives from the Pentagon. They were like prodigal sons, and the division's veterans' association had claimed them with fierce pride and possessiveness.

At Walsh's right side sat Retired Major-General Richard Gromer, resplendent in his dress uniform and chest full of battle ribbons. Gromer was in his middle sixties, a heavy man with watery blue eyes.

Constance Walsh, seated on her husband's left, wore a pale blue evening gown imported from Paris. It had cost more than her total wardrobe budget for the past three years. She was so beautiful that she glowed, Walsh noted a

little sadly. It was a glow which, as a mere man, husband, and lover, he had neglected to bring forth in recent days and nights.

Seated alongside Constance were Sergeant and Mrs. Rinkon. Lillian Rinkon was a small, dumpy woman with bleached blonde hair and a round cherubic face that was, essentially, featureless. She reminded Walsh of a Kewpie doll.

Mrs. Robert Nichols sat at Gromer's right side. Anne Nichols had turned out to be a pretty, slender girl with short auburn hair. Her black, long-sleeved evening gown emphasized her pale but lively face. Dave had met her at the airport, and during the long conversation they had been able to hold before the people from the division drove her to her hotel, she had been able to speak about her husband without grief or regrets, but with affection and with pride.

Lieutenant Delvecchio, still a bachelor, was Mrs. Nichols' dinner partner. And while nobody knew better than Dave that she was not at all the type Joe was used to, Joe being Joe was able to draw her out without any trouble at all.

Corporal Cummins, on the other side of Delvecchio, had become a captive audience for an elderly man in American Legion uniform who sat at his end of the table.

Walsh ate none of his appetizer or soup and did little more than pick at the main course, although it was his favorite dish, prime ribs. Dread of the after-dinner ceremonies had killed his appetite.

Constance and Gromer were talking across him. He paid no attention to what they said. Instead, he stared fixedly at Adam March, who was at the press table in front of the dais. March had insisted on being seated "with the rest of the working press." Every gesture March made: the way he held his fork, the way he picked up his coffee cup, the

way he lit a cigarette, infuriated Walsh and fed his hatred
of the man.

Several times March looked up at him and smiled. En-
couraging him, everybody else thought. Taunting him,
Dave Walsh knew.

Then the photographers' strobe lights were winking and
General Gromer was clearing his throat and pushing back
his chair. He rose and waited for the din of conversation to
subside in the ballroom. His voice boomed pompously out
of the loudspeakers high on the walls.

"Ladies and gentlemen—or would you prefer I address
you as fighting men of the Spearhead Division and their
women—we've come here tonight to honor *our* David."
He gestured pridefully at Walsh. "But I sincerely hope
none of you are under the impression that *I* am Goliath."
The general gazed down solemnly at his portly middle,
clapping both hands over the bulge. He waited for the
laughter to finish. Then he looked at Walsh. "Well, this is
one Goliath who doesn't want any part of *this* David!"

The applause and whistles made Walsh cringe down
lower in his chair.

Gromer plodded on: "I don't think I have to tell anybody
why we're here. If you don't know why, you haven't been
reading Adam March's nationally syndicated column. Or
should I say *Colonel* March's column?"

Two of March's stooges at the press table began to clap
loudly. And they did succeed in drumming up a generous if
not overwhelming burst of applause which March,
gracious as always, acknowledged with a smile and a
wave.

Gromer continued: "But we are not here tonight just to
honor the living. The real heroes of war are those that don't
come back. Nobody knows that better than we of the Sixteenth Division. They don't call us the Spearhead Division
for nothing. We've shed our blood in all the great wars.

The beaches and hedgerows of France ran red with our blood in World War II. Through no fault of our own, we never got the chance to fight in Korea. And that was a damn lucky thing for the Commies there, let me tell you!"

Cheers, whistles, and stomping feet.

"Most of us here tonight know what it's like to have a buddy die beside us. I don't think we can be accused of boasting if we say that we old-timers set a tradition that inspired and sustained Captain Walsh and his men on the bloody slopes of Mt. Goliath, and I don't think Captain Walsh will begrudge us our feeling—no, our certainty— that we were there with them on that mountain!"

The applause was short, sedate. The faces, which had all turned with Gromer's to the heroes on the platform, were sober, respectful, filled with reverence.

Walsh could not look at them. Instead, he glanced over at Rinkon and Cummins and found them sitting stiffly erect, chests thrown out, and jaws squared, radiating pride! Anne Nichols, biting on her lower lip, eyes downcast, her hands tearing at the small lace handkerchief in her lap, was fighting back tears. Constance! Constance glowed alongside him as if she believed every word that was being said.

Joe Delvecchio covered a yawn with his hand. Good old Joe. One sane note of reality!

Walsh forced himself to turn his mind back on what Gromer was saying:

". . . we are not here tonight just to pay tribute to the heroes who are sitting here at this table." He touched Mrs. Nichols' shoulder lightly. "For if it had not been for the heroic action of Lieutenant Bob Nichols, they wouldn't be sitting here at all!"

In the midst of the applause, Lieutenant Delvecchio began to cough into his napkin. He tried to get Walsh's attention, but Walsh refused to look at him.

"But, of course, Bob Nichols *is* here tonight. He is here in spirit, and he is here in the presence of one of the most gracious ladies I have ever had the pleasure to meet. Ladies and gentlemen, I take great honor in presenting Mrs. Robert Nichols."

With a flourish of military gallantry, General Gromer placed his steadying hand on the elbow of Lieutenant Nichols' widow and helped her to her feet.

June Nichols smiled bravely, swallowed, and touched her tongue to her dry lips. She began speaking in a low, shy voice that quivered over the first words:

"All I can say is . . . is thank you. I want to thank you . . . for Bob . . . for all those wonderful . . . tributes. And I want to thank you for myself for keeping his memory fresh and alive with these tributes." As she went on she gained poise and confidence. "I knew Robert Nichols as a good man and a loving husband. His comrades here tonight knew him, too, as a good man and a brave man."

She looked down the table to David Walsh. "I never met Captain Walsh until this afternoon, but I knew him, too, as a good man and a brave man. I knew him through my husband's letters. And I know what your friendship meant to him, Captain Walsh. It is sometimes difficult for a woman to understand why a man would lay down his life for his friends. . . . But I do believe I have gained some small understanding of why today." She averted her eyes from Walsh and sat down quickly.

The absolute quiet that attended and followed her speech was more eloquent than applause would have been.

General Gromer said gravely, "Thank you, Mrs. Nichols," and paused for a respectful moment of silence before resuming his role of genial toastmaster.

"Enlisted men like to gripe that the brass get all the gravy, but the brass know that it's the sergeants who run the Army. . . ."

There were rebel yells and a stomping of feet.

Gromer's face brightened. "We have one of 'em here tonight, and from what I hear, Captain Walsh was mighty
glad to have him aboard. All of us have served under a
tough, rock-headed topkick at one time . . . soooo, we all
know Sergeant Frank Rinkon!"

Laughter and applause greeted Rinkon as he braced his
hands on the table and hauled his thick-set body out of the
chair. He stood at his place, leaning a little to one side, red-
faced and uncomfortable, but obviously pleased by the
warm reception he was getting from the vets of the Sixteenth. Mrs. Rinkon was clapping harder than anyone else
at the head table, her pink doll's face shining with pride
and joy.

As the room quieted, Rinkon straightened up, pulled in
his gut, and hooked his thumbs inside the wide leather belt
around his waist. Frown lines creased his forehead. He was
trying his best, Walsh thought, to live up to the general's
introduction.

"Thank you. . . . Thank you. . . ." A grin replaced the
frown as he took some good-natured ribbing from the
former enlisted men at the tables.

"Hey, Frank! Who's on KP this weekend?"

"There's *his* topkick sitting next to him!"

"Yaaay! Three cheers for Lil Rinkon!"

"All right. . . . AT EASE, YOU YARDBIRDS!" Rinkon
bellowed.

Walsh shook his head from side to side, his face unsmil-
ing, as the ballroom rocked with laughter.

Over the uproar, Rinkon shouted, "I'm not very good at
making speeches, so this is going to be a short one. . . ."

An old Legionnaire at a table off to the left of the dais
got up, swaying alcoholically, and waved a bottle of
champagne.

"Hey, Frank!" he yelled. "Why didn't you save those

'short speeches' for reveille?"

Rinkon waved at him. "Sit down before you fall down, Red!"

Out of the side of his mouth, Walsh muttered to his wife. "I've got a feeling Frank's looking to play himself when they make the movie."

"Shhhh!" Constance lifted a fluttering hand to show that she didn't want to be distracted.

Order was finally restored and Sergeant Rinkon was able to continue. He was very serious now. "I couldn't agree more with what General Gromer said about the real heroes being the dead heroes. And all of us know what Mrs. Nichols meant about why a soldier would be willing to give up his life. All of us here in this room tonight know that. When we were going up that mountain, we all figured we were going to get killed. . . . I know I did. And if you think I wasn't scared, you're crazy. I want to tell you right now we didn't feel much like heroes. . . . One thing we did feel. If we were going to die, we were going to take a lot of them with us . . . cause there were a lot of them to take. . . ."

Walsh had the sensation that he was hearing words he had heard before; he had that familiar feeling that he was reliving an experience which he knew, at heart, he could not possibly have had before. It was disturbing. . . .

But, then, Rinkon himself (*the whole goddamn speech*) was downright incredible! Dave had listened at first with utter disbelief, and then with amazement and fascination. He believed it! There was no guile about the man. Frank Rinkon truly believed it!

With an effort of sheer will Dave kept himself from looking down at Adam March.

The sergeant waited for his laugh, got it, and went on: "But there's one thing everybody seems to forget. There were more than just four men on our team. Don't let any-

body underestimate those South Vietnamese troopers. They may not have been that much to start with, but when Captain Walsh got through with 'em, I'm here to tell you, believe you me, you couldn't find a better bunch of fighting men anywhere in the world."

Walsh's dismay was now total. He wondered if Adam March had, indeed, written Rinkon's speech. He braced himself for what his intuition told him was surely coming next. And sure enough, as if on cue, Sergeant Rinkon swung around and gazed straight at him.

"It made all of us over in Vietnam pretty sick to hear about all the trouble and riots you folks back home were having. All this talk about desegregation and brotherhood. Let me tell you something, over in Vietnam there's more being done to improve racial relations than all the court decisions, all the protest marches, all the sit-ins have accomplished in the past twenty years. When you're pinned down in the jungle by Charley, it don't matter what's the color of the skin of the guy next to you. All you care about is that he should be a good man and your good buddy." Rinkon reached across Constance and extended his hand. "I've served under a lot of officers in my years in the Army, but I've never met a finer leader or a more courageous man than Dave Walsh."

The thunderous applause assailed Walsh from all sides, reverberating off the walls and ceiling, beating at him so that he felt real physical pain. There was no other choice open to him. He had to take Rinkon's hand and, as Rinkon straightened up to face the cheering audience, he was virtually pulled to his feet himself. Strobe lights, all flashing at once, blinded him. The cameramen were right on the ball.

General Gromer was on his feet, holding up his hands for silence. He shook Sergeant Rinkon's hand himself, indicating in the process that he should sit down. Then he placed

a hand on Walsh's shoulder and spoke: "Sergeant Rinkon has stormed and captured the toastmaster's chair. He has already introduced our guest of honor, and probably much better than I would have. All that is left for me to say, ladies and gentlemen, is: The Sixteenth Division's own Captain David Walsh!"

They began to clap in rhythm now, that peculiar rite by which the mass public pays tribute to its athletic and political heroes. The applause went on and on relentlessly, increasing in volume, feeding on itself, while Walsh stared out, grim and unhappy. The noise against the eardrums and the steady rhythmic movement of the hands had a dizzying effect on him.

There is a line where applause ceases to be homage and becomes something quite the opposite. They had passed that line. They wanted to show that they could pay homage to a Negro hero. Which, David realized, was a way of saying that they were willing to pay homage to him even though he was a Negro.

He wondered how they'd react if he delivered his NSBE speech to them, deadpan, about a world they hardly knew existed. He wondered how they'd react to Olive's father's letter. He had no doubt at all that he could cast an instant pall over the room by opening with: "I want to tell you about these four Negro Medal of Honor winners: Olive, Charlton, Thompson. . . .

His mind clicked. . . .

Thompson!

. . . Clicked back to Rinkon's speech and that disquieting feeling that he had heard those words before. "*If we were going to die we were going to take a lot of them with us. Because there were a lot of them to take.*"

"*Maybe I won't get out,*" Thompson had said, "*but I'm going to take a lot of them with me.*"

Poor Thompson. He had the right color, and even the

right words, but he came around at the wrong time. They
weren't that interested in a black hero then.

Give the devil his due!

March had been right. Like he said: he didn't guess, he
knew. Waiting for the applause to stop, his eyes drifted to
the press table where March, alert, raised his hands high in
front of him, and, very gently pitter-pattered his hands together—a gesture so openly contemptuous of the audience and so flattering to himself for knowing just how predictable (and therefore manageable) they were, that it was
grotesque.

The real indignity.

March had bulled through with his story, after he had
saved his reputation, because he had been looking for a
black man, and he had found him. They needed a black
hero, and one black man was as good as another. What did
it matter whether he was a real hero or not?

If the Army had been looking also (particularly hard
too), they at least were looking for a Negro who had displayed the kind of valor to deserve it.

And then it hit him! Having their black hero in David
Walsh, there had been no need for them to really put out
that extra effort. By going along with the story, by accepting the publicity and the homage, he had deprived a real
Negro hero from the honor that should have been his. He
was not only a fraud, he was a thief!

He remembered the stories he had heard about the incredibly brave Negro scouts who led their squads out into
the darkness and lay like dead in the heart of the Cong.

In a frenzy of guilt, he began to wave for quiet, but that
only sent the noise level soaring again. "Please," he
shouted. "I have to tell you something!"

General Gromer shoved a hand mike at him. "You'll
have to talk over them, Captain," he shouted. "They just
won't stop. They love you too much." The general signaled

down to the technician at the far side of the press table to turn up the volume.

Gripping the microphone tightly in both hands, Walsh shouted, "Please . . . you are making a big mistake here tonight. . . . You are cheering the wrong man. . . . I am not a hero. . . ."

At the press table Adam March's face went ashen.

Behind him the ballroom exploded with applause.

Walsh screamed into the mike. "Now wait a minute! Will you people listen to me! We didn't really do anything on that mountain. . . ."

Constance reached for his elbow, and when he drew it away, she reached a second time. And a third time. From the floor it looked as if she were giving him a loving, wifely pat of approval as a reward for his becoming modesty.

From the center of the room, somebody jumped up and shouted, "Me too, lady!"

It was followed by a chorus of voices from all over the ballroom:

"Walsh and Eisenhower, they didn't do a thing!"

"That's a real hero for you!"

"Ain't he something! It makes you proud to be a member of this outfit!"

"This outfit? It makes you proud to be an American!"

A drunken Legionnaire, with a World War I tin hat on his head, clambered up onto the dais. Unsteadily, he lifted his arms high in the air. "Let's hear it, fellers, for Dave Walsh. For the Fighting Sixteenth. And for the good old U. S. A.!"

There was an infestation of other Legionnaires onto the dais, surrounding Walsh. There was a Sixteenth Division song, of uncertain melody. And new lyrics had been written to incorporate Captain Walsh's heroics.

Walsh tried once or twice to lean across to General Gromer, shouting. "*Make them listen. Make them listen.*

. . . I have to tell them about Thompson!"

The general pointed to his ear and shrugged. Walsh stared out into the crowd. At last, he put down the mike, spread his hands in resignation, and managed to pull his chair just far enough out from the table so that he was able to sit down. The singers had entered into another chorus. As he squeezed into his chair, he could not avoid Constance. There was an expression on her face that said unmistakeably:

"If you humiliate me like this, I will never forgive you."

He could have told her not to worry. He knew that his moment had passed.

When General Gromer got things under control, much later, Dave just shook his head.

"Captain Walsh," said Gromer, his face beaming, "is too moved to go on. I'm sure we can all understand his emotion."

After the ceremonies were completed, the ballroom was made ready for dancing. The tables, which had been set up all over the dance floor, were removed. The dais was changed back into a bandstand.

The Meyer Davis orchestra's opening number was "The Star Spangled Banner." Then Walsh and his wife led off the dancing to "The Waltz You Saved for Me."

General Gromer asked Constance for the second dance and Walsh retreated into the bar. Joe Delvecchio sat at one end, drinking with a group of Legionnaires. Welcoming hands clutched at Walsh's arms and shoulders as he joined the party.

"Dave, boy!"

"Here's the man, himself."

"What are you drinking, Dave?"

"Joe," Dave said. "You're just the man I want to see."

"I've got myself some sponsors," Joe said, "they keep tell-

ing me they know where the action is and they like my style. They look like trustworthy types?"

He banged on the bar. "Innkeeper! A shot of hemlock for my friend. On the rocks. That was a great speech you didn't make, Dave."

"Scotch, straight, double," Walsh told the bartender.

An old-timer, with a shiny pate and two tufts of wooly red hair sprouting around his ears, draped an arm around Walsh's shoulders.

"I was just telling Joe here, you had the right idea, Dave. The best defense is an offense. That's what Fielding Yost used to say when I was playing for him at Michigan U."

His buddy interrupted him. "Attack! That's why they call us the Spearhead Division. Attack!"

Delvecchio winked at Walsh and raised his glass. "Attack!"

The redheaded man ignored them. "We never had the fastest team in the world, Dave, but when we hit, we hit! I ran a kickoff back 98 yards against Notre Dame, and there wasn't a man standing when I crossed that line." He jabbed a finger into another Legionnaire's chest. "And those Irish could hit too, and don't you forget it!"

"You must have been quite a tiger, Red," Delvecchio needled.

"Ninety-eight yards." Red sagged against the bar. "Boy could I run then. November 12, 1920. Red Martin. Ninety-eight yards against Notre Dame. You look it up. Attack is what did it! Attack! Billy Phillips can tell you." He gazed around the room with bleary eyes as if by some miracle Billy Phillips would suddenly materialize. "Billy! Anybody here seen old Billy?"

The other men were convulsed by laughter.

"Billy Phillips has been dead ten years," one of them said.

Red drew himself up defiantly. "Tha's a damnable lie!

And a canard upon the dead departed." He grabbed two friends by the arm. "With all this booze around, Billy has got to be here someplace. Come on, let's find him."

The three of them weaved off together, calling for Billy to the attendant hoots of the others.

Delvecchio and Walsh seized the opportunity to escape to a small table in a dark corner of the bar.

"Poor Red," Delvecchio said. "By this time you'd think he'd have learned that the really beloved heroes are the modest heroes."

"Very funny!" Walsh took a healthy swallow of his drink. "Only I'm not laughing."

"Aw, Dave. They're old men reliving when they were young. I'll be like that. I picked out one old wop; short, fat, and bowlegged old guy. I swear to God I could see myself thirty years from now. And making an ass of myself like him too. You don't have to worry about that, Captain. When you're sixty you'll still think it's a sin to enjoy yourself."

"I wasn't talking about them," Walsh said. "I was talking about what went on here tonight." Even in the dim light, he could catch enough of Joe's sly grin to tell that Joe had known that all along. Leave it to Delvecchio to put you right on the defensive.

"That *Rinkon!*" he said, as if he were hurling an obscenity.

Delvecchio grinned. "Rinkon's nothing. You should have heard Cummins laying it on for Gromer when we first got there. First time I ever realized that a medic, given the right set of moral values, can win a war with a needle and syringe."

"They must be crazy."

"Naw!" Delvecchio stirred his drink with a finger. "They believe it. You want to know something? Of all the people in the world, there are only two—thee and me—who

don't believe it. And I half believe it. If you want my counsel and sympathy, you'd better move fast, because I'm planning to be a true believer before the frost sets in."

"This is all a big joke to you like everything else, isn't it?" Walsh said sharply. "But I'm the guy who has to stand up and let the President pin a medal on me."

Delvecchio's dark, bushy eyebrows went up. "You wanna change places?"

"Go to hell!"

"Look, the way I see it, it's like an accident. Suppose a truck had hit you and broke both your legs or something. Nobody would say you deserved it or didn't deserve it. It would just be something that happened. You'd be hit, that's all, and you'd end up in the hospital, wondering how you were going to pay the bill. This is the same thing, only in reverse. You got hit by good fortune. Rejoice that it's good instead of bad."

Delvecchio's handsome Latin face was serene. "Life, my son, is a succession of alternatives. One of your alternatives at the moment is to go comb your hair and stand up straight like an officer and a gentleman and let the man pin a medal on you, then slobber over you a little for the benefit of the black voters. I can understand why you wouldn't want to get that close to a politician if you could help it, but. . . ."

"Ah! But I do have that other alternative, don't I?" Walsh cut in. "And that's not to let them pin anything on me."

"Okay, so don't take it." Delvecchio's expression of indifference gradually gave way to a smile. "My God, what a renunciation scene. The likes of which has not been seen since Camille. Since Edward gave up his throne for the love of a good woman. My God, man, the Congressional Medal of Honor." He rocked back on the heel of his chair and framed the scene with his hands. "There you stand up

there in the Rose Garden, the President to the front of you, your loved ones to the back of you, your old comrades-in-arms simpering alongside, and the eyes of the world over all.

"Then you throw him a line like: 'I deem this too great an honor, too sacred a prize to be awarded mistakenly or accepted lightly.' My God . . . the photographers lined up there for a routine shot . . . that would wake them up in a hurry, wouldn't it?" He grinned slyly, the grin that always let you know that the shaft was coming. "You didn't have much luck with that approach tonight, but I don't see how they can ignore you over color television."

"Dammit, Joe, I said I wanted to talk to you. If I wait until I'm standing in the Rose Garden, a lot of people are going to get the idea that some of the real heroes were phonies too."

"You mean those dumb oxes who didn't know any better than to run into machine-gun nests? Serves 'em right."

Dave raised his eyebrows and put down his glass. "You do have a memory, don't you, Joe?"

"It comes with the deck of cards. And there are some things that just have a way of sticking in my mind. Like all those dead heroes stick in yours."

Seeing Walsh begin to bristle, Delvecchio began to laugh. He reached across the table and slapped him on the arm. "Oh hell, Dave, if you've got to worry—and I guess you got to—save it for the living people, will you? You're not the only one involved in this, you know. I can think of a few other gallant goof-ups who'll get hurt if you kill Adam March's brainchild. For one, me. But, goddamit it, Dave. . . ." His eyes brightened. "The Day Dave Walsh Told the President to Shove the Medal of Honor Up His Keister! And I'll be there! Do it, Dave! Do it."

Dave was taken so completely aback that he had to look at Joe Delvecchio afresh. "I never figured you for a martyr,

Joe."

"There are unexpected shoals and depths to my character." He was looking right through Dave. "To see March
get stepped on! To hear him go *pfffft* and watch his guts
come squirting out!"

There was a scratchy quality to his voice that Dave had
never really heard before. Two points of light seemed to be
shining out of those closely set eyes. "To show up the
Army, and the politicians, and the newspapers, and the
television folk for what they really are. I'd have all that to
comfort me in my days of exile and disgrace."

The rancor behind it came as a shock. The affable mask
had slipped down briefly. Bob Nichols had been wrong
about Joe Delvecchio. Nichols' innocent, open man who
wore no mask was all mask. The amused observer had been
revealed as a sorehead.

And what about all those innocent insults now? Cleared
the air, my eye! Filled it, rather, with vitriol.

A chill went through Dave Walsh, as chilling in its own
way, as the chill he had felt in hearing Rinkon.

Walsh sipped at his scotch, trying to decide how far he
should push this. Why not? This was his night for
discovery.

"Yeah," he said, "but what you said about you and the
others getting hurt too? I should take that into consideration, shouldn't I?"

"Do what you want, daddy-o, it's all the same to me. If
you take it, I ride the gravy train. If you blow the whistle
on March, I lead the cheering section at his wake."

"Since when did you hate March that much? I thought
you kinda liked him?"

Delvecchio started to answer, stopped. He regarded
Walsh narrowly. "Psychologists will tell you that hate and
love are kindred emotions," he said carefully.

Their eyes had caught.

"Who do you want to get stepped on, Joe? Who do you want to go *phffft?*

"Black man talk in strange riddles." He described a circle with his arms. "Must be full moon tonight." The closely set eyes were wary. The face seemed flushed.

"You win no matter what, isn't that about it, Joe? But you really want me to take it, don't you?"

"I told you, *immaterial.* . . ."

"You want me to take it so you can tell yourself, 'He's as rotten as Adam March and the rest of them.' You'd get some deep-seated confirmation out of that. Isn't that the truth?"

"You do have a way of being a very uppity nigger, Cap." The humor didn't quite come off. The careless grin and the artless air were not quite there. "I *told* you. Immaterial. You told *me*. Either way, I win."

"That's what I can't figure out. Why? If I don't take it, I go down the drain, but you go down the drain a little too. You said it yourself."

Delvecchio had recovered very quickly. "You've got to make up your mind one way or the other." The jaunty smile was back on his lips; there was a little mocking edge to the words: "If I wanted you stepped on, why would I want you to get away with it?" However he may have meant it, it did not come out as a denial; it came out as a challenge.

Dave folded his arms across the table and pushed his face toward him. "Explain it to me."

Joe pushed his lips out, thinking about it. He put his hand inside his jacket and came out with a deck of cards. "Just happen to have them on me," he said. "You should have heard those Legionnaires gasp in awe, mystification, and amazement. You'd have been proud of me, Captain." He had, with those practiced, expert motions, slipped the deck out of its box, and now he was giving it the fast

shuffles and the quick riffles Walsh had seen so often before. He cut the deck three or four times, in three or four different ways, and began to weave the cards in and out of his fingers. "Faster than the human eye can follow," he said, in a card dealer's chant. "You will notice that the deck never leaves the table, ladies and gentlemen, and the fingers never leave the hand." The full deck fanned out in a complete circle and then, with a flick of the wrist, the fan disappeared. Back and forth, in and out, like a peacock's tail opening and closing.

Dave followed it out of the corner of his eye, his own elbows never leaving the table, his own eyes never leaving Joe's face.

"Mystification and amazement," Delvecchio chanted. "Are you mystified, Captain? Are you amazed?"

Suddenly, the deck was on the table and—*slap, slap, slap*—being cut. Even more suddenly, the deck was thrust under Walsh's chin, and Delvecchio's eyes were locked with his. "Take a card. Any card."

Walsh took a card, glanced at it—the four of hearts—and put it back into the deck. He had seen Delvecchio do this dozens of times, and he never missed.

Delvecchio cut, shuffled, cut, shuffled, and turned over the nine of diamonds.

"Wrong." Walsh continued to look at him. Finally he said: "Four of hearts."

Delvecchio shrugged, put the cards back into the box and placed the box very neatly on the table in front of himself, lengthwise. He picked up his drink. "I have a little idiosyncracy. You can't always believe everything I say. As a leader of men you should have noticed that." There was that easy, cocky smile that Dave knew so well. "I didn't get any medal, Dave. I haven't made any speeches. Not even tonight. The only thing I did was to sign a statement so that I wouldn't have to blow the whistle on my good

buddies. If you ever get to read my testimony, you'll see where I made it clear, with my accustomed modesty, that my own small part in the heroic business was disgustingly unheroic. It's known as protecting your ass. You learn it in all the best military academies, college fraternities, and women's clubs."

"Tell me, Joe, what did you ever do that you think is so rotten that you have to keep showing yourself that everybody and everything else is rotten too? Or was that just something else that comes with the cards?"

"You want it, baby." Delvecchio told him, in a soft, insinuating voice. "You want it just like I'd want it." He slid the box of cards over to Walsh. "Go ahead," he hissed, "pick it up. Didn't I always tell you that the Steubenville dealer and the Harlem nigger were brothers under the skin?"

"Don't ever even breathe the word nigger in my direction again. No matter how; no matter why. I just withdrew permission."

Their eyes were still locked. A little sneering grin spread across Delvecchio's lips. Walsh lifted a warning finger. "And if you think it, Joe, don't think it loud."

"Could you be talking about Joseph Vincent Delvecchio, friend of the common man, confidante of his little black brother?" All at once the color drained out of his face. "You think you're so goddamn noble. If you're so noble, why did you want Nichols to have that medal. I don't see any difference, my moral black friend, between your getting the Medal of Honor and Nichols getting his DSM!"

Walsh had pushed his chair back. "For your information," he said deliberately, "F. Y. I. I never asked for any medal for Bob Nichols. All I ever asked for was a line in Adam March's dispatch. That's one thing you ought to know. You were there."

"We know what your line is, lady. Now we're just hag-

gling over price."

"Oh, shit!" Dave said, getting ready to walk away. "What am I doing talking to you?"

"Is it because Nichols was a white man?" Delvecchio asked. "Is it because you think you're not good enough, or because you think you're too damn good?"

Dave turned back, his fists clenched. "You son of a bitch!"

But Delvecchio was holding both hands up in front of himself, the picture of inoffensiveness and nonresistance. "Ah, ah. The seventh thing they teach us in Steubenville is to never mess around with a quiet man. I don't mind you getting the medal, Dave, I just hate to see· you get the medal and a leg up on sainthood too. One or the other, daddy-o. One or the other."

Dave gripped both sides of the table and was shifting his weight forward to flip it over into Delvecchio's lap before he was able to control himself. "I figure you're going to make this easy for me. How come you haven't blown the whistle already? What are you doing, waiting for the right time and spot?"

In a frustration of nervous energy, Dave swept the box of cards up and flipped it across the table. Reacting, Delvecchio caught it against his chest. His eyes were wide, alert for anything that might be coming. "I won't have any need of those," Walsh spat. "You pack too dirty a box."

As Walsh was stalking away, Delvecchio called out urgently, "Dave!" Instinctively, Dave looked back over his shoulder. Delvecchio was lying back easily in the chair, his legs sprawled out under the table. He was holding the box of cards up and smiling most pleasantly. "Did I ever tell you the tenth thing they taught us in Stuebenville? Nobody likes a stoolie."

The offices of Bestor, Sampson and Adams, refurbished just the year before, impressed Walsh as being vulgarly

modernistic. Too much naked, bright metal and explosive color.

"This decorator, he also majored in psychology, claimed that you got to jar the eye and mind to stimulate the creative process," Clem Bestor explained to Walsh. "Like that mural." He indicated the wall opposite his desk. "Doesn't it make you sit up and think?"

"It does, indeed," Walsh said carefully. It made him think of the fingerpainting Josh had done in kindergarten.

Bestor was a porcine little man with gray hair and pink cheeks. Walsh thought he looked more like a priest than a public relations executive, a slovenly priest at that. Lester Sampson wore his success far more convincingly than his white partner.

Bestor leaned back in his chair with his hands locked behind his thick neck, reminiscing.

"Yup, it's a far cry from that loft we started out in on Eighth Avenue, right, Lester?"

Lester chuckled. "You started out in. I didn't even have office space. Just a battered briefcase. I used to answer my mail on the pay typewriters in the Public Library."

Walsh had heard the story so many times, he was able to make all the proper responses in the right places without even following too closely what they were saying. The two had met while soliciting the same client, a small integrated repertoire theater group which was terminating its relationship with another press agent who happened to be Paul Adams. Sharing their various vicissitudes along with coffee and Danish in a luncheonette while awaiting the client's decision, they became convinced that none of them could afford to lose this business.

"So let's tie our shoestring operations together," Clem Bestor had said in, what had become, to him, a moment of historic inspiration.

"And none of us has ever regretted it, Dave," he told

Walsh. "And neither will you." He placed his hand over the contracts on his desk which Walsh had just signed, and winked at Lester. "David Walsh, Public Relations Consultant, sounds pretty fancy, eh? After you pass a million in annual billing, you don't call yourself a press agent, Dave. It's public relations."

"Remember, Dave, we just wanted you signed up," Lester assured him. "We're not pushing you to make any appearances here at the office for a couple of months."

"Not with his schedule, all them public appearances he's got to make for the Army and the NSBE," Bestor agreed, chewing on his cold cigar. "But you're on the payroll, Dave, as of today."

"Thanks, Clem, but I don't want you to do that," Walsh was adamant about it. "I wouldn't feel right accepting a paycheck until I start to earn it." He prudently did not add: *"However that may be, God only knows!"*

"I hear April 1 is being officially designated David Walsh Day in New York City by Mayor Lindsay," Lester said. He grinned slyly. "If the mayor should just happen to ask you about your plans for the future up there before the TV cameras, we won't get mad if you put in a word for Bester, Walsh, Sampson and Adams."

Walsh laughed along with the others but not at the same joke. April 1! The monumental irony of it! Now there might be the graceful way out for him. He would stand up in the official limousine and shout it out to New York's millions.

"April Fool! It was all a big joke, folks!"

Clem Bestor frowned. "April 1, isn't that a long time to wait to welcome a hero? A month after he got home?"

Lester explained that a great deal of red tape and planning was involved in these official functions these days. "It's not like when Lindbergh stepped right off the boat and into a car driving up Fifth Avenue."

"Yeah, that's right." Bestor nodded solemnly. "Even for

a lousy wedding reception my niece had to make reservations fourteen months in advance. The way things are going these days, I told my sister, they shouldn't take a chance with more than nine. You know what had me worried? She didn't laugh!"

Lester was consulting his wrist watch to signal Dave that it was getting time to leave. Lester was taking the 2 P.M. plane to the Coast, and the plan was for Dave to drive him to Kennedy, and then shoot out to Westchester to pick up Miriam so that he could drive her home for dinner. Miriam was going to sleep over and then drive Connie back to Westchester for some househunting.

"Go already, before you miss the plane," Bestor said. He held out his hand to Walsh. "At the risk of sounding like a broken record, Dave, as president of this outfit, I speak for Lester and Paul, as well as myself, in saying that we are proud and honored to have you on our team. For myself alone, I hope our association will be a long and mutually prosperous one." He scratched the side of his head rather shyly. "What do you know, it takes me as long to shake a hand as it takes your wife to make five round trips from Westchester."

Lester insisted that Dave drive his new Lincoln convertible out to Kennedy Airport to get the feel of it. The unaccustomed power and luxury of the car were irresistible. Walsh was almost ashamed of himself for the childish pleasure of power he got from commanding it.

Lester smiled knowledgeably. "Pretty quick now, you'll be driving one of your own. I can get you a deal. Listen, why don't you and Connie and Josh drive back with Miriam tomorrow and have them do their househunting from there?" He had let the servants go when he and Miriam decided to spend most of their time out on the Coast, he said, and he hated to have Miriam stay in that big

house alone.

"We'll see about it." He laughed softly, as if at some private joke.

Inexplicably, Walsh was overcome by a sudden premonition of danger. Without any conscious decision on his part, his foot eased up on the accelerator.

Lester turned his head quickly to the rear window. "What's the matter? Did you spot a cop?"

"Yeah," he said, not really knowing why he thought it necessary to lie. "He was laying there off the ramp. No sense taking any chances. You've got a plane to catch."

Two hours later, when he drove up the Sampson's circular drive, the sense of warning was stronger than ever. The $75,000 English Tudor was built on a 2-acre plot on a wooded hillside in northern Westchester. There was something about that place that always shrivelled Dave Walsh.

There was no sense kidding himself either; he knew what it was. They had always come there as poor relatives visiting. Usually on a Sunday. Constance would always dress Josh at his very best and herself at her nervous, overdressed worst. Conversation between the sisters would be alternately vivacious and strained. The trip home would be forbidding. And the next day would be hell.

Dave could find it in himself to sympathize with his wife, though. Whether she should have been jealous of her sister was beside the point. She was. Given her personality and whatever relationship had existed between her and her sister long before Dave had come to know either of them, it was probably inevitable.

Standing there at the door now, the house no longer had the cold, forbidding Sunday look about it. He rang the door chimes three times before Miriam opened the door. The reason for the delay was obvious. Miriam's hair was

plastered wetly to her head, little spikes of it pressing down flat over her forehead. She was wearing—could it be all she was wearing?—a short terry cloth robe. There were, he saw, looking closer, damp stains on the cloth where it pressed against her breasts and hips. Where, to put it more precisely, her breasts and hips pressed against it. There was no doubt about it! She was naked underneath.

She seemed startled to see him. "Dave, I'm sorry, I was in the shower. I honestly didn't expect to see you for another hour." She laughed at his discomfort, a high, tinkling laugh that was strange to him. "Don't look so scandalized. I don't usually come to the door like this. I peeked out of the bedroom window."

The laughter annoyed him. Not the laughter itself, but the implication that she looked upon him as that narrow minded, that much of a puritan.

He told her, sounding narrow and apologetic to his own ears, that he had come straight from the airport. "That was the plan, wasn't it?"

She spread out her arms in a sort of shrug, as if to say, "You're here, so it must have been."

"It was Lester and Constance who made the plans last night." The tinkling laugh again. "I'm always the last one to get the word." Taking him by the elbow, she whispered confidentially, "Anyway, I was pretty bombed last night. Which is the perfect lead-in for: Why don't you be a dear boy and mix us a drink?"

She walked ahead of him into the immense living room, the terry cloth riding up on her hips. The fine hand of her Fifth Avenue decorator was quite evident. The period was Italian Provincial. The decor, gold and white. It was splendid, Walsh thought, but too busy for his personal tastes. Maybe, as Constance claimed, Miriam didn't have any taste. (Of course, Constance always said that he didn't have any taste either.)

Miriam moved across the room, ever so lightly on her toes, the deep pile giving her a little spring, the bare feet leaving fleeting imprints on the deep-piled gold carpeting. He was acutely aware of her bare feet and bare legs, and the movement of her hips inside the terry cloth. That slightly dumpy look of women without shoes was there, of course, and yet, with Miriam, it made her somehow more sexy.

There was an armoire on one side of the fireplace that opened up into a small bar, fully equipped and stocked. There was even an ice-making machine. That was something new.

"Lester sure thinks of everything," he said, as he put the ice, neatly shaped into half-circles, into the glasses.

"Lester knows how to live. . . ." The flat, toneless way she had said it, leaving the sentence open at the end, caused him to look up, quizzically, as he handed her the drink. "Now that you're in a new position, David, you really ought to learn to enjoy life too." She made a little movement with her glass, in automatic, wordless toast. "You should get to know Lester better. We all ought to get to know each other better."

He lifted his own glass. "I'll drink to that."

She leaned back against the corner of the mantel, the fireplace off behind her. Fresh as she was from the shower, her face scrubbed and clean, totally free of cosmetics or artifice, she had the look of an innocent child. Tiny droplets of water glistened in her eyebrows and beaded in the soft indentation above her upper lip.

"Don't underestimate Lester. Lester is willing to be a white nigger on Madison Avenue, because that's the way he had to play the game. But on his own time he lives the living black life. You take Lester," she said, looking up over the rim of her glass. "Lester believes in taking what he wants. So do I." She lowered the glass and leaned back so

that the robe came apart momentarily, just long enough to reveal the rounds of both breasts. "Let me see, we're supposed to go househunting tomorrow, aren't we? Constance and I. The neighbors will love that. The black tide sweeps on. Lester got off all right?"

"Lester got off fine."

"Lester always gets off fine. He's a man of many talents. I could tell you stories about Lester that would make you see him in an entirely new light." She was moving in those little springy steps to one of the twin love seats that faced each other in front of the fireplace, inviting him with a sweep of the eyes to sit too. "And not a bad light either."

She placed her glass on the low table between them and snuggled back into the corner of the couch, her legs curled up in her characteristic pose. With a deliberation that was clearly practiced, she pulled the robe around her and arranged the skirt to cover as much of her body and legs as was humanly possible.

But when she looked over at him, it was with a direct and meaningful gaze that took his breath away.

"Now let me see, I seem to remember that we were talking about my husband," she said with a little teasing smile.

"Lester's a man who takes what he wants. So do you. I should get to know him better. . . ."

"Yes, Lester's not a man to waste any time on a woman he isn't going to bed with." She shrugged it away. "I know that."

"You got a great marriage there." He reached for his glass.

"A great marriage, baby. The first time I went out with Lester. . . ." She gave him that direct, melting look again, and this time he did not try to tell himself he hadn't seen it. "I had indicated to him, in faultless female fashion, that I might not be unreceptive to an invitation, and he told me, 'Look, baby, you want to be my gal, you got to put out. On

command. Like right away. Tonight.'" The tip of her tongue swept slowly across her upper lip. "He said, 'Make up your mind quick. There's lots of pussy prowling around the alleys.'"

She rolled her shoulders, slowly and languorously across her cushion at the side of the couch. "You're a white man, Dave." She said it affectionately: "You are, you know. I suppose they programmed you when you were a boy. You think that insults a girl?" She shook her head, her eyes gleaming. "I love it! I like a man who knows what he wants and goes after it. And *takes* it. I told you I take what I want, yes. . . ." Her voice had grown low and husky. "What I want from a man is that he take me."

So that was the way it was going to be, he told himself happily, he was going to screw the most beautiful woman he had ever seen. So that was the way it was going to be, he thought sadly. He was going to cheat on his wife with her kid sister.

She watched him with those languid cat's eyes. "Every man wants all the . . . women he can get. Black, brown, white, or yellow. The nature of the beast. It ain't bad and it ain't good. It is. These kids are on to something about middle-class morality. Middle-class morality is what tells you you don't want what you know you damn well do want. That leaves all the more for the people who do all the preaching."

He wasn't going to be taken. He was going to take. He sat back and enjoyed it, letting it build up to the glorious explosion, wondering what the final words were going to be, how he was going to say: "I'm taking," and she was going to say: "Come take."

"You're telling me, take all the women I can get, is that it? All I want. Or, anyway, all I can handle."

"I'm telling you to be good to yourself. Lester's using you. You use Lester. It does you no harm to make some

money. You're a great war hero, David, and a very attractive man. I don't know many women who wouldn't be
happy to take the good fall for you. You haven't got that
many years left, David. Gather ye rosebuds. . . ."

He didn't like much the way the conversation had
turned. He didn't much like having his wife's kid sister, his
own prospective bedmate, offering the kind of advice
you'd expect to get from an older brother.

"I don't want to mix into your private life, David, but
I've given you a look into mine, so what the hell. You'd
have a better and happier wife if you laid . . . down the
law more." She had crossed her legs, and, after carefully
rearranging the folds of the robe, she began to roll her
shoulders, once again, across the cushion. "Lester is a very
practical man. He does not expect to go plowing other
fields without expecting me to find another plowman
here and there myself. Lester was black and beautiful before these kids ever came along."

"You have an arrangement?" he said.

"We go our way."

He did see Lester in a new light, all right. He also understood that private joke Lester was laughing about. Lester,
leaving town, had given him his car and sent him home to
make love to his wife. Miriam had not misunderstood
about the time. She had planned to greet him like this.
There were, as she had said openly, few women who
wouldn't take the good fall for him.

If it removed one element of risk—who wanted an
angry husband gunning for you?—it also made this whole
seduction scene less appetizing. It was no seduction scene
at all; he was a present the good living husband was presenting his good living wife.

But she was right. He couldn't lie to himself. Underneath the clowning around, there had always been a
physical attraction between himself and his wife's younger

sister. All the squeezing and flirting that Constance had always frowned on (he was aware that Constance frowned and it pleased him) had—as it always must—a firm sexual basis. What it said was: "Oh, what a time we could have with each other if only we weren't related." It had pleased him all right. It had showed him that he was attractive to a beautiful woman and—admit it—to a beautiful woman about whom his wife was inordinately jealous.

But there had never been the slightest lustful contact between them. Not even in his imagination. Or—wait a minute now—had there? All right, there had been idle thoughts. He had wondered, idly, what she was like in bed, the way he might have wondered about any attractive, warm-blooded woman. But he could tell himself—and know that he was being absolutely honest—that he had never for one moment seriously thought of having an affair with his wife's sister.

He laughed out loud, and when Miriam looked up, quizzically, a little peevishly even, as if she wondered if he could possibly be laughing at her, he told her.

"I just thought to myself that I'd never seriously thought of having an affair with you. So I suppose you're right. A white nigger. White men have affairs. Niggers' ball."

The word made it inevitable. The word told them both that there was no longer any doubt at all that it was going to happen.

"I wonder," she said, lowering her eyes, "what the Afro-Americans do."

"Make speeches," he said. "They get themselves off making speeches about African culture."

He felt the glow that came to him from the knowledge that he was doing this well. He had never really seduced a woman before. He and Connie had got to it gradually, the kissing, and the feeling, and the petting, until it had finally reached the point of no return in a first, mechanical affair

in that old Dodge of his that always got flat tires. In the front seat yet. He had, once he knew the way, had a few girls after dances; in the cloakroom and, even, alleys. He had paid for it a few times in Tokyo and Saigon.

But not with a woman like this, and never in this kind of a setting. There was something luxurious, and superior, and civilized about it. "Shall we get to the bedroom, Miriam. I've got more clothes to get out of than you."

She lay back in the white sofa, one leg swinging across the gold carpet, and held up her arms. "Here."

She wanted a battle of wills, he could see. She wanted to be told.

"Upstairs," he said. He grabbed hold of one hand and yanked, and as she came around, her robe came undone. She cupped her hands under her breasts, holding them out to him. "Here." There was a look of pleading in her eyes. "Here, love. Lester and I have never done it here."

For the moment he was transfixed. He had never seen breasts like that before. So perfect and—this was the surprise—so much bigger than he would have ever expected.

"What does the plowman plow," he whispered, "that would make him leave his own fields?"

She glowed under the compliment and, breathing deeply, pushed them out even farther, looking down at them herself in pride.

He took one breast out of her hand and nuzzled her stiff nipples. Her breath cooled his ear, then burned it. He caught the nipple between his lips, sucking deep then, caught it between his teeth and bit down slowly until he forced her to a cry of pain. He tugged at the robe. "Off!"

In a quick, supple move she was naked and lying back on the sofa and waiting. He had never seen a body like that. In all his life, he had never thought to see such a body. "Don't move," he said, as he undressed himself. "Don't move one muscle. I want you to stay right where you are.

Right there where you are."

He came over her bursting with potency. He was powerful, indestructible. A man, a giant, and an animal.

After a minimum of nuzzling, she caught the loose flesh under his chin between her teeth. "Do it," she whispered. "Do it," she moaned. "Do it to me, love."

He flung her feet up almost over her head, but it was awkward. "Sweet Jesus," she said with a throaty laugh, "you're going to make a contortionist out of me."

But she flung them up even farther herself, when he went into her, making little sucking-kissing noises with her lips.

For some reason, he pulled out. He leaped to his feet and lifted her in his arms. "I want you where Lester had you," he said. What he didn't want was to have her where he suspected her "occasional plowman" had her.

She resisted not at all. She laid her head in the crook of his neck, her legs drawn up, her knees pressed tightly together. Half way up the stairs, he stopped to take a breath.

"Don't strain yourself, love," she said, with a little cooing laugh. "Not here. Not yet. I'm going to have a need for you."

It was so typical of her, the joke in the middle of passion, that it added to the excitement.

It was a huge bed. The long climb had served the purpose of slowing them both down, giving him a fresh opportunity to browse over that unbelievable body. But when they were ready, when he was about to go into her in earnest, she closed up. "Tell me about the war," she said.

"Hell!"

"Tell me about the men you killed. Tell me! Tell me and I'll be good to you. Tell me, you big black bloody bastard! Tell me!"

He told her a black-pajamed Vietcong had jumped out at him from behind a bush and as she opened to him, he said,

"I *shot* him with my sidearm."

She moaned as he went in, and said, "Tell me!"

"And they came at us as we neared the strip, screaming and yelling, and I *stuck* one ('Tell me!') with my knife. There was another on my back and I *jabbed* him ('Tell me!') with my elbow and *ripped* him ('Tell me!') with my knife. And then they were all around me, and I *stuck* them ('Kill him!'), and *ripped* them ('Kill him!'), and *jammed* ('Jam me!') the *pistol* ('Shoot it to me') into his *ear* ('Hear me!'), and *pulled* ('Pull me!') the *trigger* ('Trig me!'), and it *fired* ('Frig me!') and *blew* ('Blow!') *his* ('Oh!') *fuckin'* ('Ohhhh') *brains* ('Ohhhhhh!') *out* ('Eeeeeeeee!')

He could see it all very clearly. He could see it as if it had really happened. He could see it so clear. He killed seven men before he was really ready, but she had already began to scream, a high-pitched siren that would have awakened the whole house. He had never heard anything like it before. He had never had anybody like her before. When he was finished, he was covered with sweat.

"You're a good man, Charlie Brown," she said. "You sure do know how to tell a war story."

He didn't know how long he dozed off, but it couldn't have been too long because it was still light outside. Miriam, having shaken him gently, was holding a lighted cigarette out to him. "Got to get up an' at 'em, Charlie Brown. We got a dinner appointment with a close and dear relative of ours."

She must have seen the stab of pain that went through him, because she said very quickly, "Ooooh, I'm sorry, Dave. That didn't come out quite the way it was supposed to. Like Connie always says, 'I just ain't got no tact.'"

He lay on his back staring at the ceiling, inhaling stonily. He had never felt so miserable in his life. So corrupt and debased. So contemptible. It was not so much that he had been unfaithful to his wife sexually as that he

had been disloyal to her as a person. He had done to Constance who was, when you came right down to it, the only person in the world who really cared whether he lived or died, the worst thing he could possibly have done to her.

And he couldn't even plead that he hadn't understood exactly what he was doing. He had seen the battle scene he had been describing clearly, he had been aware of Miriam and the act. And yet, below it all, in one corner of Walsh's brain, a sad and huddled observer had been saying, "I'm sorry, Connie. I'm sorry. . . ."

The phone rang, startling them both. They stared, transfixed, as it rang and rang; the phone was a witness in the room, each ring an outside observer making his presence —*her* presence—felt. Accusing them. For both of them knew who it was.

They stared at each other, finally, guiltily, as if they had been caught. And then Miriam swung her legs over the side of the bed, picked up the phone, and nodded to him. Dutifully, cleverly, she said, "You can blame me, Connie. I had myself all strung up—you know the way I can get— and I just had to have a drink before I left. I hope you won't clobber me, but I zonked your poor husband into joining me. Lone drinking has always depressed me. Hold on, he's right here." She handed him the phone, looking oh so pleased with herself, and went dashing to the closet for her clothes.

"I was just wondering what was keeping you?" Connie said. Her voice sounded small to him. Timid and vulnerable. It was as if she were saying to him, "*don't do this to me.*" "I thought you were going to call me to put the roast on."

He heard himself saying, "Had a little traffic on the Expressway. And a quick drink with Miriam." He sounded to his own ears, oh so composed, oh so urbane. Miriam must be proud of him. "But we're practically out the door, hon.

Good thing you called. I'd clean forgot I was supposed to call you before we left."

"We got good soul food," he heard himself say, after he had hung up. "Roast."

Miriam was already in her bra, and she was pulling on her panties. "I've had all the soul food I can stand for one night, love. Dave. . . ." She smiled across the room. "You know what I told you about all those women waiting to outspread? Leave them be for awhile, huh? I want to keep you in the family." There was that soft shy melting look again. "There's something I want more than anything in the world right now. I want you to make me a baby." Mischievously, she held her dress in front of her, hiding her body from him. "We'll call him Hero. Nobody will ever suspect."

He was looking around for his clothes again.

"Downstairs," she said. "You done despoiled me from one floor to the other." *The spoils of war*, Adam March had said. Ring up another on the register for Adam March.

Miriam was beautiful through dinner, just beautiful. He had been afraid that, being a woman, she would somehow give something away. A lot he knew! Being a woman, she breezed through the dinner without a hitch, kidding as always with Joshua, quarreling as always with Constance, and, most remarkable of all, showing no sign of guilt in her relationship with Dave. Contrariwise, she overdid the flirting bit to prove that there couldn't possibly be anything between them or why would she risk giving it away?

Even when Connie went in to fix up the guest room and they were suddenly alone, they held a perfectly natural, cooly casual conversation.

He felt guilty about sleeping with his wife while her sister, whom he had just slept with, was in the room next door, only a few feet away. Once he was in bed, though, a

wave of tenderness for Constance swept over him which, taken together with his desperate need to purge himself, was overwhelming.

"Don't," Connie whispered, "Miriam will hear us."

It was only an automatic response, though, an obligatory female delicacy. There was no real resistance. Far from it. Things hadn't been good between them for more than a week and she was, when all was said and done, not only ready but, after the first few moments, helpless. At first he tried to be quiet so that Miriam wouldn't hear anything, but then he didn't care. It took him awhile, naturally enough, and Constance rose again and again. Through it all, Dave tried not to think of Miriam. He tried not to see her on the couch downstairs, he tried not to see himself carrying her up the stairs, he tried not to see the grand finale on the big bed, and, most of all, he tried not to have it once again all mixed up with violence, and murder, and blood. When he finally rose to the occasion himself, Constance was in a final paroxysm of pleasure. He had the terrible fear that she was going to scream like her sister, but by then it didn't really matter.

As she lay in his arm afterward, he made himself a personal vow that he would make it up to her. He would spend the rest of his life making it up to her.

As the dull, gusty March days went by, Dave knew a little of what it would be like to be in Hell. He could smell and taste the sulphur and brimstone. He was a man consumed. Consumed by his physical desire for Miriam. Consumed by guilt and remorse. Consumed by his inability to move one way or the other about the Medal of Honor.

He had always assumed that, drift though he might, something would happen before July 4 to keep him from accepting the medal. Even if it meant a positive act of renunciation by himself. For the first time, he was not sure

in his own mind that he would be able to turn the medal down. Above and beyond the problem of Miriam, there was Constance. Having betrayed her once, wouldn't he now be, in her mind at least, betraying her again? For even though the problem of the medal had been pushed into the background by Miriam, it was always there ready to push itself into the foreground whenever any related matter, no matter how peripheral, brushed against it.

More and more, his mind dwelt upon the three Negro Medal of Honor winners who had died, in acts of bravery, knowing no honors, having no women ready to fall back for them. Who knew the name of Bill Thompson, killed at Inchon, at the age of eighteen? And Cornelius Charlton, mortally wounded, incredibly brave, climbing, seizing, and securing Hill 542? Everybody knew about Mt. Goliath. Who had heard of Hill 542?

And—worst of all, worst of all—somewhere in Vietnam had died another Thompson, another Charlton, another Olive whose bravery was unknown even to his own family because the United States had found the black "hero" it was looking for in David Walsh. He knew that. As sure as he was alive—a living, breathing fraud—he knew that he had stolen a black brother's name and honor.

He would sometimes go to sleep cursing himself for not being able to accept the arguments of March, Delvecchio, Constance. What was done had been done. He had, Delvecchio had said, been hit by good fortune instead of bad. "*Suppose a truck had hit you. Nobody would say you deserved it or didn't deserve it. It would be just something that happened. . . .*"

But he was what he was. He was a middle-class black man who had been programmed with white ambitions and white values, whatever that was supposed to mean.

Wasn't honor an eternal value?

Wasn't true accomplishment the eternal goal?

Wasn't conscience conscience?

Wasn't black honor, accomplishment, and conscience as good as white?

Yes, there lay the kernal of the problem. How dare they tell him that because white was dishonorable, fraudulent, and dishonest, black had no call to be different? How dare they!

Night after night, he turned on his sweat-soaked pillow and pondered that. How dare they tell him he was anything except David Walsh. One man, husband of one woman, father of one son.

Yes, and the one-time lover of one woman. That was David Walsh too.

And that would bring on another few hours of sleeplessness.

He began to get pains in his stomach. He wondered whether he was developing an ulcer. Connie began to get after him to start right in on his job. Except for the speeches for the NSBE he was at a loss for anything to do with himself. "It isn't good for a man to be moping around the house all the time," Connie would tell him. "It isn't right. It isn't healthy."

At first, he was sure that Constance didn't have the slightest suspicion about him and Miriam. Still, Miriam and Constance were spending a lot of time together, househunting, and as his father always said, "Woman is woman!"

Miriam did have a way of calling him, "Charlie Brown," with a sidelong look that made it clear they shared a special secret. Or was that only his imagination? And while Constance never actually said anything, there was a pervading sense of sadness about her, a new tenseness in her voice. Occasionally, he caught her looking at him as if. . . . Or was that just his imagination too?

Of course it was, he told himself. Their sex life had been

reactivated since he had gone to bed with Miriam—although at times he did wonder whether, driven on as he was by his guilt, he wasn't overdoing it. Once she had even said, "Again? What are you trying to prove, Dave? For the love of God you're forty-five."

It was not until she mentioned, quite incidentally—too incidentally?—that she had decided not to look in Westchester any more that he had his first real surge of fear. Especially when she added, "Miriam's my sister, but I don't really relish the idea of having her around Josh all the time, the way she talks."

And then there began the constant digs at her, sly at first and then open and brutal. "She's my sister and I have the blood feeling for her, but she *is* such a slut. You should see how she throws it around at every man she sees. There was one real estate man there, I swear to God if I'd left them alone for five minutes they'd have run right up to the bedroom. I don't know how Lester dares to leave her alone so much."

"Oh hell," he said, mildly enough, "why do you say things like that?"

And in a rage, she said, "You don't know what a slut she is or you wouldn't always be defending her! There's a lot of things I wouldn't tell you; I've got too much family pride. She'd like to roll in the gutter! She'd like to take on the whole of Coxey's army if she could!"

And all the time April 1 was drawing closer and closer.

It was on March 31, the night before the parade, that Lyndon Johnson made his dramatic television announcement that he would not seek reelection in November.

After the initial shock had passed, Walsh was depressed out of all proportion to what his sentiments about President Johnson had always been. For some vague reason he felt a kind of personal bond with the President, some bond of defeat that he could not quite place his finger on.

"I don't know why you're getting so all-fired worked up about it," Constance said to him as they sat in the kitchen afterward drinking coffee. "You never even liked the man. You and Lester were just saying the other night what a fake he was, how he had never stood up for civil rights when he was in the Senate. And all those crooked deals in Texas that made him rich. You should be happy the country won't be stuck with him another four years."

Walsh was silent, holding his cup tightly with both hands, staring at the little ring of bubbles swirling in the middle of the black coffee. That was supposed to mean good luck. Some joke. Constance was right, though. He had never been a fan of Johnson's, even though he had voted for him. Joshua was right too; the country was going to hell. Still, tonight, seeing the President's haggard, weary, lined face on the TV tube, he had been moved to deep compassion. Something stronger even than compassion. Yes, a feeling of kinship almost.

"It certainly did come as a surprise, though," Constance said. "With that ego of his, who would have ever thought he'd give up without a fight?"

"Who said he was giving up?" Dave demanded, angrily.

"Well, Dave, what else would you call it? All the polls, like they said afterward. They showed how unpopular he's getting with the people. Just look at the mess he's got this country in. All the rioting, the student protests, the kids burning their draft cards. All those men—I don't have to tell you, Dave—being killed in Vietnam."

Yes, if there had been no war, he would have been teaching school somewhere, quietly and happily. There was no way of getting around that. "I don't care what anybody says," he said, stubborn to the end. "Lyndon Johnson did a lot for the black man while he was in the White House." Before she could say anything, he added with unaccustomed pugnacity, "More than any other President ever

did."

"Well," Constance said aimlessly, letting it fade away, "I guess it all got to be too much for him. . . ."

The sound of the phone ringing caused his hand to jerk, spilling coffee over the rim of the cup into the saucer. He was still ducking phone calls, as much to protect himself from any private conversation with Miriam at this point as from Adam March or anybody else. But this time, it had nothing to do with that. He had a premonition, ridiculous as he knew it to be, that this call was about Josh. With that burgeoning social life of his, Josh had gone to the "Casino Night" at the American Legion Hall, a form of indoor carnival featuring penny-ante games of chance—throwing baseballs at pyramids of wooden milk bottles, betting on the numbers of the glittering spinning wheel, and the like. Perfectly respectable. The proceeds were to be donated to the Community Chest. Dave knew all about it, because he'd had to beg off accepting some kind of citizenship award they'd wanted to give him to kick the evening off.

Perfectly safe. And yet, he had a bad feeling about it. And now with the news of the abdication of Lyndon Johnson sure to hit the hall like a bomb. . . .

"It's probably Miriam," Constance said, pushing herself out of her chair. "She was going to call me after they got back from the theatre."

It was Miriam all right. Dave had wandered out to the living room after her to just make sure, and he found himself eavesdropping with more than casual interest. He strained to hear what Connie was saying so that he might guess what was being said on the other end, and then, disgusted with himself, he didn't want to hear at all.

He wandered around the room restlessly, tidying up the top of the television console where Joshua had left a scarf and one glove. Joshua's schoolbooks were piled high on the coffee table too. Having nothing else to do, Walsh

gathered them up and carried them through the hall to his son's room. After placing them down on the desk, he patted the top book fondly, a little smile on his face, as if he were patting his son's head.

The Intimate Life of Alexander Hamilton, the title read.

He let the book turn open at the bookmark and read down the page idly. A phrase caught his attention. He read it once silently. Then he read, aloud:

"The people is a great beast, and it must be fed. . . ."

Wisdom from Adam March, he thought, out of Alexander Hamilton.

Out in the foyer, Constance was calling for him. He closed the book, patted it again, and walked out of the room and into the hall.

"Oh, there you are. Listen, Miriam wants to wish you well." She covered the mouthpiece with her hand and whispered, "She's all bitched up about her and Lester not being on the platform with the mayor at City Hall tomorrow. Maybe you can do something with her." The expression on her face clearly said that Lord knew *she* couldn't.

"Just what I need." He took the phone. "Hello, Miriam," he said, trying to force some enthusiasm into his voice. "What's the matter, dear, getting that left-out feeling? You can see me any old time, so I guess you really want to get next to Johnny Baby."

Constance waggled her fingers at him and pointed toward the bedroom. "I'm going to loosen myself up some."

Miriam's voice came over lower. "That was only an excuse. I really only wanted to talk to you, lover."

There was a long heavy silence, and then a soft, throaty laughter came into his ear. "Don't worry, Lester's not here. Besides, he's heard me call you 'lover' a thousand times."

"I suppose so."

"Dave, Les is flying to Miami on Friday. He'll be gone three days." She told him she would be taking a room at the

Hilton over the weekend. "From time to time," she said, "I feel the need of getting away from it all; doing some shopping, seeing the shows. I haven't done any . . . shopping for it seems, love, like ages."

"Well," he said, "I'm going to be pretty busy, I don't think I can make it."

The tone of the voice in his ear sharpened. "Well, don't make it sound like I just made you an appointment to see the dentist." He could see her pouting. "Since when did you go taking holy vows against a little . . . shopping." He wondered which phone she had called from. He wondered whether she was standing in the foyer just inside the front door or sitting on the big bed upstairs. It was the bedroom voice that came crooning over, low-down and smoky. "I thought you might be in a mood to go shopping for that fine, fair brown you once upon a time showed such a fine and Charlie Brown partiality for."

He sure wished that he could, he said, unable to bring himself to completely insult her. But he was afraid it was out of the question for now. "Listen, Miriam, I have to hang up. I've got to go pick Josh up. He's at something down at the Legion Hall and it should be just about breaking up."

"Dave, wait. What I really wanted to tell you was . . . I could be wrong, of course, but . . . I think you're going to become an uncle."

"What! That's ridiculous!" He tempered his voice. "You couldn't possibly know that. We haven't. . . . How could you possibly know that?"

It was a joke, of course, he thought, relieved. Except that it wasn't Miriam's kind of joke at all.

"Because I'm regular as clockwork. You can set your calendar by me. And I'm two days late."

"Oh, hell! You're two days crazy! I never figured you for the kind who. . . ." He glanced toward the bedroom.

"Who'd be that foolish."

"It could be . . . uh, emotional, of course. I've found myself emotionally involved, of late; but, Dave, it's never happened before. I'm regular as a clock." And then mischievously, "You can ask Constance. Constance was always all over the place, while I could call the date, time, and place. It was only one of the things she was jealous of me about." The mischievous laughter came into his ear again. Yeah, he thought, mischievous and malicious. "And, lover," she said, "I've got that feeling. Hope he doesn't look too much like Josh."

He hung up in panic. As ridiculous as it was, *it could be!*

On top of everything else, he had to have this! Why now, tonight, when he had another ordeal to live through tomorrow? Why did everything have to hit him at once!

It hit him like a revelation! It was as if a sign had been given to him. *That was why it had been now, tonight!* If he could tell Constance the truth about himself and Miriam, bring it all out into the open, he could tell the world the truth about David and Mt. Goliath.

Since he hadn't been able to do it in one great step, he was being given the chance to do it in two small ones.

Constance was sitting at her vanity, creaming her face. When Dave came into the room, she screwed the cover back on the jar and stood up, smoothing down the robe with the flat of her hands.

"Well," she asked, "did you pacify the child?"

"Connie, sit down. I want to talk to you. It's about Miriam."

"It'll keep until later, won't it?" she said, brightly. "I want to take a shower."

"No, we're going to talk about it right now. Constance, this isn't going to be easy for me, so. . . ."

"So we'll talk about it later. After my shower."

For Dave, there was that feeling once again that he was

watching a replay of a scene he had seen before. Only this
time it took no great effort to remember what it was. He
saw Connie, in her robe, sitting on that same hassock. He
saw himself standing in this same spot. He saw that same
tight, mannikin smile pasted on her face.

"*Sit down, Constance. I want to tell you something.
. . .*"

"*Not now. . . .*"

"*It's going to be now, Connie. . . . This isn't going to be
easy for me.*"

Only this time it was Constance who had determined
what she was going to do. The mannikin smile disappeared, and in its place came a cold, grim, accusing stare.
"Dave, really," she said. "I'm not interested in hearing
about Miriam or Miriam's troubles." The words came out
hard and chiseled. "Her affairs are her affairs, not mine. If
you want to let her bend your ear, you let her, but leave
. . . me . . . out of it. Especially now." A cold glint came
into her eyes. "Tonight, only one thing matters to me."

So that was it. You give me this and I'll give you that. No
quarrels, no recriminations, no questions asked. As long as
it wasn't put into words, Constance was willing to live with
it.

He walked past her and sat down on the bed. His body
was wet with perspiration underneath his clothing.

"It *is* all that matters to you, isn't it?"

"I beg of you. Don't do anything foolish tomorrow at
City Hall. Like what you tried to do at the banquet. That
would destroy us, Dave. It would destroy us."

"Oh God," he said, looking to the heavens, "let's not go
into that again."

"No, let's. Let's bring it right up front. You listen to me,
Dave." She shook a threatening finger at him. "If you say
anything to disgrace yourself and your son before the entire country, I want you to know why. You like to think it's

because you're some kind of a person better than the rest of us. More honest. . . ." She couldn't resist it, "More pure. Well, the truth of it is that you're afraid. You're afraid of The Man! You're afraid of being anything but The Man's good nigger."

She had picked her time and spot to hit him with that again, not through indirection as before but head-on. And right on target.

"Maybe you're right," he said calmly. "Maybe I am afraid. I've been in the Army three different times, and I know that they always catch up to you. Guys go AWOL for twenty years, and they still catch up with them."

But he knew that wasn't the main thing, and he could see that she knew it too. "Maybe Adam March is right," he said. "Maybe I want the medal and I'm afraid of wanting it. Maybe you're right. Maybe I put too much value in the opinion of other people. Although I don't know why that should be. You know, I've found out something very interesting in this thing, Constance. . . ." He was speaking more deliberately now, listening to himself because this, he knew, *was* true. "I always believed we were held together in this world by a common trust in each other's honesty. Maybe not in the little things, but in the big things; the things that were important. That isn't true, you know." He shook his head pensively, almost wistfully. "No, we're held together by a common trust in each other's dishonesty. You and Joe Delvecchio, you have a lot in common. Adam March too. You have to poke around inside a man until you find the worm, the hidden selfish motive crawling around inside him. You have to prove that he's really out to get his, just like everybody else."

"There!" she said triumphantly. "You said it yourself! Just like everybody else! Everybody else is out to get theirs. Why shouldn't you?"

All at once he seemed to have lost his concentration. Aware of nausea, a momentary dizziness came over him. "Bob Nichols wasn't," he said aimlessly. He took a deep breath. "But Nichols is dead, so I don't suppose he counts anymore. We got him a DSM so his wife could be proud of him. That makes it as if he deserved it, doesn't it? Because she thinks he deserved it, and she's probably the only person alive who cares whether he did or not?" He smiled at her rather foolishly, knowing that he was rambling. "Maybe Adam March is right."

"Adam March is nobody's fool," she said pointedly.

A dry, bitter laugh. "Adam March is nobody's fool, all right. And that's not the half of it." He peered across at her again. "But to say that a man might want to do something simply because he believes it's the honest, decent thing to do, that's too much to believe, isn't it? He has to be a Tom, or a liar, or a fool, is that it? You now, Constance. You've lived with me for seventeen years. Out of all those years, can't you find something—one thing, one moment—so that you can look at me right now and say: 'Yes, you are an honest, decent man. . . .'"

Her sharp intake of breath stopped him, even before she turned her head away.

"All right, Connie, *one* mistake and it will never happen again. Look at me. *Look at me!* I'm asking you to go back through seventeen years for enough good moments so that you can say, 'You are an honest, decent man. Do what you think is right and, whatever happens, we'll be all right!'"

It was at that moment they both became aware that the front door chimes were ringing.

"That must be Josh!" Relieved, she turned back to the face cream and the mirror.

Dave could only nod at her, grimly and impotently. "Okay," he said tightly, "*Don't* look at me." The chimes kept ringing, steadily and urgently, as he hurried down the

hall. Not like Josh at all. A premonition—of what?—
closed around him. Not like Josh at all.

He opened the door and saw a small, rotund black
woman with a scarf thrown over her frizzled gray hair. It
took him a few moments to place the thin-lipped, pinched-
faced woman as the building superintendant's normally
jolly and placid wife.

"Mrs. Bascomb," he said, "can I do anything for you?"

"No, sir, Mr. Walsh, I. . . ." Her eyes kept sliding away
from him. "It's just I thought I ought to tell you. . . ." She
kept swallowing, rapidly and nervously.

"Tell me what, Mrs. Bascomb?" The premonition had
clamped down on him like a cold, icy hand, straining the
cords at the back of his neck.

"It probably isn't anything I should bother you about,
but Martin. . . ." She cleared her throat. ". . . Anyway,
Martin went and walked up to the avenue just a bit ago,
you see, to have a couple of beers with some of his friends,
and play some shuffleboard like they do." She licked at her
lips. "But he come right back, you see. There's some trouble
in town, he says. A gang of boys that is having some trouble
with the police and he. . . ." She looked past his shoulder
to Constance who was coming down the hall. "Is your boy
come home?"

He had known all right. For some reason, however, it
seemed important not to let Mrs. Bascomb see that he had
known and that he was frightened. "Did Martin say my
boy was there? That he had seen him with this gang?"

Her eyes slid away again. Well, no, Martin hadn't said
that exactly. Martin wasn't that sure really. He had come
right back home, you see, before things got out of hand.

What was the poor woman to say? She had gone to the
trouble of coming up to tell him, hadn't she? And what did
that mean, if it did not mean that Martin had either seen or
thought that he had seen Josh.

Constance had shoved in beside him in the small vestibule. "Dave, what is it?" Her voice was tremulous. "Is Josh in some kind of trouble?"

"Now, that isn't what she said at all," Dave told her, trying, in soothing her, to put down his own rising panic. "There's some kind of rumble going on in town, that's all, and Mrs. Bascomb thought we ought to know about it."

He could have kicked himself for using the word rumble, which made it sound worse than he had any reason to believe—to be sure, anyway—that it was.

"Not that I thought for one minute your boy would get hisself together with a gang of toughs, Mrs. Walsh," the super's wife was saying. "But it's like Martin was saying the other night. Nowadays, you walk down the street minding your own business and trouble is looking for you at every street corner."

"Martin has a point," Walsh said. And Walsh had an idea. "Connie," he said, "Why don't you pour Mrs. Bascomb some coffee?"

"Oh, my, Mr. Walsh—Captain—you don't have to do that." She clasped her hands to her bosom, overwhelmed at being invited into the home of so great a hero.

Taking her firmly by the elbow, the great hero ushered her over the threshold. He knew exactly what he was going to do, and Mrs. Bascomb would serve very nicely to distract Constance while he was gone.

"Dave," Connie said. "Why don't you phone the Legion Hall while I'm fixing the coffee? If they've broken up over there, maybe you could walk up that way and meet him."

No sense bothering to call, he said as casually as he could manage. "I'll just walk up that way. I need some air anyway."

Mrs. Bascomb had become rooted where she stood, a tense, miserable expression across her face. "Mr. Walsh, sir," she said weakly. "That's where Martin heard it all

started, all that trouble. Down at the Legion Hall."

Just what he had been afraid of all night. "Well," he said, smiling at Mrs. Bascomb while he patted Constance on her arm. "Joshua talks some, but he's too smart a boy to go messing around with that kind of thing."

He knew better. Constance knew better. Mrs. Bascomb probably knew better. Josh had been playing the hero's son role to the hilt to reinforce what Dave had to admit was a natural taste for leadership. With all this swirling talk about black power, this affair at the Legion Hall, this damn carnival with its excitement and competition . . . yes, that was what had been festering in the back of his mind all evening. He had known all along he should have accepted the invitation just so that he'd be there, in case anything happened.

"Mr. Walsh," Mrs. Bascomb said. He looked to her, hopefully, waiting for some words of encouragement. In some ways, she'd know Josh best of all. She would have seen him out in the street, with his friends, at his worst behavior. She was, he was sure, going to tell him that he was right, there was nothing to worry about.

She must have seen the hunger in his face too, because she shrank back a little as she muttered that it was mighty cold and wintry out there and she'd presume to advise that he should wrap himself up good and warm.

Dave put his Army field jacket on over his suit jacket, feeling to his surprise rather military, rather combative; feeling, even, that it was *right* to be wearing it.

It was, as Mrs. Bascomb had said, cold and wintry, with a biting wind that whipped up shards of old newspapers, swirls of dust, and the few blackened leaves left over from the ravages of winter. But when he turned the corner and entered the deep shadows of the big, old oaks, which flung a canopy over the residential side street that led up to the avenue, the very quiet and peacefulness insinuated them-

selves into the dread that was prickling along the backs of his legs and spurred him to a quickened strike. In a block he was trotting. Another block and he began to run.

By the time he reached Hollis Avenue his lungs were raw; his armpits and the palms of his hand were damp with sweat. He was running again along the twisted jungle path that led to Flatiron Mountain, and the thought association sent a tremor through him. The terrible presentiment of mortal danger was hovering once again all around him; closing in from behind, waiting up ahead.

You damned fool! he told himself, laughing shakily. The brightly lighted thoroughfare was all but empty. Clear, clean, and empty in the cold, crisp air. There was an old white man walking a German shepherd, and, across the street, two black couples strolling home after a late movie or visit. No sight or sound of trouble anywhere.

His legs unsteady, his heart pounding, he crossed the street toward the bar in the middle of the block. What he needed now was one quick one, after which he would go on to the Legion Hall and pick up his boy. Whatever trouble had taken place over there must have been very minor, two kids swinging at each other probably, and he didn't want to embarrass Josh by walking in and pulling him out of there like a child.

He was right outside the bar when he heard the sirens coming up behind him fast. Then the two patrol cars were speeding past him, with their red beacons revolving, and busting right through the red light at the corner and turning left off the avenue, three blocks down, burning rubber on the quick, tight turn, and they were gone.

Sweet Jesus!

He started to run again as the door to the bar swung open, and through the cold, clear air he could hear, with astonishing clarity, the argument going on behind him, the men wanting to go down and see what was happening, the

women protesting and groaning that it was so darn cold out here and so nice and warm in there.

He arrived at the scene, completely out of breath. Both ends of North Sewart Street, a short and narrow street, had been blocked off by patrol cars parked in V-formation, their revolving turret beacons whipsawing long, slashing shafts of ruby light across the façades of the drab buildings and store windows, picking up, in an eerie flickering way, the people hanging out the windows of the cheap apartments above the stores and shops.

The two patrol cars that had sped past him had pulled up behind the others, their headlights and beacons contributing to the total illumination. The doors of both cars had been thrown open, and the four cops were standing alongside them, a black and white cop in each team.

As Walsh pushed through the crowd and hopped over the wooden barricade, he saw that the flickering light that had puzzled him did not come from the beacons, but from a bonfire in the middle of the street.

In the middle of the block, between the police cars closing off the intersections, a couple of dozen kids—if they were all kids; Dave couldn't be sure of their number or their age—were leaping and prancing around the bonfire in wild juvenile abandon, stopping every now and then to shout at the police or wave their arms in beckoning challenge. Empty garbage cans and Department of Sanitation trash baskets were strewn all over the street and sidewalk. (From the number of trash baskets, it was clear that they must have been collected from all over the neighborhood.)

The cops were lined up on the other side of the patrol cars, in front of a whole line of barricades stretching from one side of the street to the other, clenching their nightsticks in the palms of their hands like soldiers at a loose and ready parade rest.

As Walsh looked desperately into the mob scene to find

Josh, he could see the two cops from the open patrol car coming toward him, the white cop saying, automatically, "Just step back, Mister. We'll take care of this."

At that moment, a tall, skinny kid picked up a trash can with both hands, spun around and around with a dervish fervor and, with a final wild whoop, let it fly toward the store front. The big plate glass showcase shattered with an obscenely musical sound, followed by the even more obscene cheers and laughter from the mob of kids and—unbelievable to Walsh—the shouted encouragement and applause from the people hanging out of the windows.

The cops at the barricades clutched at their nightsticks and did nothing. By irrevocable habit, Dave turned to the black cop, a powerfully built man with a neat little mustache, to ask how come officers of the law, grown men, were standing around doing nothing while a bunch of kids were going stark, crazy wild.

The black cop looked at him more in disbelief than anything else, but the white cop, glancing past Walsh to his black partner, smiled thinly and said, "You want an answer to that one, you better write the mayor. Just tell him you're a tax-paying property owner." The expression of contempt on his face said very clearly, *Where are you guys when we need you?*

Just as he finished, another plate glass shattered, and it was then Walsh realized that the white cop apparently thought it was his window that had got busted before.

One hour earlier Dave would have sworn that he would never use the medal business for personal advantage. Under the circumstances he didn't hesitate for a second. "Now, look," he said, calling up the voice of command. "My name is David Walsh, Captain David Walsh, and I think I've got a kid in this thing. If you're not going to do anything, I damn well am."

He got, as he had anticipated, the raised eyebrows and

the measuring, approving stares he had come to know so well. A command car was screeching to a stop behind the others; followed, directly behind, by a paddy wagon. The black cop told Walsh very quickly that his name was Floyd Meader. "Stick around, Walsh," he told him. Hurrying toward them—and past them—was a slender lieutenant with graying hair and gold braid on his cap and epaulets. Meader motioned to Walsh to come along with them. "Whatever anybody else says, you just move where we move, and leave the talking up to me. Got it?"

The white cop smiled his thin smile and shrugged. It was no skin off his ass one way or the other.

The lieutenant was bawling out a sergeant for letting the thing get out of control in the first place. "All I've got to say is somebody's going to be making out a report to explain why this crowd wasn't broken up and dispersed outside Legion Hall. And it better be explained to my satisfaction!"

The sergeant, a considerably larger man than the lieutenant, explained in a slow, rather insolent drawl that they hadn't caught up to them until they had gathered here and started the fire. "When the patrol car arrived on the scene and called in, headquarters ordered us not to provoke the residents of the community or"—his expression didn't change one iota—"incite any more violence among the rioters." It did change then to become more open and innocent. "We don't want to radicalize them, do we, sir?"

Standing as he was only a few feet from the lieutenant, Walsh could see a hostility in this white man's face that was every bit as savage as anything he had seen in the black faces in the crowd. It went beyond anger, into a mistrust and fear that was both primitive and professional. Riot in the street he could always take care of, especially a small thing like this. But could he take care of both riot in the street and mutiny in the ranks?

Gathering the whole lineup of cops back in around him, the lieutenant informed them there would be no tactical police in on this unless it became absolutely necessary. "And it isn't going to become necessary for a handful of kids." He had been assured that television was going to stay away. "Thank God for small favors!" And so they were going to let youthful energies run their course and hope that when the fire burned itself out, they'd all break up and go home. If they did have to move in, there'd be no helmets, no guns, no nightsticks above the waist. He sneaked a look around the crowd. "I don't have to tell you. The Man gets his picture in the paper with a nightstick over his head, it's his ass."

Dave had been listening with half an ear, still trying to spot Joshua in the mob. He had thought, from time to time, that he did see him; but with the fire getting lower and dimmer, it was becoming increasingly more difficult to pick anybody out. "Who the hell," he heard the lieutenant say, "called for plainclothesmen?" In looking around for photographers, the lieutenant's eyes had come to rest on Walsh.

Meader and his partner took the lieutenant aside and spoke to him confidentially, their heads jerking back toward Dave. The lieutenant looked directly at him, as unhappy as a man could be, and Dave could lip-read more than hear him growl, in disgust: "Swell!" Moving in closer so that he could argue his own case if he had to, he heard the lieutenant say, ". . . if you want to take the responsibility. As long as I don't know a damn thing about it, you understand? Shit, you know Morgan. He booked his own kid."

With the fire almost completely out now, one of the kids had hopped on top of a turned-over trash basket and was beginning to harangue the crowd wildly, in the rhythm of a preacher but in the kind of language Walsh had never

heard before. The kind of language that not only sickened him, but damn well near traumatized him. Other kids, breaking away from the solid core, were advancing toward the two intersections, taunting the cops, baiting them. Most of them carried crude weapons: broken broomsticks, bottles, bricks, and knives.

"Pigs, go home!"

"White motherfucking pigs take black pigs with you!"

"Pigs eat shit!"

"I know yo' sister, pig, she come down here and suck black cock alla time, ev'y night!"

The cops stood there, holding their nightsticks lower, waiting.

"We gonna get the black fuzz," the kid on the trash basket screamed. "We gonna cut off their black traitor nuts."

Behind the police lines, the gathering crowd picked it up: "Get the black fuzz. Black pigs. . . . Black traitor's nuts!"

And from the windows and, by now, the rooftops, it bounced back down like an echo. "Yeah, yeah! Cut off their nuts!"

And then it was: "Get the honkies!"

"Yeah! Yeah! Get the honkies!"

"I want me some roasted pig tonight! Ain' nothing I like like I like roast white pig meat."

"Honky pig meat is so-o-o-o delicious!"

The kid on the basket flung out his hands in ecstasy and screamed; "Hallellujah, brothers! Tonight we got the biggest honky of 'em all!"

"Hallellujah!" from the crowd.

"Hallellujah" from the rooftops.

From the smaller group that had hung together around the embers of the fire, somewhat more timid, a bit more uncertain than the others, there came the thundering chorus:

"YEAH-YEAH-YEAYYYYY, LBJ. Who put LBJ away?"

And from all around them, came the answering chorus: "We did!"

"One-two-three-four, who ain't got LBJ any more."

"We ain't!"

"LBJ, LBJ. Who put LBJ away?"

"We did!"

"Who did?"

"We did!"

The lieutenant was still waiting, but there was a whistle in his hand. Looking across the lieutenant's shoulder, past the whistle, Dave saw his son. An instant of shocking, incredible recognition. He saw him first as a tall form racing across the enclosure from the far barricade, a fragment of brick clutched in his right hand, the hand cocked high behind him like a grenade-thrower. And then he recognized the school jacket (he hadn't worn the mackinaw after all), just as Josh let the brick fly. It arched over the head of the line of policemen and landed with a dull thud on the hood of the lieutenant's car.

It was, or might as well have been, a signal. A barrage of stones, bricks, and other projectiles filled the air; the whistle pierced the air with an incredibly strident, stirring call to action; and the helmetless policemen charged forward, shielding their heads and faces with their arms.

The rioters, as if by preconceived strategy, retreated slowly toward the rubble in the center of their island, jumping backward and forward, in and out, the braver of them dashing right up to the line of cops, to taunt or swing a stick, before scooting back.

With the police closing in from both sides, the other army in the apartment windows and the rooftops let go another barrage. Eggs. Fruit. Cans. Pots. Pans. Footstools. Bricks. Anything they could get their hands on that was mildly expendable.

Dave had started out, as directed, wedged behind Floyd Meader and his partner. But when a cop just ahead was felled by a vase that shattered against his shoulder, Dave sprinted through the gap in the line to get to Josh before the cops did. Now that he was out of the wedge, plates and glassware, the kitchen artillery from above, came smashing and clattering all around him. It was, in its own weird way, like running the gauntlet of the Commie ambush all over again. Except this was so much more personal. So much more hostile. So much more exposed. In all that light, it was as if he were on a stage.

"Josh!" he shouted, seeing him. "You little bastard, come here. . . ."

Not hearing, Josh raced back across the rubble and when Dave saw him again, he was battling with a cop from the other barricade. The cop had one of his arms twisted behind his back, and, as Josh tried to wrench away, he caught sight of his father. At the same split second another cop kicked him in the shin. The first cop's forearm clamped around Josh's neck, and the second cop scooped him up by both feet. Dave opened his mouth to yell, "Wait . . . ," but something crashed against the back of his neck and he went down, on all fours. Refocusing, he could just make out the two cops carrying Josh toward the paddy wagon. Out of his peripheral vision he saw the other form, the shadowy bulk moving to him and the swinging foot—but not soon enough to be able to jerk his head away. He caught the shoe square on the temple.

When he came to, he could see, through the blur, that he was back on the curb and Floyd Meader was hunched down in front of him. His hand went to his head and he felt the bit of gauze under the adhesive tape, and the sticky feel of the blood that had soaked through and was beginning to drip again. "I tried to get you some flesh-colored adhesive tape," Meader grinned, "and you know what they told me?

They told me, 'What's the matter with you, man? That *is* flesh colored?' "

Although Meader was concerned he was not at all displeased, Dave could see, that Captain Walsh had discovered that it was maybe tougher in the streets of New York than in the mountains of Vietnam.

It was just about over, though. The last few kids were being put into the squad cars, but the paddy wagon was gone. Presumably it had left with a full complement. The rubble and broken glass were all around him, the refuse of the battle. There was also a heavy acrid odor, sickening to the nostrils, which Walsh recognized soon enough as vomit. But the street. . . . The street was a clutter of everything, a curb-to-curb junk shop. A few yards up, in the gutter, there was a brassiere—no, the way it had kept its form, it was quite clearly a falsie. Somebody up there had given her all.

While Meader was applying a new bandage, he told Dave that he had found his kid in the paddy wagon and offered to let him go home with his father. Changing to his flat police-report voice, he said, "Subject, juvenile, responded with the words: 'Screw you, cop, I stick with my friends.' "

A horn sounded. An impatient voice called out, "What do you say, Meader? We going or aren't we?"

"That's my partner, Galluciano. He maybe feels he's put in a full day putting down this week's black insurrection." He affected the ghetto-Negro accent again. "You fell with the advancing po-lice line, Captain Walsh, suh, so ah thinks we can spare an inch or two of catgut to sew up that haid." As he helped Walsh to his feet, he said, more seriously, "And maybe you can do something about your kid."

On the way to the station, Meader told him that the whole thing had started at the Legion Hall when a couple of plainclothesmen nailed a pusher selling pot to a couple

of kids in the john. "From the downtown narco squad at that. You see what great intradepartmental communication we have? The first we heard about it was that some of our kids had jumped them and taken their prisoner away. Now that's what I call real policework! The next we heard, it was Fourth of July on North Sewart."

Galluciano, who was driving, said impassively, "The bastard is probably halfway back to Jersey by now. That's the great part of this whole grand adventure in the romance of policework. Nobody local on either side. Nothing local except the . . . uh, disturbance."

It was the only time Galluciano opened his mouth during the entire, if brief, trip to the station.

The two cops, sitting side by side, had paid so little attention to each other that, as Meader was taking Walsh downstairs to the dispensary, Dave commented that he and Galluciano must have been teamed together fairly recently.

"Mario?" He gave a hollow little laugh. "We been partners going on five years now. Used to be Floyd and Mario, and we'd eat at each other's house probably once a month, one way or the other, you know?" At the bottom of the stairs, he nudged him to turn right. "Second door there, you'll smell it. I'd still count on Mario to cover me on a rooftop, and I know he could count on me, but it's Galluciano and Meader now, not Mario and Floyd. I feel like hell about it and so does he, I can tell." He shook his head sadly. "Why does everything have to be black and white these days, Dave?"

"I don't know, Floyd." Dave managed a smile. "But all of us have got to keep our cool, that's for sure. Like my old man's been saying all of his life, 'There's better days ahead.' And you know something, he's been right. Things are better now than when I was growing up, listening to my old man say it."

"Yeah." Meader clamped a hand on Dave's shoulder as they entered the dispensary and winked. "My old man used to have a saying too: 'It's a great life if you don't weaken.'"

The doctor was seated in back, alongside the examining table, drinking coffee with a couple of cops. One of the cops had a patch on the back of his head, the other had a splint on his finger. Both of them continued to stare at Dave while the doctor, who looked young enough to be a medical student, sat him down and cleaned off the wound. Squinting and grunting, he pinched at the skin around the temple and finally told him he'd apply a butterfly bandage instead of stitches. "It will hold you through the parade tomorrow," he said, "and after that, if I were you, I'd go see my own doctor."

"That's special treatment," Meader told him, cheerful as always. "The usual surgical procedure around here for a split skull is iodine and aspirin."

"Glad you reminded me," the doctor grinned. "You've got a sweet little contusion there, Walsh." He reached into his pocket and came out with a little white packet. "If you feel any pain take a couple of these." Dave took a couple of them right there.

He had not missed the point that the medic had been expecting him. Nor that they did not want any nosy newspaperman to be able to say that David Walsh had been injured so badly he had needed stitches. If you were stitched up at a police station, there was always the presumption of police brutality.

Remembering that Floyd Meader had taken full responsibility for him, he could understand why he was sticking so close to him. Poor Floyd must have had some bad moments back there while he was waiting for Dave to regain consciousness.

While Meader was escorting him back upstairs through

the long corridor to the booking room, Walsh told him if there was any chance of him catching any static about this, he'd be happy to start signing waivers absolving anybody of any responsibility.

"What the hell you talking about?" Meader said. "Officially, you weren't even there."

It was the first time Walsh had ever been inside a police station, and the look of the booking room surprised him. It reminded him of a business office with banks of desks arranged in a neat geometric pattern, except that the majority of the workers busy at their typewriters and telephones wore police uniforms.

A middle-aged white couple was seated on the long wooden bench outside, the man staring off into space, the woman, her arms folded resolutely, glaring at them as they entered as if she were daring anybody to make her move.

A slender, dark officer with sergeant's stripes on his blue shirt sat behind the desk just inside the low wooden ballustrade (a desk somewhat larger and higher than the others). He looked up at Meader and Walsh with the mildest interest and jerked his thumb over his shoulder.

Meader asked him if they were booking them all.

The sergeant tapped the big ledger on his desk. "They send 'em in, we write 'em up. Every last mother of them." The thumb jerked over the shoulder again. "They're back there now being mugged and printed." They went through the swinging gate to the back of the receiving office and turned into a large studio. One side was crammed with photoflood lamps and photographic equipment. The kids were lined up along the opposite wall, all of them standing, there being not a chair in the entire room.

What impressed Dave immediately was the good nature of it all. The kids were loose and laughing, and not with any particular sense of bravado either, and the half-a-dozen cops who were standing guard over them did not

seem at all upset with them. It was like a PAL locker room after the game; a winning locker room, in which everybody knew he had performed well.

He had, of course, seen immediately that Josh was not among them. Meader nodded and went back to the phone alongside the fingerprinting desk, directly behind the camera.

The mugging camera, an old-fashioned box-like device sat on a tripod. It was pointed into the intersection of two aluminum reflectors angled to cast the maximum amount of illumination. The photographer was a short, stout, sweating cop with his sleeves rolled up above the elbow. "O.K.," he called out, "I'm looking for Dolly Burns."

A little, wide-mouthed kid, who looked no more than fourteen to Dave, came strutting out from the line, saying, "All right, C. B., this may be the Big Time for you, go git yo'self together. These snapshots, they going right on to J. Edgar Who. . . ."

"Stand right on the painted line," the cop chanted. "And close your mouth, and look to the front, right at the camera. This must be the first time you've had your mouth shut all day. And turn to the right like you seen the others do. . . . And now to the left. . . ."

"This my good side you're messing with now," Dolly said, turning his left profile to the camera. "Be especial tender of this side 'cause if you do a good job I'm gonna order me a dozen, one fo' each of my girl friends. . . ."

"And close your mouth," the cop said in the same monotone. "And now you're immortal. Step across the room and say hello to Corporal Nevers." He glanced down. "O.K., I'm looking for Sammy Dockins. . . ."

Across the room, directly in front of Meader, Corporal Nevers, dressed in civilian clothes, was holding another kid's hand and pressing each finger down hard, first on the inked metal plate and then onto the indicated box on the

NOTES

NOTES

NOTES

NOTES

NOTES

NOTES

booking card. "Now just relax," he'd say each time, "and hang easy and let me do the work."

The kids had been studying Walsh from the time he came in, nudging each other and whispering, but it wasn't until Meader came back and told him that Josh was down in Chief Morgan's office that they were sure it was he. As he went through the door, they were calling after him, in a happy chorus: Josh had been thrown in solitary on bread and water, but they weren't going to mess around with Captain Walsh; no, what that big-ass chief was going to do was kiss Captain Walsh's ass, and smack his lips, and swear it tasted like milk and honey.

It was all very jolly, and the only thing sad about it was that all those comedians now had records.

Entering Chief Morgan's office, Walsh found himself surprised again. Instead of the starred and beribboned police official he expected to find, erect and impressive behind the desk, he found a chubby, gray-haired man, wearing a tweed jacket and smoking a pipe, slouched easily on a couch at the side of the room.

"Your boy's in back," Morgan said. "In the holding cage. All by his lonesome. I'm letting him sweat a little. Might not do him any good, but it sure as hell won't do him any harm."

It was obvious to the naked eye that the chief was a weary man. He had been called out for this—which probably meant that somebody had thought it might get a lot worse than it had or, more probably, that somebody wanted to know what to do about David Walsh's kid.

"I'd like to see him," Dave said, wondering whether it would be a good or bad idea to cite some kind of constitutional right.

"I'm going to give him to you, Captain Walsh," Morgan said, almost as if he had been reading Dave's mind. "In return, all I ask is for you to be a little patient with me." He patted the worn leatherette cushion beside him. "Why don't you sit down and we'll talk a while, Captain?"

"Thanks." Dave sat down tensely on the edge of the couch and lit a cigarette. Automatically, his eyes went to the white man's face, searching for some sign to clue him in to what to expect. Was Chief Morgan going to play the benign white father to him?

At once the chief disarmed him with his next words: "I've been sitting here communing with myself this past hour, and the thought that came to me most forcibly was that one of the troubles with this job is that there aren't too many people you can talk to." He was talking to Dave in the tone of one leader of men to another, as men who understood the problems of command and could, therefore, proceed as equals.

He put a match to his pipe to get it started again. "My father was a desk sergeant," he said, puffing. "And a better man than his son. Not here, the Bronx. Not this Bronx. The old Irish and Italian Bronx."

In the old days, Chief Morgan told him, the desk sergeant ran his precinct just about, he would imagine, the way a good top sergeant ran an infantry outfit. He knew every kid in the neighborhood who was going to be a problem, and he'd pick the time to throw the fear of God into him. "The fear of God or the fear of Chet Morgan, I'm not sure which. They were probably about the same. The timing, though, that was the important thing."

He shifted himself wearily as if he were trying to make himself more comfortable. "Now you'll hear people today bragging about how they never take their jobs home with them? That wasn't my old man. My old man didn't talk about much at the supper table except police business. I grew up with police business and sauerkraut, know what I mean? A lot of it was about this timing: A lot of it was whether it was too soon to let a boy see what serving time was like, and a lot of it was that the time had come. And, sure, sometimes it was that he had waited too long. But not that often. I want to tell you something; my old man, he was pretty damn good at it."

He chuckled reminiscently. "The kids he saved, he figured he was entitled to hang them on his belt like prizes. Some of them became pretty big men. Most of them, they figured he was a dumb Irish cop who used to pick on them all the time."

He closed his eyes for a moment. "The old order changeth," he said, sighing heavily. "And who's to say it isn't all for the best, huh? You can't go leaving the administration of the law in the hands of unschooled desk sergeants, now, can you?"

He knocked the ashes out into a glass ashtray on the table alongside him. No, even those dumb old cops knew better than that. The old cops sent their sons to college, only some of the sons decided that being a cop wasn't so bad. Some of them even might have thought that being a cop, just like their old man, was about the greatest thing you could be in the world.

"But, there's this about it, Walsh. There's some things they can't teach you in college. Timing is one." He tapped his heart. "And heart. My old man knew when it was better to let them walk out, but he also knew that he could keep them from walking out when the time came to put the fear in them. That's the difference, Captain Walsh. Latitude, Captain Walsh, latitude. Latitude is what we don't have any more. Without latitude, the administration of the law can put a very great strain on the brain."

"It seems to me," Walsh said, "that every once in a while the parents have to do it themselves."

"Yes, I've thought that too from time to time." He bit down hard on the pipe. "Mr. Walsh, I have a 15-year-old myself. I don't think we're going to have a third-generation cop in the family, having observed at the supper table that he doesn't think for one second that being a cop is the greatest thing anybody could be in the world."

It came to Walsh then what the lieutenant had said to Floyd Meader back at the barricade about Morgan booking his own kid, and suddenly they were looking across the room at each other in mutual sympathy and recognition. In recognition, if nothing else, of the common bond all fathers had these days.

"Oh, hell, Captain," Morgan said. "I don't know what kind of a kid you've got. He seems no worse than most." He started to push himself off the couch, his hands pressing down on his thighs, and just wasn't quite able to make it. This man was intolerably weary. "Tomorrow's a big day for you. Why spoil it? If he's going to get into trouble, we'll see him again soon enough." He pushed himself up on his second try, stretched himself, and moved off toward his desk. "One more kid more or less on the ledger isn't going to hurt us," he said, yawning. "We made our quota today easy."

He shuffled some papers aimlessly on his desk. "I don't have my old man's feel for these things, but maybe it won't happen again." Still standing, he dropped his eyes to Walsh. "It won't do him any good to go through life tagged as the kid who ruined his father's big day. Once he gets to thinking he's the bad Walsh kid he just might get to thinking he's got to live up to his billing."

The same little mocking note Dave had noted when he first entered had crept back into Morgan's voice. "They teach us psychology and everything in college, know what I mean? Too bad," he said, tapping his heart, "they can't teach us this."

The chief had been skirting along the edges of something so personal that Dave didn't know quite what to say. Fortunately, he didn't really have to say anything.

"And frankly, Captain," Morgan said, "I don't see that it would do us any good to book him either. The way things stand, there was some trouble after the casino let out, and some kids got a little out of hand. With David Walsh's son in it, it becomes, with all respects, Captain, an uprising of black youth."

So that was it. With all that talk about timing, with all that sweet nostalgia and those obscure, passing glances at whatever mistake he might have made with his own kid, when you got right down to the gristle it was Chief Morgan and Chief Morgan's own problems he was concerned about. That and that alone. The rest of it might be true enough, the rest of it might make him feel better about it, but the rest of it really didn't matter. If Josh had been the rottenest kid in town, Chief Morgan would still have let him go.

"So . . . ," Morgan was saying, "your assurance that he'll behave himself in the future will be sufficient warranty in the view of the department to release him in your custody."

But what did it matter? When your own kid was in the balance, what the hell else really mattered?

The chief picked up a file card from the desk, tore it slowly in half, and dropped the two pieces into the basket beside his desk. He picked up the phone and told whoever he had called to bring the Walsh kid out to the desk. "His father will be there to pick him up. And, Sergeant, have a patrol car there to drive them home."

Dave told him he'd just as soon he forget about the patrol car, and it seemed to him that Morgan understood. "You can do me another favor, though. I'd like to call home and let my wife know that everything's all right."

They left the station house by the side entrance, their route taking them past the booking room where Dave could see—and not without a sense of guilt—the hunched, frightened group of parents who had already begun to gather.

The wait in the holding cage didn't have the desired effect on Josh, mostly because he never doubted for one moment that his father was going to spring him. "Man," he said, "you should have been in that paddy wagon with us. It went around like wildfire. Everybody was saying, 'David Walsh is with us. Did you see how David Walsh took on that whole police force.' Everybody there was saying that once word got out the pigs had beat and brutalized David Walsh, there was going to be a shake-up in the entire police department of the entire city."

With an enormous effort at self-restraint, Walsh informed his son that he was wrong on a few of his basic points. First of all, he could tell his friends that his father wasn't with *them;* he was against them. Secondly, he hadn't been hit by the police; he had been knocked down by a hunk of crockery thrown from one of the windows, then stomped by one of Josh's friends in the street. Thirdly, he never wanted to hear him use the word pigs for cops in his presence again.

"And I didn't spring you. This chief, who I guess is one of the heads you want to roll, thought it might ruin my big day tomorrow to have everybody read in the paper that my son had been picked up in a riot over taking some dope pusher away from the police."

That last piece of information really came as a surprise to Josh. It wasn't any dope pusher, he protested virtuously. It was a bookie who was just trying to write a little business like the Legion Hall was doing itself, because what were all those games of chance, if they weren't legalized gambling?

It was a dope pusher, Dave told him. The scum of the earth. Although he would be damned if he could understand why anybody would want to get into a fight over somebody they thought was a bookie. Unless, of course, they were spoiling for a fight to begin with.

Josh bridled. "Because you don't notice that they pull in any white bookies, do you? They're in cahoots with the white Syndicate to squeeze the black bookies out."

It was not as cold as it had been. That late at night the wind had already died. Josh was walking with his hands stuffed into the slash pockets of his jacket, his head down, noticeably unhappy. Pouting.

"What are you going to be, Josh?" Walsh said. "That's what's got me worried. A cop fighter? A part of a mob? I want to understand why this happened. Make me understand."

And saying it, David Walsh had made himself understand something. Before they got home, he would have to tell Josh the truth about himself too. It was not possible to have this kind of conversation with his son and then have his son find out, somehow, at some later date, that the paternal lecturer, the stern moralist, was a fraud. Timing, Chief Morgan had said was everything in these things. The time was upon him.

Josh had stopped in his tracks. His hand came up stiffly, as if he were fending his father off. "I'm gonna be me, pop. I'm gonna be *me*." It had come first as a declaration, then as a warning, and now, his fist closing over, it was a howl: *"I'm gonna be me!"*

"Good enough," Dave told him. He had asked an honest question and got an honest answer and he thanked him for it. They walked on a while longer. "And was that you I saw out there tonight? A hoodlum throwing rocks at police cars?" It wasn't cold at all. In the Army jacket and all, he was beginning to feel warm.

"If that's what I got to do for them to look at me, yeah. If that's what I got to do to get my own, yeah." He cast a sidelong, painful look at his father which said: *Do you really want to talk? Do you really want to TALK about where it's at?* "If the only way to overthrow this corrupt society is to throw rocks at the cops, yeah, that's me."

"By breaking the law you get your manhood, is that it?" He was holding his temper very tightly in check. He was picking his words with care, because he was very well aware that this had better be done right. "I was taught different than that and I think you're wrong. But I know *you* think you're right. So explain it to me."

"Aw, pa. You're not going to give me that about law and order. The kind of law and order that was made to deny the black man his rights! It's not law and order, pop. I'm talking about justice. That's where it's at. It's justice."

"I've heard The Speech, Josh. I think justice is the most important thing there is too. We're in pretty good company." In all the languages he had learned, Walsh told his son, he had found that the most revered and ancient philosophers always had a particular concern with the meaning of justice. "I think," he said, "my favorite is Plato's. Plato said that justice is the right of every man to perform up to the limit of his capacities."

Josh slammed his fist into the palm of his hand. "Yes," he said. "Yes."

"To be himself."

"*Yes!*"

"All right, then. I heard you yelling 'black pig' at a man tonight. It happens that it was a man who's one helluva man, maybe we'll have him over for supper some night for you to meet." He was happy to see Josh wince. "Now you're telling that black man he can't be a cop, if that's what he is and wants to be, because you don't like it. I want you to tell me the justice in that."

"Because he's a lackey of the White Power Structure who was hired to hold down his own people."

"And you really think that, do you? Really?"

"It's not only me, pop," Josh said eagerly. "You ask anybody."

"You mean the Black Power Structure's got a right to do what the White Power Structure hasn't? Maybe they have. But we were talking about every man being himself. I'm not asking what *everybody* thinks. I'm asking you, as yourself, all by yourself. Only you."

An involuntary grunt was expelled from Josh. He walked along, his head down, his brow furrowed.

His father said: "Do you really think a black cop is so bad, or are you only repeating what you hear? Is that being what you are, Josh, just repeating the words that somebody hands down to you and says, 'All right, man, here's the word for this week.' Or do you have to ask yourself: 'What do I think? Me, Joshua Walsh? Not everybody else. Me.'"

"I never thought about it like that. . . ."

Walsh was taking him home, the long way around, because he wanted to take Josh past North Sewart. Something told him—some instinct, some small change in Josh's bearing and attitude—that a look at the damage was not what Josh needed right now. Considering the confession Dave himself had to make before they got home, it might even be harmful. Abruptly, he cut back across the street for a more direct route home.

"To be yourself," he said. "That isn't an easy thing. You'd be surprised how hard it is. It's maybe the hardest thing in the world." He passed a hand over his eyes. "I don't say agree with me. All I say is think it through. If it suits a man to be a Tom—by what you think or what I think or, for that matter, what everybody else in the world thinks—if he can get through life most comfortable that way, given where he came from and what he went through, who are you, all 15-years old of you, to tell him he has to be somebody else? Or the President of the United States either. If that's what he is, Josh, that's what he is. He hasn't got any way to be anything else."

They were passing under a street light, so he was not unaware of the look of sheer admiration that came over Josh, a look which stated very clearly that he had never thought his father could have such thoughts or, having them, could explain them so well. "But I can hate who did it to him," Josh said fiercely. "And I can tell them they ain't gonna do to me like they did to him!"

"Sure you can. But who did it to him? That black cop? Those white cops? We're talking about each man, remember. And each man being himself." It came out then, quite naturally, about Floyd and Mario, riding silently through the night in their patrol car. "That's where we're at right now, and are you going to tell me one of them is to blame or the other?" (My God, he thought, there was a symbolism in that story he hadn't recognized himself until he heard himself telling it out loud. Just as there were things about himself that he was understanding more clearly by hearing what he was saying to his son. One thing you had to give these kids, they sure did make you think.)

"What got them there is the same thing we're talking about," Josh insisted. "Injustice. What got them there is that law and order won't work any more in the middle of injustice because, pop . . . we . . . won't . . . let . . . it." He opened his mouth to say something else, and instantly decided against it.

"Go ahead, Josh," Dave said, deliberately. "I started this. Let's let it take us wherever it takes us."

Josh still couldn't bring himself to look at his father. "You know what I mean, pop," he said, his throat constricting. "I don't mean you, but . . . well, look at grandpa."

He could have gladly whacked him! He could have. . . . "Don't know so much so soon!" he snapped. "History didn't start when you learned how to read. Nothing you've said hasn't been said for years. Nothing you've said wasn't said by me and my friends when we were your age . . . or maybe a little older."

"Only we're doing something about it," Josh shot back, "that's the difference. Well, you told me to tell you the truth." There was a look of accusation in his eyes. "You said to let it take us all the way." Of disappointment too. "I didn't want to, pop. You did."

He was right, of course.

What he was trying to tell him, Dave said patiently, was that he and his generation hadn't created this thing, fully hatched. "You didn't change the times. The times changed. You said something about your grandfather. Did you know your grandfather was one of the first members of the Brotherhood?" And realizing with an inner grimace of his own, that Josh probably didn't even know what the Brotherhood was, he explained that it was the Brotherhood of Sleeping Car Porters.

"A Negro union in those days, Josh. Do you have any idea what that meant? It meant that every hand was turned against you. It meant that you were alone. There were no laws protecting unions then. The company didn't want a union, and the other unions didn't want a Negro union either."

He told Amos Walsh's grandson what it meant. To be an officer of the Brotherhood meant that you were automatically fired. You didn't go to court for your rights, because you had no rights. The company had all the power and the company had all the rights. You didn't have strike benefits because the Brotherhood had no money. You didn't even have any way to carry off a strike, because you lived from one week's salary to the next. He remembered those days all right. He saw himself as a small boy listening to his father at the supper table, and suddenly his mind went to Chief Morgan—if it was possible to imagine Chief Morgan as a little boy—sitting at the supper table listening to his father too.

"You didn't have a rumble and go on home to a hot supper in those days," he told Josh. "You lost your job and watched your family starve. You were black, and you had no rights, and you were alone. If it was you, like tonight, they'd have thrown you in jail and thrown away the key. Not just fingerprinted you and given you back to your folks."

No, history hadn't started the day before yesterday. "And they fought them, Josh. They fought them all, all by themselves, with nothing but their determination. And they won, Joshua, they won." He was stirred by his own words, stirred by the memory of it. "Not in a month or a year. Years! It took them ten years before the company would even recognize them. And longer still before the other unions would recognize them." He had forgotten it himself in the succeeding years; he had let himself forget it.

"And your grandfather was one of them. Remember that the next time you talk to him." He nodded gently and said, more to himself than to Joshua. "I should have told you about that before. But I forgot."

"I'm glad you told me now."

And those kids down south, the students who started it all with the sit-ins, did he think they came out of nothing? Nothing came out of nothing. Just maybe there were some parents who gave them the courage to go ahead. Just maybe there were some black teachers in those black colleges—he realized that Josh had him saying black now too —who had given them something to hold onto, something that told them it was all right.

He was talking more easily now, less self-consciously, for he had stopped listening to his own words. He was talking for both of them now. "If Swahili is what you want, fine. What it means to you it means to you. If I can't understand it, that doesn't make it wrong. If I can't understand it, it doesn't make *me* wrong either. I'll tell you what I think. I think our black culture is here in this country. I think we've built something in this country, by ourselves, starting from nothing." From slavery, he thought. "From less than nothing," he said. History couldn't be changed, but accomplishment was to be measured and measured proudly.

They had stopped briefly at a red light, even though there wasn't a car in sight.

"Pop," Josh said, "I didn't mean to spoil anything about the parade tomorrow. I wasn't thinking of that. I just didn't think."

Well, there it was. He had the same sense of stepping off into the void (the same tingling hollowness in the groin) that he had experienced as he sat in the empty barracks, his bags packed, waiting to ship over to Vietnam.

He stepped off the curb and said, "There isn't going to be any parade tomorrow." And now it was irrevocable.

Thank God, it flowed naturally from everything that had gone before. Not easily, but naturally.

"Remember what we were saying about Plato? About getting what you deserved? Well, if you want what you deserve, you can't take what you don't deserve, can you? Because then you're taking it from someone who really deserves it."

"That's where it's come to, pop." He didn't take his eyes off him.

"Well, I don't deserve any Medal of Honor. Or any other medal either."

He told him about the Red ambush.

He told him about the hasty-unto-panicky retreat.

He told him about Bob Nichols, and how they had found refuge in the cavern on top of Flatiron Mountain.

He told him about the arrival of Adam March, out of

mists.

He told his son everything without stint or apology.

The streets were silent, except for the sound of his measured voice and the rhythm of their footsteps on the cold pavement. Josh listened, running his hand over his hair, surprised and intent at first, then frowning, solemnly and finally, his hands jammed inside his jacket, with a wholly inscrutable attentiveness.

"It doesn't matter, pop."

"It matters," Dave said sharply. "Believe me, it matters."

"Not to me. What did them Vietcongs ever do to you?"

Groaning, Dave flung his arms into the air. He had just told his son he was a fake, and his son wanted to argue the merits of the war with him. And then, with a little snort, he said, "Don't tell me I was an embarrassment to you, all your friends thinking I'd killed all them friendly Vietcongs and you had to apologize for me?"

"No. It's like you say. They do a lot of talking, but they were damned impressed. Believe-you-me-Bob."

Believe-you-me-Bob? Was that coming back? He looked at his son again. He had better not go underestimating this kid of his, he thought. With all the ranting and screaming, with all the theatrics, he did see the difference between the talk and the reality.

The thing about it, Josh said, with that juvenile pomposity that was for once not maddening, the thing about it was that they weren't going to be taking scraps from Whitey's table any more. "Most especially we don't take the pat on the head and the 'good nigger.'"

"The Speech goes," Dave continued, "that he treats us as well as he can imagine any pet dog being treated, and he can't understand why the dog keeps complaining." Dave paused for just a second. "And maybe that part of The Speech isn't all that wrong."

"Hey, pop." Grinning, looking incredibly young and

coltish, Josh bounded back a step, his features arranged into a look of pleased and exaggerated astonishment. "You're not bad for a black boose-wah-sie. We might make something out of you yet."

"You might get a whack across your backside, that's what you might do."

It was said on both sides with broad grins, the son letting it be known that he was being outrageously patronizing to the father who could whack him at will, and the father letting him know that he knew it.

There wasn't anything funny about this, Dave told him, sternly. What was going to happen now was going to change Josh's life. "It can be the difference between your going to college or not. It's the difference between better or worse. The difference between easy and hard."

"Pop. I've been telling you. Bite me and I bite back."

Dave started to place his hand tentatively and shyly on Josh's shoulder but very quickly let it fall.

"Pop. . . . You don't have to win any medal to make me proud of you." He started to reach out himself, even more tentatively, more shyly, but his hand fell back too. He turned his head away and for the first time there was a tremor in his voice. "You're my father." He looked back out of the sides of his eyes and tried to smile. "Aside from which I kind of like you."

Dave made a little cough to clear the thickness out of his throat. "Yeah, I kind of like you too."

They walked the rest of the way in a warm and comfortable silence, lengthening their strides, both of them understanding that they were closer in silence than they could ever be in words.

As they got to the house and into the hallway, Josh hung back for a moment while Dave fumbled for the key.

"Pop? . . . It's us against the world, huh?"

Walsh put his arm around his son's shoulder and gave

him a gruff little squeeze. "It's us against the liars. Yeah, the cheaters, and the hypocrites, and the liars."

With a boyish giggle, Josh was the prancing, coltish boy again. "There's the difference between us," he said, fighting to keep a straight face. "I'm just a militant and you're one of those gawd-damn extremists I keep hearing about!"

Out of some sixth sense, Constance flung the door open just as they were coming out of the elevator. "Well," she said, crossly, trying to hide her relief, "it's about time. Just don't think I don't know what happened down on North Sewart. I've got sources of information too."

That "sources of information" sounded so ominous that, against his will, Dave had to smile. Not Joshua. The way his mother was glowering at him, he had the good sense to look as shamefaced as possible.

"You bad boy," she said, shaking her finger in his face. "You bad, bad boy."

"You *bad*, boy," she said, throwing her arms around him and hugging him fiercely. "Oh, you're such a bad boy," she said, her voice breaking. "You'll be the death of me, not that you care."

Joshua sent an appeal for help over her head to his father, who shook his head firmly to let him know that their compact against the world didn't extend to this. When she released him finally with a little shove so that she could wipe her eyes, Josh took advantage of the opportunity to go skittering out of the vestibule and into the parlor. Constance, who had perhaps come to the conclusion that she hadn't been quite the firm, inflexible disciplinarian she had intended to be, shouted after him, "And don't think I can't still put you across my knee," a picture of such absurdity that she immediately felt it necessary to add, with great dignity, "as big and ungainly a boy as you've got to be."

But that only served to bring on another association in her mind, the other fear that had been tormenting her as she waited. "They didn't hurt you down at the station, did they . . . you bad boy?" The little smile that curled at the corners of his lips while he was shaking his head told her that he knew he was out of the woods.

She turned on Dave, "And I don't see anything so funny either. You're two of a kind. . . . Hey!" She was gaping at the bandage on his forehead, and he had to assure her that while it was good of her to notice that he was there too, it was only a scratch.

"Not that you'd tell me the truth, anyway," she said, affecting her best martyr voice. "Either of you." She had caught something else. She had caught the masculine camaraderie, and she seemed to understand instinctively that it was part of her role, at this moment, to continue to play the fussy woman whom they willingly and affectionately tolerated, in their masculine fashion, together.

She took another look, a quizzical, heart-stopping look that saw something else, something she didn't want to see or admit to seeing.

There was a glass of milk on the kitchen table for him, she told Josh, and he'd better not think he was going to bed without drinking every drop of it. "And you finish that wedge of cake there too, every crumb of it, you hear me!" And, she yelled, while he was disappearing gratefully into the kitchen. "You be sure and use that fork, not eat it with your hands like you're some animal off of the street. You've had some bringing up, even if," she said pointedly, "I've had to do it all alone."

Now that she'd got it all out of her, the whole thing hit her. She put her hands to her face, her shoulders shaking, her knees gave way and she sank into the parlor chair. Dave lit a cigarette for her, but she pushed his hand away. Yes, she had caught something else, all right. She had watched for and caught the look that had passed between them again just before Joshua had headed for the kitchen.

What she didn't know, she sure as hell suspected.

"I told him about the medal," Dave said, watching her closely. "He said it was all right. And, you know . . . he meant it."

Connie twisted her head away, as if she didn't want to give him the satisfaction of seeing her wiping her eyes again. She rose with a weary sigh, still not looking at him. "Why is it me," she said, far more composed than he had expected, "who has to have a crazy husband and a crazy son?"

She fussed around the house for the rest of the night, making it clear, without quite saying it, that she didn't want to talk any more about it yet.

It was, in fact, as if nothing had happened. She came out, quite pleasantly, to tell him that he wouldn't believe it but Joshua had washed both the fork and the plate before he went to bed. "What in the world do you suppose is going to happen next?" she asked him, as if that were the most remarkable thing that had happened that night. As if that were the greatest care they had in the world.

She even urged Dave to have some milk and cake himself—it was a rich chocolate layer cake—before he went to bed. Dave had no appetite for anything at all, but it was clearly her way of showing him that while they weren't talking about it, they weren't fighting about it either.

He knew her so well. He knew she wouldn't be coming right to bed. He also knew it would be better all around if he did go to bed and waited for her. He knew exactly what she'd do. She'd iron some clothes. She'd do whatever sewing she had been saving up. If there was nothing else for her to do, she'd wash the floor. He knew her like a book. She had to come to terms with it, and this was her way. Just knowing that he knew her that well—and knowing the heartache this was causing her—endeared her to him.

Fighting to stay awake, he let his mind dwell on the following morning. He'd have to call the mayor's office first to get that parade canceled. He'd have to call Lester. And then he'd call Bobby Coleman so that he'd know he was about to have the rug pulled out from under him.

It was too much to hope that Coleman wouldn't immediately call Adam March, but there was nothing he could do about that. And, he mused, it was too much to hope that Adam March wouldn't somehow figure out a way of landing on his feet. There was no sense kidding himself. When he took the fall, he was going to be taking it all by himself.

Oddly enough, Miriam didn't particularly worry him any more. She had, after all, been waiting for him that afternoon, and he didn't really believe she'd have been foolish enough, despite all her talk, to take any chances. No matter, he told himself, he had all the trouble he could handle right now without looking for still more.

Get in line and wait your turn, troubles. One at a time.

Eventually, he heard the shower running in the bathroom (he must have dozed off after all), and he knew Connie would be coming to bed with her hair net on to make it clear to him that there would be no great making-up scene *that way* tonight. Yes, he thought, smiling to himself in the darkness, he knew that woman like a book.

She lay in bed alongside him for a time, just as he had known she would, before she said, "Just don't think I didn't know all along that you wouldn't take it."

She had, as he should have expected, come to grips with it by making herself superior to it. Good enough.

"You want to know why? Because you're you! And," she said, triumphantly, "I know you like a book."

"Yes," he said, mildly, "I guess you do." She would never know, he supposed, that she had never been dearer to him than she was at that moment.

"I'd wake up in the night and look at you and I'd say to myself, 'He'll never take it.' I'd say to myself, 'Not with my luck he won't. Just my luck,' I'd say to myself, 'I had to go marry an honest, decent man.' "

She had answered his question. In her own way, in her own good time, spitting out praise like a curse, accepting whatever virtue he had as if *it* were a curse. And still, Dave knew what it had cost her to say it. He could hope that she did know him well enough to know that he knew.

"Just your luck," he said, in a gentle teasing tone.

"Just my luck," she said, squeezing his hand. And that, he knew, was as close as she was ever going to come to saying that it was all right.

Because although she was letting him know that she was accommodating herself to his stupidity, it would never be all right with her. He didn't doubt for one moment that she would be throwing it up to him for the rest of their lives. Yes, he knew this woman like a book. With the best will in the world, she wouldn't be able to resist it.

In a matter of seconds, she said, "Just don't think everybody's going to be so easy on you, that's all."

"That's my girl," he said.

"You think you know people? You don't know people!" Her voice went hard as stone. "Don't think it's going to be easy," she said, "Not on any of us."

"No," Dave said. "I don't think it's going to be easy." He squeezed her hand back and said a crazy thing, but both of them understood exactly what he meant by it:

"It isn't going to be easy," he said, squeezing his wife's hand, "but now it's going to be easy."

Epilogue

The official explanation released jointly by the White House and the Department of Defense was short and discreet, wisely deemphasizing Dave's decision not to accept the Medal of Honor. In 1899, the War Department had established a military board of review to screen all candidates for the medal, and had set a three-year time limit before the approval of recommendations became final. Captain David Walsh had submitted a personal request to the board of review to reconsider the application made in his behalf by Major-General Randolph Ritter and his staff. After reappraising the eye-witness statements describing the action in which Captain Walsh and his command had participated in the sector of Flatiron Mountain on the dates for the medal, and had set a three-year time limit before the approval of recommendations became final. tions of this same action, the board of review's decision was that Captain Walsh's name should be removed from the list of candidates *at his own personal recommendation*.

The President of the United States extolled ". . . the virtue, integrity, and honor of this fine American. . . ." and praised ". . . his courage in the face of this difficult and soul-searching decision. . . ."

The same day the story broke, Lester phoned the apartment, late at night. He was subdued and sympathetic, and Dave could detect in his voice some of the polite condescension of the successful man toward his not-too-well-endowed brother-in-law that had characterized their relationship before the medal had become a factor in all of their lives.

"It took courage to do what you did, Dave," he said, imitating the President's sermonizing voice. "I mean that."

Dave knew that what Lester really believed was that he was a goddamn fool.

"Miriam didn't fill this lighter," Lester muttered. "Just a sec." Dave could almost see him acting out the pompous ritual of lighting his cigar. Idly he studied the silk-screen print that hung on the wall above the dry sink on the opposite wall of the small vestibule. A favorite of Connie's, a fierce-looking Japanese samurai warrior.

"Dave? You there?" As if Lester had forgotten who he was talking to.

"I'm here."

"How's Connie?"

"Lying down. She took some aspirin and a tranquilizer."

"Yeah . . . yeahhhh." Lester knew how it was. "Well . . . don't worry about that girl, kid. She's aces high, we both know that. A winner."

"That she is, Les."

Lester cleared his throat. "We were all set to drive down and take you all out to eat tonight. . . ."

"Thanks, but it's just as well," Dave rescued him.

"No, no!" Lester protested vehemently. "It's Miriam. She got bombed on two drinks and went to bed without supper."

"I'm certainly a trial to the women in this family," Dave said wryly.

"Jesus, Dave, I didn't mean anything like that." He gave a small, embarrassed snort. "She was late this month. That always makes her bitchy. And well . . . the shock today . . . reading it in the papers always makes it seem worse than it really is . . . the shock brought her around. That and the drinks just pooped her out."

"*. . . it brought her around.*"

The announcement was stunning. Like the time when he was twelve years old and the manager of the Merrick Theater in Jamaica called his number playing "Screeno." Twelve half-dollars he had won. It was magic.

Laughing, loose as a snake, Dave slithered off the uncomfortable chair Constance kept next to the telephone table and sprawled on the floor. On the far wall the samurai leered at him.

"So, what's funny?" Lester asked.

"Women. . . . Miriam and Connie. Women, they're all funny. All nerves and contradictions."

"That's a fact." Lester gave his unqualified approval. There was a lengthy, tense pause. Dave knew what was coming.

"Dave . . . the reason I called. . . ." Lester was a funeral director arranging an interment. "I spoke with Clem Bestor a little while ago. In spite of what has happened today, Bestor, Sampson and Adams are solidly behind you. (Whatever happened to *Bestor, Walsh, Sampson and Adams?*) Once this mess blows over, we feel you could be a very positive asset to the firm. So, don't worry about a thing. The contract guarantees you a year's salary with a mutual option to renew. . . ."

Dave stopped him. "Lester, don't play games with me. You and I are too close for that. We both know that my value as chief handshaker for your firm has diminished considerably since I'm not getting any Medal of Honor. In fact, it is a big fat zero! You and Clem don't owe me a gift of a year's salary; that's all it would be, and you know it, a gift."

"Now, you're exaggerating, Dave. I'm sure we can work something out."

But Dave could sense the relief in Lester's voice. The same sense of lightness that had infected him when he heard about Miriam having her period.

"Look, Les, we'll talk about it another time. I got a pot of coffee perking in the kitchen."

"Sure we will, boy. Now take care and give our love to Connie and Josh. Remember, we're with you all the way on this thing."

Dave hung up, feeling an enormous affection for Lester in spite of the brush-off. No five-figure check from Bestor, Sampson and Adams could come close to matching the gift Lester had unwittingly presented to him. *Miriam had come around! You lose a few, you win a few.*

He lost more than he won in the days that followed. The phone calls came, sometimes one after the other, night and day, most of them anonymous hate calls.

Nigger!

Black lying bastard!

Not all of them were from white bigots though. As he had expected, as Adam March had warned him, a considerable cross section of the black community was outraged by his renunciation of the medal. They believed he had sold out his people. By making himself vulnerable to ridicule and censure, he had reflected discredit on the whole black race. White or black, he did not hang up on a single caller. He listened to what they had to say.

"You take that infernal instrument off the hook or I'll tear it out of the wall," Constance kept threatening. "It's driving me crazy."

In defense, Josh would shut himself up in his room and turn up his stereo to full volume to drown out the fiendish ringing of the phone.

Dave realized he was acting out a role like a penitent monk sleeping on the cold stone flags of his lonely cell. It was masochistic, but he indulged his need.

The newspapers, and television, and radio had a predictable field day, picturing March and Dave as the biggest hoaxter team since P. T. Barnum and the Cardiff

Giant. What perplexed Dave the most was Adam March himself. He was "unavailable for comment"—as his rival newshounds kept pointing out with malicious glee—conspicuous by his absence from the clubs and cafes, which always had been his nightly haunts, for days following the White House announcement. One tabloid ran a tongue-in-cheek headline on the second page:

IS ADAM MARCH WITH JUDGE CRATER?

It was Bobby Coleman of the NSBE who finally solved the mystery for him. When Dave had originally phoned him to inform him that he had decided not to take the medal, Coleman had been shocked, then infuriated, and then, before Dave could lay out all of his reasons, he had rudely hung up. But, near the end of the week, Coleman phoned him, and, to Dave's surprise, he was almost cordial.

"I'm not apologizing for what I said the other night, Dave," he said solemnly. "You had no right to pull the rug out without giving the boys in our 'think tank' a couple of weeks to work out an angle. We could have eased you out of it before the Fourth of July without all this bad press. Christ, man! You let fly with a bag of shit like this and we all get dirty.

"Anyway, it could have been worse. You must carry a rabbit's foot in your back pocket like my old grandpa." He actually allowed himself a gay little chuckle. "You may not come out of this as badly as it first seemed. Now that we've taken the plunge, the water isn't so cold after all. . . ."

Dave puckered up his forehead. Coleman had lost him right after the chuckle. "What do you mean, Bobby?" he asked.

"Laying the whole business back on this Lieutenant Nichols, it could work out pretty well all around. It won't be the same as if you had won the medal, but. . . ."

"Laying what back on Lieutenant Nichols?" Dave said

in bafflement.

"Just what you said all along. You wanted to get him a medal."

"I didn't *want* to get him a medal. I didn't want any of us to get a medal."

Coleman hesitated. "Well. . . . You wanted his wife and his parents to think he died a hero's death." There was another silence. Dave experienced a warning before the next words came out. Coleman's voice was cold and flat. "When the truth is, he was shot running away, a coward."

Dave's fingers tightened on the phone. He was still too stunned by what Coleman had said to feel any negotiable emotions. "Where did you hear that?" he asked.

"From Adam March," Coleman said brightly. "I had drinks with him earlier today. They can say what they want about Adam March, but the man is in a class by himself. A giant. And Adam March wants you to know that he holds no ill will toward you, Dave, for what you did to his story. He told me how he's been sort of father confessor to you all the while you were battling this thing out with your conscience. He knew how you felt because Adam was doing a lot of soul-searching of his own. The two of you were really caught in the middle, like in one of those Greek tragedies, you know that, Dave? You wanting to protect the good name of your friend Nichols. Your *white* friend. Adam wanting to protect you because of the color issue. Of course, if you had been white, he would have killed those first stories they printed about you on the spot. What the hell, it's water under the bridge. We make do with what we have. Now, as we see it at the NSBE, the image of a courageous black captain trying to save the honor of his cowardly white lieutenant. . . ."

Dave missed the rest of it. He crashed the phone down, breaking the connection. He leaned back against the wall unsteadily and closed his eyes.

Adam March and Alexander Hamilton had the real goods. The public was a "great beast." And it wasn't particular what it fed on. War, famine, pestilence, presidential assassinations, police brutality, rape, or murder in the streets. All the more to salivate over.

Yesterday Adam March had fed it David and Goliath. Today it was slavering over the carcass of David Walsh. Tomorrow Adam March would feed it poor Bob Nichols.

Tomorrow Adam March would be back in favor, the perennial darling of the mass communication media.

For the first time, the full realization and comprehension of the rough times that lay ahead of him hit Dave. And the impact was crushing.

THE END